Taste of Home

Backyard grilling

RECIPES AND TIPS TO GRILL LIKE A PRO

Taste of Home
B O O K S

REIMAN MEDIA GROUP, INC. · GREENDALE, WISCONSIN

Taste of Home. Reader's Digest

A TASTE OF HOME/READER'S DIGEST BOOK

©2006 Reiman Media Group, Inc.
5400 S. 60th St., Greendale WI 53129
All rights reserved.

Taste of Home and Reader's Digest are registered trademarks
of The Reader's Digest Association, Inc.

Editors: Jennifer Olski, Julie Schnittka
Art Directors: Edwin Robles, Jr., Maribeth Greinke
Layout Designer: Emma Acevedo
Proofreader: Jean Steiner
Editorial Assistant: Barb Czysz
Recipe Testing and Editing: Taste of Home Test Kitchen
Food Photography: Reiman Photo Studio

Senior Editor, Retail Books: Jennifer Olski
Vice President/Executive Editor, Books: Heidi Reuter Lloyd
Creative Director: Ardyth Cope
Senior Vice President/Editor in Chief: Catherine Cassidy
President: Barbara Newton
Founder: Roy Reiman

Pictured on front cover: Portobello Mushroom Burger (p. 74)

Pictured on back cover (clockwise from top): Grilled Asparagus Medley (p. 31),
Chicken Satay (p. 11), Lemon Grilled Salmon (p. 197) and Sesame Steaks (p. 101)

Pictured on front flap and spine: The Perfect Hamburger (p. 69)

International Standard Book Number (10): 0-89821-557-9
International Standard Book Number (13): 978-0-89821-557-1

Library of Congress Control Number: 2006931747

For other Taste of Home books and products, visit
www.tasteofhome.com.
For more Reader's Digest products and information,
visit our website
www.rd.com (in the United States)
www.rd.ca (in Canada)

Printed in China 9 10 8

Table of Contents

·Grilling Basics·

You'll be grilling like a pro after reviewing the helpful information in this chapter! Begin with the basics of choosing a grill, starting a charcoal grill and testing a grill's temperature.

For more advanced grilling techniques, learn about direct and indirect cooking methods and ways to add flavor with wood chips.

Great Grilling Tips

- Always place your grill on a solid, level surface away from fences, shrubs, grass and overhangs. Grill in a well-ventilated area.

- Store charcoal in a dry place. Damp or wet charcoal may not ignite.

- Never add lighter fluid to lit coals. Never use gasoline or kerosene to light briquettes.

- Have two pairs of long-handled tongs—one for moving the coals and one to turn food.

- Bring food to a cool room temperature before placing on the grill. Cold food may burn on the outside before the interior is cooked.

- Don't allow raw meat and fish to come into contact with other food. Use separate cutting boards and utensils. Thoroughly wash your hands and surfaces with hot soapy water after handling uncooked food. Don't carve cooked meat on the same board used to handle raw meat.

- Don't crowd food on the grill. Allow some space around each piece for even cooking.

- Protect yourself from the heat with long barbecue mitts and long-handled tools. Use tongs for turning to avoid piercing the food and losing juices. (Spatulas should be used for hamburgers.)

- Use a meat or instant-read thermometer to check the internal temperature of meat and poultry before the recommended cooking time is up. Don't leave an instant thermometer in food while grilling.

- Allow more cooking time on cold or windy days or at higher altitudes. On extremely hot days, allow less time.

- To avoid flare-ups, trim excess fat from meat or use lean ground meat or place a drip pan directly under meat, stacking coals on either side. Have a water bottle handy to extinguish flare-ups.

- Opening and closing vents in a covered charcoal grill helps regulate coal temperature. When vents are open, more air flows through the grill and coals burn hotter. When vents are closed, the coals are deprived of fresh air (oxygen) and will eventually extinguish themselves.

- Don't discard the ashes until they are completely cooled. Cover the grill, close the vents and let stand until cold.

Choosing a Grill

Charcoal or gas—which one to choose? Actually, it is a matter of preference. Both types of grills will give you delicious results. Factors to consider when purchasing a grill are: price, ease of use, grilling needs and frequency.

Both types of grills are available in a wide range of prices, but in general, gas grills cost more than charcoal grills. Gas grills ignite immediately, take just minutes to heat up and allow you to easily control the grilling temperature.

Charcoal grills take about 30 minutes for the briquettes to get hot, and the coals start off hot and cool down during cooking. The ash from coals can also be messy to clean up. If you don't plan to grill often or grill only small amounts, then an inexpensive charcoal grill or a small hibachi might be good choices.

Starting a Charcoal Grill

The number of briquettes needed to grill will depend on the amount of food you're grilling, the size of the grill and weather conditions. Adverse weather conditions—high winds, cold temperatures and high humidity—will require you to use more briquettes. About 30 briquettes are needed to cook 1 pound of meat.

There are three ways to start a charcoal grill. (If you are using briquettes that just need to be lit with a match, follow package directions for lighting.)

Pyramid Style. Arrange the briquettes in a pyramid in the grill. Pour lighter fluid over the

briquettes. Recap the fluid and place away from the grill. Light the briquettes.

Chimney Starter. Crumple newspaper or waxed paper and place a chimney starter over

the paper in the grill. Fill the chimney starter with the briquettes. Light the paper. When the coals are ready, dump them out of the chimney starter and spread out.

Electric Starter. Arrange the briquettes in a pyramid in the grill. Insert the electric starter in

Greasing a Grill

Spray the food grate with non-stick cooking spray before starting the grill. Never spray directly over the fire (gas or coal) as you can cause a fire. To grease a hot grate, fold a paper towel into a small pad. Holding the pad with long-handled tongs, dip in vegetable oil and rub over the grate.

the middle of the coals. Plug the starter into an outlet. If using an extension cord, use a heavy-duty one. It will take 8 to 10 minutes for the ash to start to form on the coals. At that point, unplug the electric starter and remove from briquettes.

The starter will be very hot, so place it out of the way on a heatproof surface. The briquettes need to continue heating until they are covered with a light gray ash.

Depending on your grill, the briquettes will go on a charcoal grate or the bottom of the grill. The coals are ready when they are covered with a light gray ash—this takes about 25 to 30 minutes. Once they are ready, spread them out for direct or indirect heat. Never pour lighter fluid on coals that have already been lit.

Preparing a Grill for Direct and Indirect Heat

You can grill foods with two cooking methods—direct or indirect. Consult the instructions from your grill's manufacturer for specific details about your grill and follow these general guidelines:

Direct heat is used for foods that take about 30 minutes or less, such as steaks, hamburgers, kabobs, boneless chicken breasts, fish, hot dogs and vegetables. The food is cooked directly over an even heat source. The food is turned halfway through cooking time. Cover or uncover the grill while cooking according to recipe directions.

For a charcoal grill, spread out the preheated coals in an even layer (see illustration A).

For a gas grill, preheat the grill with all the burners on high. Place food on cooking grate, then adjust temperature to the one recommended in the recipe.

Indirect heat is used for foods that take longer than 30 minutes to cook, or are high in fat or are usually cooked in the oven rather than on the stovetop, such as roasts, ribs, thick steaks, whole chickens and bone-in chicken pieces.

Foods cooked with the indirect method do not need to be turned. Sometimes recipes call for first searing the meat over direct heat for a nice brown exterior before placing over indirect heat.

For a charcoal grill, bank half of the coals on one side of the grill and the other half on the other side. Place a foil drip pan in the center of the grill (see illustration B), replace the cooking grate and place the meat over the drip pan. Cover and grill according to recipe directions.

Note that for every 45 minutes of grilling, you should add more briquettes to the bank of coals. For a small grill (14 inches), add about four per side; for a large grill (26 inches), add about nine per side.

For a gas grill, preheat the grill with all the burners on high. Turn the center burner off and place a drip pan in the center. Place food on cooking grate over the drip pan. Adjust temperature to the one recommended in recipe, then cover and grill for the recommended time. If the gas grill has only two burners, turn one burner off and place the drip pan on that side.

A) Direct Grilling   **B) Indirect Grilling**

Adding Flavor with Wood Chips

Wood imparts wonderful flavor and richness to grilled foods. Remember…a little goes a long way. Before using, place the wood in a food-safe container; cover with water. Soak blocks of wood at least 1 hour and chips for 20 to 30 minutes; drain.

For a charcoal grill, place the wood directly on the hot coals. For a gas grill, place the wood in your grill's smoker box if available and use according to your manufacturer's directions. If no smoker box is available, place wood in a disposable foil pan or create a foil pouch for chips and set on the grill before preheating.

Wood Type	Flavor	Use With
Alder	Delicate and sweet	Fish and poultry
Apple	Slightly sweet and fruity	Poultry, pork and fish
Black Birch	Delicate, touch of mint	Lamb, chicken, swordfish, vegetables
Butternut	Sweet, nutty	Steak, venison, buffalo
Cherry	Mild, slightly sweet and fruity	Poultry, pork and fish
Grapevine	Rich, fruity	Fish, especially salmon and swordfish
Hickory	Hearty, smoky bacon-like flavor	Most red meats, pork, poultry and vegetables
Maple	Mild, smoky and sweet	Poultry, ham and vegetables
Mesquite	Strong, sharp earthy flavor	Beef, most other meats and vegetables
Oak	Rich, yet mellow	Steak, ribs, pork, venison
Peach	Mellow, fruity, sweet	Duck, goose, turkey
Pecan	Mellower than hickory	Chicken, duck
Sassafrass	Mellow, smoky	Suasage, hot or mild

Making a Foil Pouch for Chips

1. Place the soaked wood chips on a large piece of heavy-duty foil.

2. Bring up two edges over the center of chips and fold down twice.

3. Fold the side edges over twice.

4. Poke holes in top of packet with a knife or long handled fork and place on the grill.

Testing the Temperature of Your Grill

Check the temperature of your grill by cautiously holding the palm of your hand 3 to 4 inches above the grate. Count the number of seconds you can hold your hand in that position before the heat forces you to pull it away. (To check the temperature of a covered grill, have the cover down on the grill and open the vent slightly. Insert a grill thermometer through the vent.) The color of the coals also indicates the approximate temperature.

Temperature	Number of Seconds	Color of Coals
Hot (at least 450°)	2 seconds	coals glow red
Medium-hot (400°)	3 seconds	coals are gray with a red underglow
Medium (350°)	4 seconds	coals are gray with a hint of red
Medium-low (300°)	5 seconds	coals are gray with a faint red glow

Dial or Digital — What's the Difference?

The main difference between dial and digital food thermometers is where they sense temperature. Dial types have a metal stem that must penetrate the food about 2 inches. (A dimple or groove on the stem marks this depth.) For accurate readings on thin cuts like hamburgers, steaks and chicken breasts, the probe must be inserted from the side.

A digital thermometer's sensor is in the tip, making it ideal for thinner cuts.

Either type works fine for larger cuts of meat, like roasts or whole chickens. Just insert the thermometer into the thickest part of the meat. Be sure to avoid touching fat or bone; doing so will result in an inaccurate reading.

Food thermometers ensure perfect results every time.

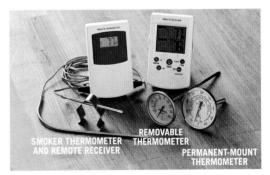

Dial-type units measure grill temperature. Digital units are available for smokers.

·Appetizers·

Get the party started at your next outdoor gathering by inviting guests around back to sample a savory selection of from-the-grill hors d'oeuvres. This chapter showcases a slew of sizzling starters...from classics such as Bruschetta from the Grill to newfound favorites like Japaleno Chicken Wraps.

Chicken Satay

(Pictured at left)

These golden skewered chicken snacks are marinated and grilled, then served with a zesty Thai-style peanut butter sauce.
—Sue Gronholz, Beaver Dam, Wisconsin

2 pounds boneless skinless chicken breasts
1/2 cup milk
6 garlic cloves, minced
1 tablespoon brown sugar
1 tablespoon *each* ground coriander, turmeric and cumin
1 teaspoon salt
1 teaspoon white pepper
1/8 teaspoon coconut extract
PEANUT BUTTER SAUCE:
1/3 cup peanut butter
1/3 cup milk
2 green onions, chopped
1 small jalapeno pepper, seeded and finely chopped
2 to 3 tablespoons lime juice
2 tablespoons soy sauce
1 garlic clove, minced
1 teaspoon sugar
1 teaspoon minced fresh cilantro

1 teaspoon minced fresh gingerroot
1/8 teaspoon coconut extract

Flatten chicken to 1/4-in. thickness; cut lengthwise into 1-in.-wide strips. In a large resealable plastic bag, combine the milk, garlic, brown sugar, seasonings and extract. Add chicken; seal bag and turn to coat. Refrigerate for 8 hours or overnight.

In a bowl, whisk the sauce ingredients until blended. Cover and refrigerate until serving. Drain and discard marinade. Thread two chicken strips each onto metal or soaked wooden skewers.

Grill, uncovered, over medium-hot heat for 2-3 minutes on each side or until chicken juices run clear. Serve with peanut butter sauce. **Yield:** 8 servings (1 cup sauce).

Editor's Note: When cutting or seeding hot peppers, use rubber or plastic gloves to protect your hands. Avoid touching your face.

Bruschetta from the Grill

(Pictured below)

Dijon mustard, mayonnaise and oregano make a savory spread for chopped tomatoes, garlic and fresh basil in this fun twist on a favorite appetizer.
—Mary Nafis, Chino, California

- 1 pound plum tomatoes (about 6), seeded and chopped
- 1 cup finely chopped celery *or* fennel bulb
- 1/4 cup minced fresh basil
- 3 tablespoons balsamic vinegar
- 3 tablespoons olive oil
- 3 tablespoons Dijon mustard
- 2 garlic cloves, minced
- 1/2 teaspoon salt

MAYONNAISE SPREAD:

- 1/2 cup mayonnaise
- 1/4 cup Dijon mustard
- 1 tablespoon finely chopped green onion
- 1 garlic clove, minced
- 3/4 teaspoon dried oregano
- 1 loaf (1 pound) French bread, cut into 3/4-inch slices

In a large bowl, combine the first eight ingredients. Cover and refrigerate for at least 30 minutes. In a small bowl, combine the mayonnaise, mustard, onion, garlic and oregano; set aside.

Grill bread slices, uncovered, over medium-low heat for 1-2 minutes or until lightly toasted. Spread mayonnaise mixture over toasted side. Grill 1-2 minutes longer or until bottom of bread is toasted. Drain tomato mixture; spoon over top. **Yield:** 8-10 servings.

Grilled Glazed Drummies

My family prefers these mild-tasting chicken wings more than the traditional hot wings. They are great for any gathering.
—Laura Mahaffey, Annapolis, Maryland

- 1 cup ketchup
- 1/3 cup soy sauce
- 4 teaspoons honey
- 3/4 teaspoon ground ginger
- 1/2 teaspoon garlic powder
- 3 pounds chicken drumettes (about 24)

In a bowl, combine the ketchup, soy sauce, honey, ginger and garlic powder; mix well. Pour 1 cup marinade into a large resealable plastic bag; add the chicken. Seal bag and turn to coat; refrigerate for at least 4 hours or overnight. Cover and refrigerate remaining marinade for basting.

Drain and discard marinade from chicken. Grill chicken, covered, over medium heat for 5 minutes. Turn and baste with reserved marinade. Grill 10-15 minutes longer or until chicken juices run clear, turning and basting occasionally. **Yield:** 2 dozen.

Jalapeno Chicken Wraps

(Pictured above)

These easy appetizers are always a hit at parties! Zesty strips of chicken and bits of onion sit in jalapeno halves that are wrapped in bacon and grilled. Serve them with blue cheese or ranch salad dressing for dipping.
—Leslie Buenz, Tinley Park, Illinois

 1 **pound boneless skinless chicken breasts**
 1 **tablespoon garlic powder**
 1 **tablespoon onion powder**
 1 **tablespoon pepper**
 2 **teaspoons seasoned salt**
 1 **teaspoon paprika**
 1 **small onion, cut into strips**
 15 **jalapeno peppers, halved and seeded**
 1 **pound sliced bacon, halved widthwise**
Blue cheese salad dressing

Cut chicken into 2-in. x 1-1/2-in. strips. In a large resealable plastic bag, combine the garlic powder, onion powder, pepper, sea-soned salt and paprika; add chicken and shake to coat. Place a chicken and onion strip in each jalapeno half. Wrap each with a piece of ba-con and secure with toothpicks.

 Grill, uncovered, over indirect medium heat for 18-20 minutes or until chicken juices run clear and bacon is crisp, turning once. Serve with blue cheese dressing. **Yield:** 2-1/2 dozen.

Editor's Note: When cutting or seeding hot peppers, use rubber or plastic gloves to pro-tect your hands. Avoid touching your face.

■ ■ ■

Polynesian Kabobs

With their explosion of flavors and textures, these kabobs make a quick, satisfying snack.
—Chris Anderson, Morton, Illinois

 1 **can (8 ounces) unsweetened pineapple chunks**
 1 **package (12 ounces) pork breakfast sausage links**
 1 **can (8 ounces) whole water chestnuts, drained**
 1 **large sweet red pepper, cut into 1-inch chunks**
 2 **tablespoons honey**
 2 **teaspoons soy sauce**
 1/8 **teaspoon ground nutmeg**
Dash pepper

Drain pineapple, reserving 1 tablespoon juice (discard remaining juice or save for another use). Thread the sausages, water chestnuts, pineapple and red pepper alternately onto 12 metal or soaked wooden skewers.

 Grill kabobs, uncovered, over medium-hot heat for 7 minutes. In a small bowl, combine the honey, soy sauce, nutmeg, pepper and reserved pineapple juice. Turn the kabobs; brush with honey mixture. Grill 5-6 minutes longer or until the sausages are browned. **Yield:** 12 kabobs.

Artichoke Mushroom Caps

(Pictured below)

These crumb-topped mushrooms never last long at our get-togethers. The rich filling of cream cheese, artichoke hearts, Parmesan cheese and green onion is terrific.
—Ruth Lewis, West Newton, Pennsylvania

- 1 package (3 ounces) cream cheese, softened
- 1/4 cup mayonnaise
- 1 jar (6-1/2 ounces) marinated artichoke hearts, drained and finely chopped
- 1/4 cup grated Parmesan cheese
- 2 tablespoons finely chopped green onion
- 20 to 25 large fresh mushrooms, stems removed
- 1/4 cup seasoned bread crumbs
- 2 teaspoons olive oil

In a mixing bowl, beat cream cheese and mayonnaise until smooth. Beat in the artichokes, Parmesan cheese and onion. Lightly spray tops of mushrooms with nonstick cooking spray. Spoon cheese mixture into mushroom caps. Combine bread crumbs and oil; sprinkle over mushrooms.

Grill, covered, over indirect medium heat for 8-10 minutes or until mushrooms are tender. **Yield:** about 2 dozen.

■ ■ ■

Roasted Corn Salsa

(Pictured at right)

This colorful salsa is worth the extra time it takes to grill the ears of corn. The flavor goes well with barbecued meats, but it's also delicious served with chips.
—Nancy Horsburgh, Everett, Ontario

- 2 medium ears sweet corn in husks
- 2 medium tomatoes, chopped
- 1 small onion, chopped
- 2 tablespoons minced fresh cilantro
- 1 tablespoon lime juice
- 1 tablespoon finely chopped green pepper
- 1 tablespoon finely chopped sweet red pepper
- 1 teaspoon minced seeded jalapeno pepper
- 1/4 teaspoon salt

Dash pepper
Tortilla chips

To clean fresh mushrooms, you can simply brush them with a damp towel if they aren't too dirty. If they must be washed, do so quickly under cool running water; do not soak.

For stuffed mushrooms, remove stems. Scoop out some of the inside with a round 1/8 or 1/4 teaspoon. Then use the teaspoon to easily stuff the filling into the caps.

Peel back husks of corn but don't remove; remove silk. Replace husks and tie with kitchen string. Place corn in a bowl and cover with water; soak for 20 minutes. Drain. Grill corn, covered, over medium-high heat for 20-25 minutes or until husks are blackened and corn is tender, turning several times. Cool.

Remove corn from cobs and place in a bowl. Add tomatoes, onion, cilantro, lime juice, peppers, salt and pepper. Serve with tortilla chips. **Yield:** about 2-1/2 cups.

Editor's Note: When cutting or seeding hot peppers, use rubber or plastic gloves to protect your hands. Avoid touching your face.

■ ■ ■

Grilled Pork Appetizers

(Pictured at right)

Marinated in a sauce that is slightly sweetened with honey, these party-starters also make a wonderful entree when served over rice.
—*Susan LeBrun, Sulphur, Louisiana*

  1 pound boneless pork loin roast
  3 tablespoons soy sauce
  3 tablespoons honey
  1 tablespoon lemon juice

  1 tablespoon vegetable oil
  3 garlic cloves, minced
1/2 teaspoon ground ginger

Cut the pork into 1/8-in. slices, then cut each slice widthwise in half. In a large resealable plastic bag, combine the remaining ingredients; add the pork. Seal the bag and turn to coat; refrigerate for 2-4 hours, turning occasionally.

Drain and discard the marinade. Thread the pork onto metal or soaked wooden skewers. Grill, uncovered, over medium heat for 2-3 minutes on each side or until meat juices run clear, turning once. **Yield:** 8 servings.

Bacon-Wrapped Stuffed Jalapenos

(Pictured above)

Sunday is grill-out day for my husband, Cliff, and these zesty peppers are one of his specialties. We usually feature them at our annual Daytona 500 party. They disappear from the appetizer tray in no time.
—Therese Pollard, Hurst, Texas

- 24 medium jalapeno peppers
- 1 pound uncooked chorizo sausage *or* bulk spicy pork sausage
- 2 cups (8 ounces) shredded cheddar cheese
- 12 bacon strips, cut in half

Make a lengthwise cut in each jalapeno, about 1/8 in. deep; remove seeds. Combine the sausage and cheese; stuff into jalapenos. Wrap each with a piece of bacon; secure with toothpicks.

Prepare grill for indirect heat, using a drip pan. Place jalapenos over pan; grill, cov-ered, over indirect medium heat for 17-20 minutes on each side or until a meat ther-mometer inserted into filling reads 160°. Grill, covered, over direct heat 1-2 minutes longer or until bacon is crisp. **Yield:** 2 dozen.

Editor's Note: When cutting or seeding hot peppers, use rubber or plastic gloves to pro-tect your hands. Avoid touching your face.

■ ■ ■

Mushroom Cheese Bread

(Pictured at right)

This savory grilled bread is delightful with steak, baked potatoes and corn on the cob. My family prefers it to rolls at Sunday dinners. For variation, we sometimes use half cheddar cheese and half mozzarella.
—Dolly McDonald, Edmonton, Alberta

- 1 cup (4 ounces) shredded part-skim mozzarella cheese
- 1 can (4 ounces) mushroom stems and pieces, drained
- 1/3 cup mayonnaise
- 2 tablespoons shredded Parmesan cheese
- 2 tablespoons chopped green onion
- 1 loaf (1 pound) unsliced French bread

Seeding a Jalapeno Pepper

To reduce the heat of jalapenos and other hot peppers, cut the pep-pers in half; remove and discard the seeds and membranes. If you like very spicy foods, add the seeds to the dish you're making instead of discarding them.

In a bowl, combine the mozzarella cheese, mushrooms, mayonnaise, Parmesan cheese and onion. Cut bread in half lengthwise; spread cheese mixture over cut sides. Grill, covered, over indirect heat or broil 4 in. from the heat for 5-10 minutes or until lightly browned. Slice and serve warm.**Yield:** 10-12 servings.

■ ■ ■

Grilled Potato Skins

(Pictured at right)

Just about everyone loves these delicious appetizers. They're nice to serve outside when friends and family are over.
—Mitzi Sentiff, Alexandria, Virginia

2 large baking potatoes
2 tablespoons butter, melted
2 teaspoons minced fresh rosemary
  or 1/2 teaspoon dried rosemary, crushed
1/2 teaspoon salt

1/2 teaspoon pepper
  1 cup (4 ounces) shredded cheddar cheese
  3 bacon strips, cooked and crumbled
  2 green onions, chopped
Sour cream

Cut each potato lengthwise into four wedges. Cut away the white portion, leaving 1/4 in. on the potato skins. Place skins on a microwave-safe plate. Microwave, uncovered, on high for 8-10 minutes or until tender. Combine the butter, rosemary, salt and pepper; brush over both sides of potato skins.

Grill potatoes, skin side up, uncovered, over direct medium heat for 2-3 minutes or until lightly browned. Turn potatoes and position over indirect heat; grill 2 minutes longer. Top with cheese. Cover and grill 2-3 minutes longer or until cheese is melted. Sprinkle with bacon and onions. Serve with sour cream. **Yield:** 8 appetizers.

Editor's Note: This recipe was tested in a 1,100-watt microwave.

Grilled Pizza Bread

(Pictured above)

These fun French bread pizzas are great picnic fare for both kids and adults. Tasty on the grill, they can just as easily be baked in the oven.
—Edna Hoffman, Hebron, Indiana

- 1 **pound ground beef**
- 1/2 **cup chopped onion**
- 1 **can (8 ounces) tomato sauce**
- 1/2 **teaspoon salt**
- 1/2 **teaspoon dried oregano**
- 1 **loaf (1 pound) French bread**
- 1 **cup (4 ounces) shredded part-skim mozzarella cheese**
- 1 **can (2-1/4 ounces) sliced ripe olives, drained**

Sliced pepperoni, optional

In a skillet over medium heat, cook beef and onion until meat is no longer pink and onion is tender; drain. Stir in the tomato sauce, salt and oregano; simmer for 5-10 minutes.

Cut bread in half lengthwise and then widthwise. Spread meat mixture on cut side of bread; sprinkle with cheese, olives and pepperoni if desired. Loosely wrap bread individually in pieces of heavy-duty foil (about 24 in. x 18 in.); seal. Grill, covered, over medium heat for 15-20 minutes or until heated through. **Yield:** 4-6 servings.

Barbecued Hot Wings

(Pictured at left)

My husband can't get enough of these spicy chicken wings. They're excellent appetizers at cookouts. We serve them with blue cheese dressing and celery sticks.
—Anita Carr, Cadiz, Ohio

- 12 whole chicken wings (about 2-1/2 pounds)
- 1 bottle (8 ounces) Italian salad dressing
- 1/2 to 3/4 cup hot pepper sauce
- 1/8 to 1/2 teaspoon cayenne pepper
- 2 tablespoons butter, melted

Cut chicken wings into three sections; discard wing tips. In a bowl, combine salad dressing, hot pepper sauce and cayenne. Remove 1/2 cup for basting; cover and refrigerate. Place remaining sauce in a large resealable plastic bag; add chicken. Seal bag and turn to coat; refrigerate overnight. Drain and discard the marinade.

Grill wings, covered, over medium heat for 12-16 minutes, turning occasionally. Add butter to the reserved sauce; brush over wings. Grill, uncovered, 8-10 minutes longer or until juices run clear, basting and turning several times. **Yield:** 6-8 servings.

Editor's Note: 2-1/2 pounds of uncooked chicken wing sections may be substituted for the whole chicken wings. Omit the first step of the recipe.

■ ■ ■

Appetizer Shrimp Kabobs

(Pictured at right)

Talk about fuss-free! I love this appetizer because the skewers are simple to assemble, and they grill to perfection in minutes. Guests enjoy them alongside spicy seafood sauce.
—Dianna Knight, Clayton, North Carolina

- 3 tablespoons olive oil
- 3 garlic cloves, crushed
- 1/2 cup dry bread crumbs
- 1/2 teaspoon seafood seasoning
- 32 uncooked medium shrimp (about 1 pound), peeled and deveined

Seafood sauce

In a shallow bowl, combine the oil and garlic; let stand for 30 minutes. In another bowl, combine bread crumbs and seafood seasoning. Dip shrimp in oil mixture, then coat with crumb mixture.

Thread onto metal or soaked wooden skewers. Grill kabobs, covered, over medium heat for 2-3 minutes or until shrimp turn pink. Serve with seafood sauce. **Yield:** 8 servings.

·Salads·

When you're looking to keep the heat out of the kitchen on sweltering summer days, a refreshing salad fills the bill. While the beef, chicken, seafood or pork are grilling, assemble some cool, crisp greens and veggies. Then bring the hot and the cold together for a refreshingly tasty lunch or dinner.

Sirloin Caesar Salad

(Pictured at left)

A tangy sauce that combines bottled salad dressing, lemon juice and Dijon mustard flavors this filling, main-dish salad. You save on cleanup time because both the steak and bread are cooked on the grill.
—*Carol Sinclair, St. Elmo, Illinois*

1 boneless top sirloin steak (1 pound)
1 cup Caesar salad dressing
1/4 cup Dijon mustard
1/4 cup lemon juice
6 slices French bread (1 inch thick)
12 cups torn romaine
1 medium tomato, chopped

Place steak in a large resealable plastic bag. In a bowl, combine salad dressing, mustard and lemon juice; set aside 3/4 cup. Pour remaining dressing mixture over steak. Seal bag and refrigerate for 1 hour, turning occasionally.

Brush both sides of bread with 1/4 cup of the reserved dressing mixture. Grill bread, uncovered, over medium heat for 1-2 minutes on each side or until lightly toasted. Wrap in foil and set aside.

Drain steak, discarding marinade. Grill, covered, for 5-8 minutes on each side or until meat reaches desired doneness (for medium-rare, a meat thermometer should read 145°; medium, 160°; well-done, 170°). Place romaine and tomato on serving platter. Slice steak diagonally; arrange over salad. Serve with the bread and remaining dressing. **Yield:** 6 servings.

Pork Fajita Salad

(Pictured above)

For a refreshing take on fajitas, try this savory salad. Your crowd will love the festive layers and creamy guacamole.
—Iola Egle, McCook, Nebraska

- 1/4 cup olive oil
- 2 tablespoons lime juice
- 1 teaspoon dried oregano
- 1 teaspoon chili powder
- 4 boneless pork loin chops (1 inch thick, about 1-1/2 pounds)
- 2-1/4 cups chicken broth
- 1 cup uncooked long grain rice
- 2 ripe avocados, peeled
- 1 tablespoon lemon juice
- 1 medium tomato, seeded and chopped
- 1 jalapeno pepper, seeded and chopped
- 2 tablespoons minced fresh cilantro
- 1 tablespoon finely chopped onion
- 1 head iceberg lettuce, shredded
- 1 can (15 ounces) black beans, rinsed and drained
- 1 cup (4 ounces) shredded sharp cheddar cheese
- 1 jar (11 ounces) salsa
- 2 cups (16 ounces) sour cream

Sliced ripe olives and green onions

In a large resealable plastic bag, combine the first four ingredients. Add pork chops. Seal and turn to coat; refrigerate overnight, turning occasionally. Drain, discarding marinade. Grill chops, uncovered, over medium heat for 12-14 minutes or until meat juices run clear, turning once. Thinly slice pork; set aside.

In a saucepan, bring broth to a boil; stir in rice. Return to a boil. Reduce heat; cover and simmer for 15 minutes or until rice is tender. Cool.

Meanwhile, for guacamole, mash avocados with lemon juice. Stir in the tomato, jalapeno, cilantro and onion. In a 5-qt. glass salad bowl, layer the lettuce, beans, cheese, pork and guacamole. Spread with salsa. Combine the rice and sour cream; spread over the salsa. Garnish with olives and green onions. **Yield:** 6 servings.

Editor's Note: When cutting or seeding hot peppers, use rubber or plastic gloves to protect your hands. Avoid touching your face.

■ ■ ■

Chicken Caesar Salad

(Pictured right)

When I ask my husband what he wants for dinner, he usually requests this hearty salad!
—Kay Anderson, Bear, Delaware

- 2 boneless skinless chicken breast halves (1/2 pound)
- 2 teaspoons olive oil

1/8 teaspoon dried basil
1/8 teaspoon dried oregano
1/4 teaspoon garlic salt
1/4 teaspoon pepper
1/4 teaspoon paprika
  4 cups torn romaine
  1 small tomato, thinly sliced
Caesar salad dressing
Caesar salad croutons

Brush the chicken with oil. Combine basil, oregano, garlic salt, pepper and paprika; sprinkle over chicken. Grill, uncovered, over medium-low heat for 12-15 minutes or until juices run clear, turning several times.

Arrange romaine and tomato on plates. Cut chicken into strips; place on top. Drizzle with dressing. Sprinkle with croutons. **Yield:** 2 servings.

■ ■ ■

Grilled Salmon Salad

For a cool summer supper, try this fresh-tasting salmon salad, created by our Test Kitchen staff. Lightly dressed with tangy raspberry vinegar, it gets a little crunch from onion and celery.

  2 salmon fillets (about 1-1/2 pounds)
  2 celery ribs, chopped
1/2 cup finely chopped red onion
  2 tablespoons snipped fresh dill
    or 2 teaspoons dill weed
DRESSING:
1/4 cup raspberry vinegar
  1 tablespoon olive oil
1-1/2 teaspoons sugar
1/2 teaspoon salt
1/4 teaspoon pepper

Coat grill rack with nonstick cooking spray before starting the grill. Cut salmon fillets widthwise into 4-in. pieces; place skin side down on grill. Grill, covered, over medium-hot heat for 12-15 minutes or until fish flakes easily with a fork. Cover and refrigerate for 1 hour.

Bone, skin and flake salmon; place in a bowl. Add celery, onion and dill. Combine the dressing ingredients; pour over salad and gently toss to coat. Serve or refrigerate; stir before serving. **Yield:** 4 servings.

Grilled Chicken and Pear Salad

(Pictured below)

A homemade vinaigrette pairs well with grilled chicken, pears and Brie in this salad.
—Janet Duran, Des Moines, Washington

- 5 boneless skinless chicken breasts (4 ounces *each*)
- 7 cups torn mixed salad greens
- 2 ounces Brie *or* Camembert cheese, cubed
- 2 medium pears, chopped
- 1/4 cup chopped pecans, toasted
- 1/4 cup apple juice concentrate, thawed
- 2 tablespoons canola oil
- 4-1/2 teaspoons cider vinegar
- 2 teaspoons Dijon mustard
- 1/4 teaspoon salt
- 1/8 teaspoon pepper

Coat grill rack with nonstick cooking spray before starting the grill. Grill chicken, covered, over medium heat for 6-8 minutes on each side or until juices run clear.

Arrange the salad greens, cheese, pears and pecans on individual plates. Slice chicken; arrange over salad. In a jar with a tight-fitting lid, combine the apple juice concentrate, oil, vinegar, mustard, salt and pepper; shake well. Drizzle over salad and serve immediately. **Yield:** 5 servings.

Pineapple Chicken Salad

(Pictured at right)

Although I love to cook, I appreciate recipes that have me out of the kitchen so I can spend time with my family. We love this main-dish salad.
—Stephanie Moon, Green Bay, Wisconsin

- 4 boneless skinless chicken breast halves (1-1/4 pounds)
- 1/4 teaspoon lemon-pepper seasoning
- 1 can (8 ounces) unsweetened sliced pineapple
- 3 tablespoons vegetable oil
- 2 tablespoons soy sauce
- 1 tablespoon white vinegar
- 1 tablespoon honey
- 1/4 teaspoon ground ginger
- 8 cups assorted vegetables (lettuce, red onion, carrots, sweet red pepper and broccoli)

Salted peanuts, optional

Sprinkle chicken with lemon-pepper. Grill over medium-hot heat for 15-18 minutes or until juices run clear, turning once. Set aside and keep warm.

Drain pineapple, reserving 2 tablespoons juice (discard remaining juice or save for another use); set pineapple aside. In a jar with a tight-fitting lid, combine oil, soy sauce, vine-

1 bottle (16 ounces) Italian salad
dressing
1 to 2 tablespoons minced fresh
rosemary *or* 1 to 2 teaspoons dried
rosemary, crushed
7 medium ears sweet corn, husks
removed
7 plum tomatoes, sliced
7 cups torn fresh spinach

Coat grill rack with nonstick cooking spray before starting the grill. In a large resealable plastic bag, combine the dressing and rosemary; add corn. Seal bag and turn to coat; remove corn from marinade. Seal bag and refrigerate marinade.

Grill corn, covered, over medium heat for 15-18 minutes or until tender, turning occasionally. Return corn to the marinade; add tomatoes. Seal bag and turn to coat; refrigerate for at least 4 hours or overnight.

Drain corn and tomatoes, reserving marinade. Cut corn off the cob. Arrange spinach on salad plates; top with tomatoes and corn. Drizzle with reserved marinade. **Yield:** 7 servings

gar, honey, ginger and reserved pineapple juice; shake well. Brush some of the dressing over pineapple; grill for 2 minutes.

Cut chicken into strips. Arrange vegetables on serving plates; top with pineapple and chicken. Sprinkle with peanuts if desired. Serve with remaining dressing. **Yield:** 4 servings.

■ ■ ■

Grilled Corn Salad

(Pictured at right)

Our family and friends always rave over this dish at Sunday afternoon barbecues. We usually grill the corn the night before. I especially like this recipe because it lets me share the cooking with my husband, Rich. We call him "King of the Grill!"
—Patty Cook, West Palm Beach, Florida

Beef Tenderloin Salad

(Pictured above)

Slices of tender beef, fresh asparagus and juicy tomatoes highlight this attractive, main-dish salad from our Test Kitchen staff.

- 1/4 cup mayonnaise
- 2 tablespoons Dijon mustard
- 1 tablespoon milk
- 2 teaspoons white wine vinegar
- 1 teaspoon prepared horseradish
- 1-1/4 teaspoons sugar
- 3/8 teaspoon salt, *divided*
- 1/4 teaspoon pepper, *divided*
- 8 cups water
- 1 pound fresh asparagus, cut into 2-inch pieces
- 4 beef tenderloin steaks (4 ounces *each*)
- 1 large garlic clove, peeled and halved
- 6 cups torn mixed salad greens
- 2 large ripe tomatoes, cut into wedges

For salad dressing, in a bowl, whisk the mayonnaise, mustard, milk, vinegar, horseradish, sugar, 1/8 teaspoon salt and 1/8 teaspoon pepper. Cover and refrigerate. In a large saucepan, bring water to a boil. Add asparagus; cover and boil for 3 minutes. Drain and immediately place asparagus in ice water; drain and pat dry. Cover and refrigerate.

If grilling the steaks, coat grill rack with nonstick cooking spray before starting the grill. Rub steaks with garlic; discard garlic. Sprinkle with remaining salt and pepper. Grill steaks, covered, over medium heat or broil 4-6 in. from the heat for 6-8 minutes on each side or until meat reaches desired doneness (for medium-rare, a meat thermometer should read 145°; medium, 160°; well-done, 170°).

On four serving plates, arrange the greens, tomatoes and asparagus. Thinly slice beef; place over salad. Drizzle with dressing. **Yield:** 4 servings.

■ ■ ■

Citrus Pork Salad

During our hot summers, I rely on salads. In this recipe, the pork is grilled so I can stay out of the kitchen.
—Roberta Whitesell, Phoenix, Arizona

DRESSING:
- 1/2 cup orange juice
- 2 tablespoons olive oil
- 2 tablespoons cider vinegar
- 1 tablespoon grated orange peel
- 2 teaspoons honey
- 2 teaspoons Dijon mustard
- 1/2 teaspoon coarsely ground pepper

SALAD:
- 1 pork tenderloin (1 pound), trimmed
- 10 cups torn salad greens
- 2 seedless oranges, peeled and sliced
- 1/4 cup chopped pistachios *or* cashews, optional

In a small bowl, combine all dressing ingredi-

ents; cover and chill. Grill pork, covered, over medium heat for 15-20 minutes or until a meat thermometer reads 160°, turning occasionally. Let stand for 5 minutes; thinly slice tenderloin.

To serve, line large platter with greens; top with orange sections and tenderloin. Sprinkle with nuts if desired. Drizzle with dressing. **Yield:** 5 servings.

■ ■ ■

Grilled Three-Pepper Salad

(Pictured above)

I'm always trying new recipes. This one's both flavorful and colorful.
—*Ruth Wickard, York, Pennsylvania*

2 **each large green, sweet red and yellow peppers, cut into 1-inch pieces**
1 **large red onion, halved and thinly sliced**

1 **pound bulk mozzarella cheese, cut into bite-size cubes**
1 **can (6 ounces) pitted ripe olives, drained and halved**
VINAIGRETTE:
2/3 **cup olive oil**
1/3 **cup red wine vinegar**
2 **tablespoons lemon juice**
2 **tablespoons Dijon mustard**
1 **tablespoon minced fresh basil or 1 teaspoon dried basil**
1/2 **teaspoon cayenne pepper**
1/2 **teaspoon garlic powder**

Thread peppers onto metal or soaked wooden skewers; grill over medium heat for 10-12 minutes or until edges are browned. Remove from skewers and place in a large bowl. Add onion, mozzarella and olives; toss gently. Cover and refrigerate.

Combine vinaigrette ingredients in a jar with tight-fitting lid; shake well. Pour over the pepper mixture just before serving; toss to coat. **Yield:** 10-12 servings.

Pasta Salad with Steak

(Pictured at left)

While there are quite a few ingredients in this recipe, it doesn't take too long to make —and cleanup afterward's a snap.
—*Julie DeRuwe, Oakville, Washington*

- 3/4 cup olive oil
- 2 tablespoons lemon juice
- 2 teaspoons dried oregano
- 1 tablespoon Dijon mustard
- 2 teaspoons red wine vinegar
- 1 teaspoon sugar
- 1/2 teaspoon salt
- 1/2 teaspoon pepper
- 3 cups cooked small shell pasta
- 1 sirloin steak (1 pound)

RUB:

- 1 tablespoon olive oil
- 3 garlic cloves, minced
- 2 teaspoons dried oregano
- 2 teaspoons pepper
- 1 teaspoon sugar

SALAD:

- 2/3 cup diced cucumber
- 1/2 cup crumbled blue *or* feta cheese
- 1/4 cup sliced ripe olives

Against the Grain

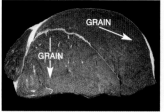

National Cattlemen's Beef Assoc. and Cattlemen's Beef Board

Bundles of long muscle fibers give meat its texture; the "grain" refers to the direction these fibers run.

Cutting in the opposite direction of the fibers, or "against the grain," shortens them. This makes the meat tender to chew. Cutting against the grain is important when carving roasts or preparing meat for stir-fries and kabobs.

Not all cuts of meat have fibers that run vertically or horizontally. Some fibers run diagonally, while others, like the beef round tip steak above, have multiple muscle sections. The fibers on the left side run vertically, while the fibers on the right diagonally. To slice this cut of meat, carve both sections separately against the grain.

1/4 cup chopped red onion
1/4 cup minced fresh parsley
  1 jar (2 ounces) diced pimientos,
    drained
Iceberg *or* romaine lettuce

In a bowl, combine the first eight ingredients; set half of the dressing aside. Place pasta in another bowl; add remaining dressing. Toss to coat; cover and refrigerate.

Pierce steak with a fork. Combine rub ingredients; rub over steak. Cover and refrigerate for at least 15 minutes. Grill steak, uncovered, over medium heat for 9-10 minutes on each side or until meat reaches desired doneness (for medium-rare, a meat thermometer should read 145°; medium, 160°; well-done, 170°). Let stand for 10 minutes.

Meanwhile, add the cucumber, cheese, olives, onion, parsley and pimientos to the pasta; mix well. Spoon onto a lettuce-lined platter. Slice the steak and arrange over salad. Serve with reserved dressing. **Yield:** 4 servings.

■ ■ ■

Italian Grilled Chicken Salad

(Pictured at right)

Simple yet elegant, this entree salad is one of my husband's favorites.
—*Lisa Rawski, Milwaukee, Wisconsin*

  3 tablespoons balsamic vinegar
  3 tablespoons olive oil
  1 teaspoon dried rosemary, crushed
  1 garlic clove, minced
1/2 teaspoon salt
1/2 teaspoon coarsely ground pepper
  4 boneless skinless chicken breast
    halves (4 ounces *each*)
  4 ounces Italian bread, sliced
  4 cups torn romaine

  2 cups chopped seeded tomatoes
  1 cup white kidney *or* cannellini beans
1/3 cup minced fresh basil

In a jar with a tight-fitting lid, combine the first six ingredients; shake well. Remove 1 tablespoon vinegar mixture; brush over chicken. Cover and refrigerate for 30 minutes. Set aside remaining vinegar mixture.

Coat grill rack with nonstick cooking spray before starting grill. Grill chicken, covered, over medium heat for 4-6 minutes on each side or until juices run clear. Brush bread slices with 1 tablespoon reserved vinegar mixture. Grill bread, uncovered, over medium heat for 2 minutes on each side or until toasted. Slice chicken and cut bread into cubes; set aside.

In a large bowl, combine the romaine, tomatoes, beans, basil and bread cubes. Drizzle with remaining vinegar mixture; toss to coat. Arrange on salad plates. Top with chicken. Serve immediately. **Yield:** 4 servings.

·Sides·

Although side dishes may often take a back seat to main courses, their supporting role is just as award-worthy! After all, what's a juicy steak without Lemon Garlic Mushrooms and Skewered Potatoes? And an all-American meal of hamburgers and brats isn't complete without Grilled Sweet Corn.

Grilled Asparagus Medley

(Pictured at left)

This colorful veggie recipe happened by accident. One evening, I didn't have room on the grill for all the things I wanted to prepare, so I threw two of the dishes together and came up with this medley. It goes great with any grilled meat.
—Pam Gaspers, Hastings, Nebraska

1 pound fresh asparagus, trimmed
1 *each* sweet red, yellow and green pepper, julienned
1 cup sliced fresh mushrooms
1 medium tomato, chopped
1 medium onion, sliced
1 can (2-1/4 ounces) sliced ripe olives, drained
2 garlic cloves, minced
2 tablespoons olive oil
1 teaspoon minced fresh parsley
1/2 teaspoon salt
1/2 teaspoon pepper
1/4 teaspoon lemon-pepper seasoning
1/4 teaspoon dill weed

In a disposable foil pan, combine the vegetables, olives and garlic; drizzle with oil and toss to coat. Sprinkle with parsley, salt, pepper, lemon-pepper and dill; toss to coat. Grill, covered, over indirect medium heat for 20-25 minutes or until vegetables are crisp-tender, stirring occasionally. **Yield:** 8 servings.

Vegetable Grilling Chart

There's no better way to bring out the naturally delicious taste of garden produce than by grilling them. Follow these guidelines. Grill vegetables until tender. Turn halfway through grilling time for even cooking.

Type	Weight or Thickness	Heat	Approximate Cooking Time (in minutes)
Asparagus	1/2 in. thick	medium/direct	6 to 8
Sweet peppers	halved or quartered	medium/direct	8 to 10
Corn	in husk	medium/direct	25 to 30
	husk removed	medium/direct	10 to 12
Eggplant	1/2-in. slices	medium/direct	8 to 10
Fennel	1/4-in. slices	medium/direct	10 to 12
Mushrooms	Button	medium/direct	8 to 10
	Portobello, whole	medium/direct	12 to 15
Onions	1/2-in. slices	medium/direct	8 to 12
Potatoes	whole	medium/indirect	45 to 60

Barbecued Olive Bread

We cook on the grill all year long, so this zesty olive-topped bread accompanies everything from pork to beef to chicken.
—Patricia Gasper, Peoria, Illinois

> 1 can (4-1/2 ounces) chopped ripe olives, drained
> 1/2 cup chopped stuffed olives
> 3/4 cup shredded Colby/Monterey Jack cheese
> 3/4 cup grated Parmesan cheese, *divided*
> 1/4 cup butter, melted
> 1 tablespoon olive oil
> 2 garlic cloves, minced
> 3 drops hot pepper sauce
> 2 cups biscuit/baking mix
> 2/3 cup milk
> 2 tablespoons minced fresh parsley
> Paprika

In a bowl, combine the olives, Colby/Monterey Jack cheese, 1/2 cup Parmesan cheese, butter, oil, garlic and hot pepper sauce; set aside. In another bowl, combine the biscuit mix, milk, 2 tablespoons Parmesan cheese and parsley just until moistened. Press into two greased 9-in. disposable aluminum pie pans. Top with the olive mixture; sprinkle with paprika and remaining Parmesan cheese.

Grill bread, covered, over indirect heat for 8-10 minutes or until bottom crust is golden brown when edge of bread is lifted with a spatula. **Yield:** 2 loaves (6-8 servings each).

■ ■ ■

Eggplant Mexicano

Salsa gives fun flavor to eggplant slices in this side dish that goes together fast and grills in minutes.
—Alyce de Roos, Sarnia, Ontario

1/2 cup vegetable oil
1 teaspoon garlic powder
1 teaspoon dried oregano
1 medium eggplant, peeled and cut into 1/2-inch slices
2/3 cup salsa, warmed
1/2 cup shredded Monterey Jack cheese

In a bowl, combine the oil, garlic powder and oregano; brush over both sides of eggplant. Grill, uncovered, over indirect medium heat for 2 minutes on each side or until tender. To serve, spoon a small amount of salsa into center of each; sprinkle with cheese. **Yield:** 6 servings.

■ ■ ■

Grilled Vegetable Skewers

(Pictured at right)

Seasoned with fresh herbs, these colorful kabobs showcase the best of summer's bounty. They complement any meaty entree.
—Susan Bourque, Danielson, Connecticut

1 medium ear fresh *or* frozen sweet corn, thawed and quartered
1 small zucchini, quartered
1/4 small red onion, halved
4 cherry tomatoes
1/4 teaspoon dried basil
1/4 teaspoon dried rosemary, crushed
1/4 teaspoon dried thyme
1/8 teaspoon garlic powder
1/8 teaspoon salt
1/8 teaspoon pepper

Place corn on a microwave-safe plate. Cover with waxed paper. Microwave on high for 2 minutes. Coat grill rack with nonstick cooking spray before starting grill. On two metal or soaked wooden skewers, alternately thread corn, zucchini, onion and tomatoes. Lightly coat vegetables with nonstick cooking spray.

In a small bowl, combine seasonings; sprinkle over vegetables.

Grill, covered, over medium heat for 3 minutes on each side or until vegetables are tender, turning three times. **Yield:** 2 servings.

How do you choose which skewers are right for your kabobs?

Wood (bamboo) skewers are inexpensive and disposable and are widely available in lengths from 4 to 10 inches. They don't absorb heat so they can go from the grill to your guests' plates. But wood skewers may ignite over a hot flame. To avoid this, first soak them in water for about 30 minutes.

If you plan on cooking kabobs often, invest in reusable stainless steel skewers. Find ones that are squared or flat. These hold food more securely, and the food won't turn on them as you rotate the skewers while grilling. Metal skewers get hot during cooking, and the food may cook faster, so keep a close eye on them. Remove food from them before serving. Treat metal skewers with a light coat of cooking spray before threading on food. This makes the food easier to remove when cooked.

Special Grilled Veggies

(Pictured below)

I fixed this colorful side dish on Father's Day one year and it's been requested many times since. It goes well with any grilled meat, chicken or seafood.
—Kimberly Hennes-Skar, Minot, North Dakota

1/2 cup red wine vinegar
1/4 cup olive oil
2 garlic cloves, minced
1/2 teaspoon dried basil
1/2 teaspoon dried thyme
1/2 teaspoon lemon-pepper seasoning
1 pound fresh asparagus, trimmed
1 large red onion, sliced and separated into rings
1 large sweet red pepper, cut into 1-inch strips

1 large sweet yellow pepper, cut into 1-inch strips

In a large resealable plastic bag, combine the first six ingredients; mix well. Add the vegetables and turn to coat. Seal and refrigerate for 1 hour or overnight, turning once.

Drain and reserve marinade. Place vegetables in a grill basket or disposable foil pan with slits cut in the bottom. Grill, uncovered, over medium-high heat for 5 minutes. Turn; baste with reserved marinade. Grill 5-8 minutes longer or until the vegetables are tender. **Yield:** 4-6 servings.

■ ■ ■

Cabbage on the Grill

My father first fixed these bacon-wrapped cabbage wedges a few years ago. Now I make them for my family when we put steak and potatoes on the grill. Even our three daughters like them.
—Demi Rice, Macks Creek, Missouri

1 medium head cabbage (about 2 pounds)
4 teaspoons butter, softened
1 teaspoon salt
1/2 teaspoon garlic powder
1/4 teaspoon pepper
2 tablespoons grated Parmesan cheese
4 bacon strips

Cut cabbage into four wedges; place each on a piece of double-layered heavy-duty foil (about 18 in. square). Spread cut sides with butter. Sprinkle with salt, garlic powder, pepper and Parmesan cheese. Wrap a bacon strip around each wedge.

Fold the foil around the cabbage wedges and seal tightly. Grill, covered, over medium heat for 40 minutes or until the cabbage is tender, turning twice. **Yield:** 4 servings.

Grilled Peppers And Zucchini

(Pictured above)

This versatile side dish is so simple and quick that I had to share it. Grilling the colorful veggies in a foil packet means one less dish to wash, but I sometimes stir-fry the mixture on the stovetop.
—Karen Anderson, Fair Oaks, California

1 medium green pepper, julienned
1 medium sweet red pepper, julienned
2 medium zucchini, julienned
1 tablespoon butter
2 teaspoons soy sauce

Place the vegetables on a double layer of heavy-duty foil (about 18 in. x 15 in.). Dot with butter; drizzle with soy sauce. Fold foil around vegetables and seal tightly. Grill, covered, over medium heat for 10-15 minutes or until vegetables are crisp-tender. **Yield:** 3-4 servings.

Bacon Potato Bundles

Cut cleanup by grilling this versatile side dish in foil packets. Wrap the bacon around the veggies and secure it with a toothpick for a fun presentation. Add carrots, squash or whatever vegetables you wish.
—Dorothy Sutherland, Seven Points, Texas

4 large baking potatoes, peeled and quartered
8 onion slices
8 green pepper slices
4 bacon strips
Salt and pepper to taste

Place potatoes on four pieces of greased heavy-duty aluminum foil. Place onion and green pepper between potato quarters; top with bacon. Sprinkle with salt and pepper. Wrap in foil. Grill, covered, over medium-high heat for 40-50 minutes or until the potatoes are tender, turning once. **Yield:** 4 servings.

Vegetable Kabobs

(Pictured below)

*This recipe's savory marinade shines through
because it's brushed on while grilling.*
—Deb Anderson, Joplin, Missouri

    2   tablespoons orange juice
        concentrate
    2   tablespoons soy sauce
4-1/2   teaspoons honey
    1   teaspoon vegetable oil
  1/4   teaspoon salt
  1/8   teaspoon crushed red pepper
        flakes
    2   medium red potatoes, cut into
        1-1/2-inch chunks
    1   teaspoon water
    1   medium zucchini, cut into 1/4-inch
        slices
    1   medium sweet yellow pepper, cut
        into 1-inch pieces
   14   cherry tomatoes

In a bowl, combine the first six ingredients; mix well and set aside. Place potatoes and water in a 1-1/2-qt. microwave-safe bowl. Cover and microwave on high for 3-4 minutes; drain.

On metal or soaked bamboo skewers, alternately thread potatoes, zucchini, yellow pepper and tomatoes. Grill, uncovered, over medium heat for 8-10 minutes or until tender, turning and basting frequently with orange juice mixture. **Yield:** 7 servings.

■ ■ ■

Grilled Garlic Bread

(Pictured at right)

*Until several years ago, I'd never thought of
making garlic bread outdoors, but Grilled
Garlic Bread turns out nice and crispy.*
—Priscilla Weaver, Hagerstown, Maryland

    1   loaf (16 ounces) French bread
  1/4   cup butter, softened
    1   teaspoon garlic powder

Cut the bread into eight slices. In a small bowl, combine the butter and garlic powder. Spread on one side of each slice of bread. Place bread, buttered side up, on a grill over medium heat for 2 minutes or until browned. Turn and grill 2 minutes longer or until browned. **Yield:** 8 servings.

■ ■ ■

Colorful Grilled Veggies

I put this combination together one day when trying to serve a side dish other than mushrooms in butter. Everyone loves this pleasantly seasoned medley.
—Susan Jesson, Oro Station, Ontario

- 10 **cherry tomatoes, halved**
- 2 **celery ribs, thinly sliced**
- 1 **medium green pepper, sliced**
- 1 **medium sweet red pepper, sliced**
- 1 **medium red onion, sliced and separated into rings**
- 1 **cup sliced fresh mushrooms**
- 1 **tablespoon red wine vinegar**
- 1 **tablespoon olive oil**
- 1 **teaspoon lemon juice**
- 1 **garlic clove, minced**
- 1 **teaspoon dried basil**
- 1/2 **teaspoon salt**
- 1/2 **teaspoon pepper**

Divide the vegetables between two pieces of heavy-duty foil (about 18 in. square). In a small bowl, combine the remaining ingredients; drizzle over vegetables. Fold foil around vegetables and seal tightly. Grill, covered, over medium heat for 10-15 minutes or until the vegetables are crisp-tender. **Yield:** 6 servings.

 If you're short on time, give firm vegetables, like potatoes and carrots, a jump-start by cooking them halfway done in the microwave. Then you can finish them on the grill.

Lemon Garlic Mushrooms

(Pictured above)

I baste whole mushrooms with a lemony sauce to prepare this simple side dish. Using skewers or a grill basket makes it easy to turn these mushrooms.
—Diane Hixon, Niceville, Florida

1/4 cup lemon juice
3 tablespoons minced fresh parsley
2 tablespoons olive oil
3 garlic cloves, minced
Pepper to taste
1 pound large fresh mushrooms

In a small bowl, combine the first five ingredients; set aside. Grill mushrooms, covered, over medium-hot heat for 5 minutes. Brush generously with lemon mixture. Turn mushrooms; grill 5-8 minutes longer or until tender. Brush with remaining lemon mixture before serving. **Yield:** 4 servings.

Grilled Greek-Style Zucchini

I made this side dish for my Women's Health Initiative Group at our local university, and everyone loved it. The grilled vegetables pick up a pleasantly mild flavor from the lemon juice and herb seasonings. Serve this alongside a meaty main course.
—Betty Washburn, Reno, Nevada

4 small zucchini, thinly sliced
1 medium tomato, seeded and chopped
1/4 cup pitted ripe olives, halved
2 tablespoons chopped green onion
4 teaspoons olive oil
2 teaspoons lemon juice
1/2 teaspoon dried oregano
1/2 teaspoon garlic salt
1/4 teaspoon pepper
2 tablespoons grated Parmesan cheese

In a bowl, combine the zucchini, tomato, olives and onion. Combine oil, lemon juice, oregano, garlic salt and pepper; pour over vegetables and toss to coat.

Place on a double thickness of heavy-duty foil (about 23 in. x 18 in.). Fold foil around vegetables and seal tightly. Grill, covered, over medium heat for 10-15 minutes or until vegetables are tender. Sprinkle with Parmesan cheese. **Yield:** 6 servings.

■■■

Grilled Potato Fans

(Pictured at right)

If you're looking for a change from plain baked potatoes, try these tender and buttery potato fans seasoned with oregano, garlic powder, celery and onion. To cut down on grilling time, I sometimes microwave the potatoes for 5-6 minutes before slicing them.
—Jennifer Black-Ortiz, San Jose, California

> 6 medium baking potatoes
> 2 medium onions, halved and thinly sliced
> 6 tablespoons butter, cubed
> 1/4 cup finely chopped celery
> 1 teaspoon salt
> 1 teaspoon dried oregano
> 1/4 teaspoon garlic powder
> 1/4 teaspoon pepper

With a sharp knife, make cuts 1/2 in. apart in each potato, leaving slices attached at the bottom. Fan the potatoes slightly. Place each on a piece of heavy-duty foil (about 12 in. square).

Insert onions and butter between potato slices. Sprinkle with celery, salt, oregano, garlic powder and pepper. Fold foil around potatoes and seal tightly. Grill, covered, over medium-hot heat for 40-45 minutes or until tender. **Yield:** 6 servings.

Fast Potato Fans

To create an attractive potato fan, set a clean uncooked potato on a cutting board. Place two wooden spoons on opposite sides of the potato, nesting its length between their handles.

With one hand holding the vegetable and the spoons in place, use a sharp knife to slice the potato widthwise. The knife should touch the handles of the spoons at every slice, leaving the slices attached at the bottom of the potato.

Marinated Grilled Vegetables

(Pictured above)

We camp out often in summer and do a lot of cooking over charcoal. These veggies go great with any grilled meat. Sometimes I also thread brown-and-serve rolls on skewers, brush with melted butter and cook them over the coals for 10-15 minutes. They get crusty on the outside, yet stay soft in the center.
—Marian Platt, Sequim, Washington

  6 small onions, halved
  4 carrots, cut into 1-1/2-inch chunks
1/3 cup olive oil
1/2 teaspoon dried rosemary
1/4 teaspoon dried marjoram
Dash pepper
  6 small pattypan *or* sunburst squash
  1 medium zucchini, cut into 1-inch chunks
  1 medium green pepper, cut into 1-inch pieces
  1 medium sweet red pepper, cut into 1-inch pieces

In a saucepan, cook onions and carrots in water for 10 minutes or until crisp-tender; drain. In a large bowl, combine oil and seasonings; add all of the vegetables and mix well. Cover and refrigerate for at least 1 hour.

Drain and reserve the marinade. Thread the vegetables alternately onto skewers. Grill, uncovered, over medium heat for 15-20 minutes or until tender. Turn and baste with the marinade every 5 minutes. **Yield:** 6 servings.

Campfire Potatoes

(Pictured below)

The onion, cheddar cheese and Worcestershire sauce combine to make a super side dish for any grilled entree. Plus, cooking in the foil makes cleanup a breeze.
—JoAnn Dettbarn, Brainerd, Minnesota

> 5 **medium potatoes, peeled and thinly sliced**
> 1 **medium onion, sliced**
> 6 **tablespoons butter**
> 1/3 **cup shredded cheddar cheese**
> 2 **tablespoons minced fresh parsley**
> 1 **tablespoon Worcestershire sauce**
> **Salt and pepper to taste**
> 1/3 **cup chicken broth**

Place the potatoes and onion on a large piece of heavy-duty foil (about 20 in. x 20 in.); dot with butter. Combine the cheese, parsley, Worcestershire sauce, salt and pepper; sprinkle over potatoes. Fold foil up around potatoes and add broth. Tightly seal the edges of foil. Grill, covered, over medium heat for 35-40 minutes or until potatoes are tender. **Yield:** 4-6 servings.

■ ■ ■

Oregano Onions

My dad, who enjoys onions, invented this tasty side dish many years ago. The tender seasoned onions go well with all types of grilled meat, so we have them often, especially during the warm grilling season.
—Marcia Preston, Clear Lake, Iowa

> 5 **large onions, sliced**
> 6 **teaspoons butter**
> 1-1/2 **teaspoons dried oregano**
> **Pepper to taste**

Divide onions between two pieces of double-layered heavy-duty foil (about 22 in. x 18 in.) coated with nonstick cooking spray. Top each with butter, oregano and pepper. Fold foil around the mixture and seal tightly. Grill, covered, over indirect heat for 30-40 minutes or until onions are tender. **Yield:** 10 servings.

Grilled Three-Cheese Potatoes

(Pictured below)

While this is delicious grilled, I've also cooked it in the oven at 350° for an hour. Add cubed ham to it and you can serve it as a full-meal main dish.
—Margaret Hanson-Maddox, Montpelier, Indiana

- 6 large potatoes, sliced 1/4 inch thick
- 2 medium onions, chopped
- 1/3 cup grated Parmesan cheese
- 1 cup (4 ounces) shredded sharp cheddar cheese, *divided*
- 1 cup (4 ounces) shredded part-skim mozzarella cheese, *divided*
- 1 pound sliced bacon, cooked and crumbled
- 1/4 cup butter, cubed
- 1 tablespoon minced fresh *or* dried chives
- 1 to 2 teaspoons seasoned salt
- 1/2 teaspoon pepper

Divide the potatoes and onions equally between two pieces of heavy-duty foil (about 18-in. square) that have been coated with nonstick cooking spray. Combine Parmesan cheese and 3/4 cup each cheddar and mozzarella; sprinkle over the potatoes and onions. Top with bacon, butter, chives, seasoned salt and pepper.

Bring opposite ends of foil together over filling and fold down several times. Fold un-sealed ends toward filling and crimp tightly. Grill, covered, over medium heat for 35-40 minutes or until potatoes are tender. Remove from the grill. Open foil carefully and sprinkle with remaining cheeses. **Yield:** 6-8 servings.

■ ■ ■

Sweet Onions with Radish Sauce

I stir up a light, creamy sauce to complement sweet grilled onions. This side dish is a special treat in spring, when Vidalia onions are in season.
—Phyllis Schmalz, Kansas City, Kansas

- 2 large sweet onions, cut into 1/2-inch slices
- 1/4 cup olive oil
- 1/2 teaspoon salt
- 1/8 teaspoon pepper
- 1/2 cup plain yogurt
- 1 tablespoon mayonnaise
- 1/4 cup chopped radishes
- 2 tablespoons snipped fresh dill *or* 2 teaspoons dill weed

Brush both sides of onion slices with oil; sprinkle with salt and pepper. Place the onions directly on grill rack. Grill, covered, over indirect heat for 8 minutes on each side or until crisp-tender. In a small bowl, combine the yogurt, mayonnaise, radishes and dill. Serve with the onions. **Yield:** 4 servings.

Zucchini with Salsa

(Pictured above)

I top zucchini slices with chunky homemade salsa to make this scrumptious side dish that cooks on the grill. I fix it often in the summer when I have the fresh vegetables on hand from my garden.
—Carole Hildebrand, Kelseyville, California

- 4 medium zucchini, sliced
- 3 medium tomatoes, diced
- 1 medium onion, diced
- 3 green onions, sliced
- 2 jalapeno peppers, seeded and minced
- 2 garlic cloves, minced
- 1 tablespoon minced fresh cilantro

Salt and pepper to taste

Divide zucchini between two pieces of heavy-duty foil (about 20 in. x 18 in.). In a bowl, combine the remaining ingredients; spoon over zucchini. Fold foil around vegetables and seal tightly. Grill, covered, over indirect heat for 15-20 minutes or until vegetables are tender. **Yield:** 10 servings.

Editor's Note: When cutting and seeding hot peppers, use rubber or plastic gloves to protect your hands. Avoid touching your face.

When making foil

packets to use on the grill, fold the foil around the ingredients and double-fold all of the seams, leaving enough room in the packet for steam to circulate. Place the packets on the grill with the seam side up to prevent leaks and to avoid possible flare-ups.

Open the cooked packets very cautiously to allow the steam to escape and to prevent burns.

1 large sweet red pepper,
  cut into 1-inch pieces
1 envelope onion soup mix
3 tablespoons minced fresh basil
  or 1 tablespoon dried basil
1 tablespoon olive oil
1/4 teaspoon pepper
1 tablespoon butter

In a large bowl, combine the first nine ingredients. Toss to coat. Place on a double thickness of heavy-duty foil (about 28 in. x 18 in.). Dot with butter. Fold foil around the vegetable mixture and seal tightly. Grill, covered, over medium heat for 25-30 minutes or until potatoes are tender, turning once. **Yield:** 6 servings.

■ ■ ■

Grilled Garlic Cheese Grits

Grits are an everyday food here in the South. I came up with this recipe one day when I ran out of potatoes but needed a satisfying side dish. It's a great alternative to baked potatoes when served with grilled steak or chicken.
—Holly Bonds, Smyrna, Georgia

4 cups water
1 cup uncooked old-fashioned grits
1 teaspoon salt
1 cup (4 ounces) shredded cheddar
  cheese
1 to 2 garlic cloves, minced
1 tablespoon olive oil

In a saucepan, bring water to a boil. Slowly add grits and salt, stirring constantly. Reduce heat; simmer, uncovered, for 40-45 minutes or until thickened, stirring occasionally. Add cheese and garlic; stir until cheese is melted. Pour into a 9-in. square baking dish coated with nonstick cooking spray. Cover and refrigerate for 2 to 2-1/2 hours or until firm.

Onion-Basil Grilled Vegetables

(Pictured above)

As the caretaker for a private home, I sometimes cook for the young family who lives there. Everyone enjoys these grilled veggies seasoned with onion soup mix and basil.
—Jan Oeffler, Danbury, Wisconsin

3 medium ears fresh corn,
  cut into 3 pieces
1 pound medium red potatoes,
  quartered
1 cup fresh baby carrots
1 large green pepper, cut into
  1-inch pieces

Before starting the grill, coat grill rack with nonstick cooking spray. Cut grits into 3-in. squares; brush both sides with oil. Grill, covered, over medium heat for 4-6 minutes on each side or until lightly browned. **Yield:** 9 servings.

■ ■ ■

Snappy Peas 'n' Mushrooms

(Pictured below)

I make this delightful dill-seasoned dish in mere minutes. Just wrap the fresh vegetables in foil, seal tightly and grill until tender. It's that easy.
—Laura Mahaffey, Annapolis, Maryland

1 pound fresh sugar snap *or* snow peas
1/2 cup sliced fresh mushrooms
2 tablespoons sliced green onions
1 tablespoon snipped fresh dill *or* 1 teaspoon dill weed
2 tablespoons butter
Salt and pepper to taste

Place the peas and mushrooms on a piece of double-layered heavy-duty foil (about 18 in. square). Sprinkle with the onions and dill; dot with butter. Fold foil around the mixture and seal tightly.

Grill, covered, over medium-hot heat for 5 minutes. Turn; grill 5-8 minutes longer or until vegetables are tender. Season with salt and pepper. **Yield:** 8-10 servings.

Grilled Dijon Summer Squash

(Pictured below)

A niece gave this mustard-seasoned squash recipe to me. My husband, Doug, and our three grandchildren love the zesty flavor and slightly crunchy texture. The kabobs are perfect partners to any grilled meat.
—Ruth Lee, Troy, Ontario

1/2 cup olive oil
1/4 cup red wine vinegar
  1 tablespoon minced fresh oregano
    or 1 teaspoon dried oregano
  1 tablespoon Dijon mustard
  2 garlic cloves, minced
1/2 teaspoon salt
1/4 teaspoon pepper
  4 medium zucchini, cut into
    1/2-inch slices
  4 medium yellow squash, cut into
    1/2-inch slices
  2 medium red onions, quartered
  1 large sweet red pepper, cut into
    2-inch pieces
  1 large sweet yellow pepper, cut into
    2-inch pieces
12 to 16 whole fresh mushrooms
12 cherry tomatoes

In a jar with a tight-fitting lid, combine the oil, vinegar, oregano, mustard, garlic, salt and pepper. Place the vegetables in a shallow baking dish. Add marinade and toss to coat. Let stand for 15 minutes.

    Drain and discard marinade; arrange vegetables on a vegetable grill rack. Grill, covered, over indirect heat for 10-12 minutes or until tender. **Yield:** 16-18 servings.

■ ■ ■

Potato Floret Packet

This side dish was developed by my daughter, Betsey, who worked in a group home. When they would grill out, this attractive veggie medley was a favorite of the residents there.
—Janet Hayes, Hermantown, Minnesota

  5 medium red potatoes, cubed
  1 cup fresh broccoli florets
  1 cup fresh cauliflowerets
  1 small onion, chopped
1/4 teaspoon garlic salt *or* garlic
    powder
Pepper to taste
1/4 cup shredded cheddar cheese

In a bowl, combine the potatoes, broccoli, cauliflower, onion, garlic salt and pepper. Place on a double thickness of heavy-duty foil (about 17 in. x 12 in.). Fold foil around potato mixture and seal tightly.

    Grill, covered, over medium heat for 30 minutes or until potatoes are tender. Sprinkle with cheese before serving. **Yield:** 6 servings.

Grilled Corn and Peppers

(Pictured above)

Every Fourth of July, we invite family and friends to our houseboat for a cookout. We always have corn on the cob prepared this way. The onions and peppers add fantastic flavor to the corn.
—Cindy Williams, Fort Myers, Florida

3 **cups Italian salad dressing**
8 **large ears fresh corn, husks removed and cleaned**
4 **medium green peppers, julienned**
4 **medium sweet red peppers, julienned**
2 **medium red onions, sliced and separated into rings**

Place salad dressing in a large resealable plastic bag. Add the corn, peppers and onions; turn to coat. Seal and refrigerate for 30 minutes.

Drain and discard marinade. Place vegetables in a grill pan or disposable foil pan with holes punched in the bottom. Grill, covered, over medium heat for 25 minutes or until corn is tender, turning frequently. **Yield:** 8 servings.

Grilled Onion Potatoes

My mother often fixed these potatoes when we grilled outdoors during the warm summer months. The tasty treatment requires just a few ingredients, so you can have them sizzling on the grill in no time at all.
—Janet Gioia, Broadalbin, New York

> 5 **medium baking potatoes**
> 1 **small onion, sliced**
> **Salt and pepper to taste**
> 1 **bottle (8 ounces) zesty Italian salad dressing**

Cut each potato into five slices. Place onion between slices and sprinkle with salt and pepper. Reassemble each potato; place on a double layer of heavy-duty foil (about 12 in. square).

Pour about 2-4 tablespoons of salad dressing over each potato. Wrap foil around the potatoes and seal tightly. Grill, covered, over medium heat for 50-60 minutes or until the potatoes are tender. **Yield:** 5 servings.

Grilled Asparagus

(Pictured above)

Our Test Kitchen staff came up with the recipe for these savory spears. They'll be a surefire success at your next barbecue.

> 1 **cup water**
> 1 **pound fresh asparagus, trimmed**
> 1/4 **cup barbecue sauce**

In a large skillet, bring water to a boil; add asparagus. Cover and cook for 4-6 minutes or until almost tender; drain and pat dry. Cool slightly.

Thread several asparagus spears onto two parallel soaked wooden skewers. Repeat. Grill, uncovered, over medium heat for 2 minutes, turning once. Baste with barbecue sauce. Grill 2 minutes longer, turning and basting once. **Yield:** 4 servings.

Grilling Asparagus

For foods that could fall into the grill (like asparagus) or that would twist around on a skewer (like mushrooms), thread on two parallel skewers. Allow 1/4 inch between items to ensure even heating. Then simply turn for even grilling.

Grilled Sweet Corn

(Pictured at right)

Since we have plenty of fresh sweet corn available in our area, we use this recipe often in summer. Parsley, chili powder and cumin accent the corn's just-picked flavor.
—*Connie Lou Hollister, Lake Odessa, Michigan*

- 8 large ears sweet corn in husks
- 6 tablespoons butter, softened
- 1 tablespoon minced fresh parsley
- 1 to 2 teaspoons chili powder
- 1 teaspoon garlic salt
- 1/2 to 1 teaspoon ground cumin

Carefully peel back husks from corn to within 1 in. of bottom; remove silk. Combine remaining ingredients; spread over corn. Rewrap corn in husks and secure with string. Place in a large kettle; cover with cold water. Soak for 20 minutes; drain.

Grill the corn, covered, over medium heat for 10-15 minutes or until tender, turning frequently. **Yield:** 8 servings.

■ ■ ■

Summer Squash Bundles

We love zucchini, and my husband enjoys cooking summer meals on the grill, so I came up with this idea to add to our outdoor dining menu. The recipe can be doubled or tripled when you're entertaining.
—*Juanita Daugherty, Cadet, Missouri*

- 1 green onion
- 1 medium yellow squash
- 1 medium zucchini
- 1/4 cup chopped leek
  (white portion only)
- 2 tablespoons grated Parmesan cheese

- 2 teaspoons Italian seasoning
- 2 teaspoons butter, melted
- 1/4 teaspoon salt

Remove white portion of green onion (save for another use). Trim the onion top to 8- or 9-in. lengths. In a saucepan, bring water to a boil. Add onion tops; boil for 1 minute or until softened. Drain and immediately place in ice water. Drain and pat dry; set aside.

Cut squash and zucchini in half lengthwise. Scoop out pulp from zucchini halves, leaving a 3/8-in. shell. Discard pulp. In a bowl, combine the remaining ingredients; fill zucchini shells. Place yellow squash halves, cut side down, over filled zucchini halves. Tie each bundle with a blanched onion top.

Wrap each bundle in a double thickness of heavy-duty foil (12 in. square). Fold foil around squash and seal tightly. Grill, covered, over medium heat for 15-20 minutes or until tender. **Yield:** 2 servings.

Cheddar Herb Bread

(Pictured above)

This delicious bread is a fun accompaniment to any meal you make on the grill—the garlic flavor really comes through.
—*Ann Jacobsen, Oakland, Michigan*

- 1 **cup (4 ounces) shredded cheddar cheese**
- 1/2 **cup butter, softened**
- 1/4 **cup minced fresh parsley**
- 1 **garlic clove, minced**
- 1/2 **teaspoon garlic powder**
- 1/2 **teaspoon paprika**
- 1 **loaf (1 pound) French bread, sliced**

In a mixing bowl, combine the first six ingredients; beat until smooth. Spread on both sides of each slice of bread; reassemble the loaf. Wrap bread in a large piece of heavy-duty foil (about 28 in. x 18 in.) and seal tightly. Grill, covered, over medium heat for 15-20 minutes or until heated through, turning once. **Yield:** 10-12 servings.

Editor's Note: Bread may also be heated in a 375° oven for 15-20 minutes.

■ ■ ■

Veggies on the Grill

(Pictured above)

I like to experiment a bit with marinades and sauces that combine different spices and herbs. This particular mix of seasonings really perks up garden-fresh vegetables.
—*H. Ross Njaa, Salinas, California*

1/3 cup vegetable oil
1-1/2 teaspoons garlic powder
1/2 teaspoon salt
1/4 teaspoon pepper
1/8 teaspoon cayenne pepper
3 medium carrots, halved lengthwise
3 large potatoes, quartered lengthwise
3 medium zucchini, quartered lengthwise

In a small bowl, combine the oil, garlic powder, salt, pepper and cayenne. Brush over vegetables. Grill carrots and potatoes, covered, over medium heat for 10 minutes. Baste with the seasoning blend. Add the zucchini. Cover and grill 10-15 minutes longer, basting and turning every 5 minutes or until the vegetables are tender. **Yield:** 6 servings.

■ ■ ■

Grilled Hash Browns

(Pictured at right)

Since my husband and I love to grill meats, we're always looking for easy side dishes that cook on the grill, too. So I came up with this simple recipe for hash browns.
—Kelly Chastain, Bedford, Indiana

3-1/2 cups frozen cubed hash brown potatoes, thawed
1 small onion, chopped
1 tablespoon beef bouillon granules
Dash *each* seasoned salt and pepper
1 tablespoon butter, melted

Place potatoes on a piece of heavy-duty foil (20 in. x 18 in.) coated with cooking spray. Sprinkle with onion, bouillon, salt and pepper; drizzle with butter.

Fold foil around the potatoes; seal tightly. Grill, covered, over indirect medium heat for 10-15 minutes or until the potatoes are tender, turning once. **Yield:** 4 servings.

Grilled Sweet Potatoes

I love trying new recipes, so when my son-in-law suggested we grill sweet potatoes, I said yes. Served with steak, they're a great change of pace from traditional baked potatoes...and pretty, too.
—Lillian Neer, Long Eddy, New York

2 large sweet potatoes, halved lengthwise
2 tablespoons butter, softened
Garlic salt and pepper to taste
2 teaspoons honey

Cut two pieces of heavy-duty foil (about 18 in. x 12 in.); place a potato half on each. Spread cut side with butter. Sprinkle with garlic salt and pepper. Top each potato with another half.

Fold foil over potatoes and seal tightly. Grill, covered, over medium-hot heat for 30 minutes or until tender, turning once. To serve, fluff potatoes with a fork and drizzle with honey. **Yield:** 4 servings.

Summer Vegetable Medley

(Pictured above)

This swift side dish is as beautiful as it is delicious. Red and yellow peppers, zucchini, corn and mushrooms are seasoned with garden-fresh herbs.
—Maria Regakis, Somerville, Massachusetts

1/2 cup butter, melted
1-1/4 teaspoons *each* minced fresh
   parsley, basil and chives
3/4 teaspoon salt
1/4 teaspoon pepper

3 medium ears sweet corn, husks
   removed, cut into 2-inch pieces
1 medium sweet red pepper, cut into
   1-inch pieces
1 medium sweet yellow pepper,
   cut into 1-inch pieces
1 medium zucchini, cut into 1/4-inch
   slices
10 large fresh mushrooms

In a large bowl, combine the butter, parsley, basil, chives, salt and pepper. Add the vegetables; toss to coat. Place vegetables in a disposable foil pan. Grill, covered, over medium-high heat for 5 minutes; stir. Grill 5 minutes longer or until the vegetables are tender. **Yield:** 6-8 servings.

Savory Grilled Potatoes

These tasty potato packets are easy to prepare ahead of time and toss on the grill when needed.
—Darlene Brenden, Salem, Oregon

- 1/4 cup mayonnaise
- 1 tablespoon grated Parmesan cheese
- 1 garlic clove, minced
- 1/2 teaspoon minced fresh parsley
- 1/4 to 1/2 teaspoon salt
- 1/4 teaspoon paprika
- 1/4 teaspoon pepper
- 2 medium baking potatoes, cut into 1/4-inch slices
- 1 small onion, sliced and separated into rings
- 2 tablespoons butter

In a large bowl, combine the first seven ingredients. Add potatoes and onion; toss gently to coat. Spoon onto a double thickness of greased heavy-duty foil (about 18 in. square). Dot with butter. Fold foil around potato mixture and seal tightly. Grill, covered, over medium heat for 30-35 minutes or until potatoes are tender, turning once. **Yield:** 2 servings.

■ ■ ■

Rice on the Grill

My husband loves to barbecue, so when it's hot outside, we do entire meals on the grill. Since our kids love rice, we often include this tangy side dish as part of the menu.
—Shirley Hopkins, Olds, Alberta

- 1-1/3 cups uncooked instant rice
- 1/3 cup sliced fresh mushrooms
- 1/4 cup chopped green pepper
- 1/4 cup chopped onion
- 1/2 cup chicken broth
- 1/2 cup water

- 1/3 cup ketchup
- 1 tablespoon butter

In a 9-in. round aluminum foil pie pan, combine the first seven ingredients. Dot with butter. Cover with heavy-duty foil; seal edges tightly. Grill, covered, for 14-15 minutes or until liquid is absorbed. Fluff with a fork and serve immediately. **Yield:** 6 servings.

■ ■ ■

Open Fire Bread

My husband and I were introduced to this bread at a street fair in Africa.
—Kathy Thye Dewbre, Kimberley, South Africa

- 2 packages (1/4 ounce *each*) active dry yeast
- 2 teaspoons honey
- 3 cups warm water (110° to 115°), *divided*
- 2 teaspoons salt
- 1 tablespoon vegetable oil
- 7 to 8 cups all-purpose flour

In a mixing bowl, combine yeast, honey and 2/3 cup water; mix well. Let stand 5 minutes. Add salt, oil, remaining water and 6 cups flour; mix well. Add enough remaining flour to form a soft dough. Turn onto a floured surface; knead until smooth and elastic, about 6-8 minutes. (Dough will be soft and slightly sticky.) Place in a greased bowl, turning once to grease top. Cover and let rise in a warm place until doubled, about 1 hour.

Punch dough down. On a floured surface, roll out dough to 3/4-in. thickness. Cut into 4-in. x 1-in. strips with a pizza cutter; sprinkle with flour. Place on a floured baking sheet. Let rise until doubled, about 25-30 minutes. Place strips directly on grill. Grill, uncovered, over medium-hot heat until golden brown, about 6-8 minutes, turning often. **Yield:** about 3 dozen.

Pesto-Corn Grilled Peppers

(Pictured below)

We grill almost daily and enjoy using produce from our garden. These pepper halves filled with a basil-seasoned corn mixture is my husband's favorite.
—Rachael Marrier, Star Prairie, Wisconsin

- 1/2 cup plus 2 teaspoons olive oil, *divided*
- 3/4 cup grated Parmesan cheese
- 2 cups tightly packed fresh basil
- 2 tablespoons sunflower kernels *or* walnuts
- 4 garlic cloves
- 1/2 cup finely chopped sweet red pepper
- 4 cups whole kernel corn
- 4 medium sweet red, yellow *or* green peppers
- 1/4 cup shredded Parmesan cheese

For pesto, combine 1/2 cup of oil, grated Parmesan cheese, basil, sunflower kernels and garlic in a blender or food processor; cover and process until blended. In a skillet, saute red pepper in remaining oil until tender. Add corn and pesto; heat through.

Halve peppers lengthwise; remove seeds. Place, cut side down, on grill over medium heat; cover and cook for 8 minutes. Turn; fill with corn mixture. Grill 4-6 minutes longer or until tender. Sprinkle with shredded Parmesan cheese. **Yield:** 8 servings.

■ ■ ■

Skewered Potatoes

Here's a unique way to prepare red potatoes. Cooking them in the microwave ensures they're tender inside, while grilling gives them a crisp outside.
—Sarah Steinacher, Geneva, Nebraska

- 2 pounds small red potatoes, quartered
- 1/3 cup cold water
- 1/2 cup mayonnaise
- 1/4 cup dry white wine *or* chicken broth
- 2 teaspoons dried rosemary, crushed
- 1 teaspoon garlic powder

Place potatoes and water in a 2-qt. microwave-safe dish. Cover and cook on high for 10-15 minutes or until tender, stirring halfway through; drain. In a large bowl, combine the remaining ingredients. Add potatoes; stir gently to coat. Cover and refrigerate for 1 hour. Drain, reserving marinade.

Thread the potatoes on metal or soaked wooden skewers. Grill, covered, over hot heat for 6-8 minutes or until the potatoes are golden brown. Turn and brush occasionally with reserved marinade. **Yield:** 6-8 servings.

Editor's Note: This recipe was tested in an 850-watt microwave.

Grilled Veggie Mix

(Pictured above)

This tempting veggie dish is the perfect accompaniment to any barbecue fare. To make the recipe even more satisfying, I often use my homegrown vegetables and herbs in the mix.
—Janet Boulger, Botwood, Newfoundland

2 medium zucchini, cut into
  1/2-inch slices
1 large green pepper, cut into
  1/2-inch squares
1 large sweet red pepper, cut into
  1/2-inch squares
1 pound fresh mushrooms, halved
1 large onion, cubed
6 medium carrots, cut into
  1/4-inch slices
2 cups small broccoli florets
2 cups small cauliflowerets

DRESSING:

1/4 cup olive oil
1/4 cup butter, melted
1/4 cup minced fresh parsley
2 garlic cloves, minced
1 teaspoon dried basil
1/2 teaspoon dried oregano
1/2 teaspoon salt
1/4 teaspoon pepper

Place all of the the vegetables in the center of two pieces of double-layered heavy-duty foil (about 18 in. square). Combine all of the dressing ingredients; drizzle over vegetables.

Fold foil around mixture and seal tightly. Grill, covered, over medium heat for 30 minutes or until vegetables are tender, turning once. **Yield:** 10 servings.

Santa Fe Corn On the Cob

(Pictured above)

Corn is my all-time favorite food, and this is the best way I've found to fix it. The zesty grilling sauce has Southwestern flair, but it's not too hot or spicy.
—Laurie Meaike, Audubon, Iowa

6 medium ears sweet corn in husks
1 tablespoon butter
2 garlic cloves, minced
1/4 cup steak sauce
3/4 teaspoon chili powder
1/4 teaspoon ground cumin

Soak corn in cold water for 1 hour. Meanwhile, in a microwave-safe dish, combine butter and garlic. Cover and microwave on high for 2 minutes or until garlic is softened, stirring once. Stir in steak sauce, chili powder and cumin; set aside.

Carefully peel back husks from corn to within 1 in. of bottom; remove silk. Brush corn with sauce. Rewrap corn in husks and secure with kitchen string. Coat grill rack with nonstick cooking spray before starting the grill. Grill corn, covered, over medium heat for 25-30 minutes, turning occasionally. **Yield:** 6 servings.

Grilled Vegetable Potato Skins

(Pictured below right)

People just love these stuffed spuds in the summer as an alternative to heavier grilled fare. Topped with a colorful vegetable medley, the tender potato skins are light yet satisfying.
—Karen Hemminger, Mansfield, Massachusetts

  2 large baking potatoes
  1 cup sliced yellow summer squash
  1 cup sliced zucchini
  1/2 large sweet red pepper, julienned
  1/2 large green pepper, julienned
  1 small red onion, cut into 1/4-inch
      wedges
  1/4 cup olive oil and vinegar salad
      dressing *or* Italian salad dressing
1-1/2 teaspoons olive oil
  1/2 teaspoon salt, *divided*
  1/4 cup shredded cheddar cheese

Pierce potatoes several times with a fork and place on a microwave-safe plate. Microwave on high for 18-20 minutes or until tender, rotating the potatoes once. Let stand until cool enough to handle.

Meanwhile, in a large resealable plastic bag, combine the summer squash, zucchini, peppers and onion. Pour salad dressing over vegetables. Seal bag and turn to coat; marinate for 20 minutes.

Cut each potato in half lengthwise. Scoop out pulp, leaving a thin shell (discard the pulp or save for another use). Brush inside of shells with oil and sprinkle with 1/4 teaspoon salt.

Coat grill rack with nonstick cooking spray. Place potato shells skin side up on grill rack. Grill, covered, over indirect medium heat for 10 minutes or until golden brown.

Drain vegetables, reserving marinade. Grill vegetables in a grill basket, uncovered, over medium heat for 10 minutes or until ten-der, basting with reserved marinade.

Sprinkle potato skins with cheese. Fill with grilled vegetables; sprinkle with remaining salt. Grill 5 minutes longer or until cheese is melted. **Yield:** 4 servings.

■ ■ ■

Cheese-Topped Tomatoes

This tasty side with tangy blue cheese is perfect served with grilled chicken or steak.
—Arlene Risius, Buffalo Center, Iowa

  8 plum tomatoes, halved lengthwise
  3/4 teaspoon salt
  1/4 cup dry bread crumbs
  1/2 cup crumbled blue cheese *or*
      shredded cheddar cheese
  1/4 cup grated onion
  2 tablespoons butter, melted

Sprinkle cut side of tomatoes with salt, bread crumbs, cheese and onion. Drizzle with butter. Grill, covered, over indirect medium heat for 6-8 minutes or until cheese is melted. **Yield:** 8 servings.

·Sandwiches·

It used to be that a burger was simply a ground beef patty seasoned with salt and pepper, topped with a slice of American cheese and placed on a bun. This chapter will reshape the way you think! Burgers and sandwiches are now works of edible art starring an assortment of meats, a bounty of seasonings and a variety of bread products.

Barbecued Burgers

(Pictured at left)

I can't take all the credit for these winning burgers. My husband's uncle passed down the special barbecue sauce recipe. We love it on everything… it was only natural to try it on, and in, burgers.
—Rhoda Troyer, Glenford, Ohio

SAUCE:
- 1 cup ketchup
- 1/2 cup packed brown sugar
- 1/3 cup sugar
- 1/4 cup honey
- 1/4 cup molasses
- 2 teaspoons prepared mustard
- 1-1/2 teaspoons Worcestershire sauce
- 1/4 teaspoon salt
- 1/4 teaspoon Liquid Smoke
- 1/8 teaspoon pepper

BURGERS:
- 1 egg, beaten
- 1/3 cup quick-cooking oats
- 1/4 teaspoon onion salt
- 1/4 teaspoon garlic salt
- 1/4 teaspoon pepper
- 1/8 teaspoon salt
- 1-1/2 pounds ground beef
- 6 hamburger buns, split
- Toppings of your choice

In a small saucepan, combine the first 10 ingredients. Bring to a boil. Remove from the heat. Set aside 1 cup barbecue sauce to serve with burgers.

In a bowl, combine the egg, oats, 1/4 cup of the remaining barbecue sauce, onion salt, garlic salt, pepper and salt. Crumble beef over mixture; mix well. Shape into six patties.

Grill, covered, over medium heat for 6-8 minutes on each side or until a meat thermometer reads 160°, basting with 1/2 cup barbecue sauce during the last 5 minutes. Serve on buns with toppings of your choice and reserved barbecue sauce. **Yield:** 6 servings.

Grilled Beef Gyros

(Pictured above)

A spicy marinade adds zip to these grilled beef slices tucked inside pita bread. Friends from Greece gave us their recipe for the cucumber sauce, which provides a cool contrast to the hot beef.
—*Lee Rademaker, Hayfork, California*

  1 **medium onion, cut into chunks**
  2 **garlic cloves**
  2 **tablespoons sugar**
  1 **tablespoon ground mustard**
1/2 **teaspoon ground ginger *or***
      2 teaspoons minced fresh gingerroot
1-1/2 **teaspoons pepper**
1/2 **teaspoon cayenne pepper**
1/2 **cup soy sauce**

1/4 **cup water**
  1 **boneless beef sirloin tip roast (2 to 3 pounds), cut into 1/4-inch-thick slices**
CUCUMBER SAUCE:
  1 **medium cucumber, peeled, seeded and cut into chunks**
  4 **garlic cloves**
1/2 **teaspoon salt**
1/3 **cup cider vinegar**
1/3 **cup olive oil**
  2 **cups (16 ounces) sour cream**
  8 **to 10 pita breads, warmed and halved**
Thinly sliced onion
Chopped tomato

In a blender or food processor, place the onion, garlic, sugar, mustard, ginger, pepper and cayenne; cover and process until onion is finely chopped. Add soy sauce and water; process until blended. Place the beef in a large resealable plastic bag. Add marinade. Seal bag and turn to coat; refrigerate for 1-2 hours.

For sauce, combine the cucumber, garlic and salt in a blender or food processor; cover and process until cucumber is chopped. Add vinegar and oil; process until blended. Transfer to a bowl; stir in sour cream. Refrigerate until serving.

Drain and discard marinade. Grill beef, covered, over medium-hot heat until meat reaches desired doneness. Place beef in pita halves. Top with cucumber sauce, sliced onion and chopped tomato. Refrigerate any remaining sauce. **Yield:** 8-10 sandwiches.

If you're looking for a way to give a gourmet touch to your homemade hamburgers, try this tasty idea...serve them on toasted buns! Simply butter both sides of the buns; place butter-side-down on the grill for about 5 minutes or until golden brown. Top with your favorite hamburgers.

Garden Turkey Burgers

(Pictured below)

These moist burgers get plenty of color and flavor from onion, zucchini and red pepper. I often make the mixture ahead of time and put it in the refrigerator. Later, I can put the burgers on the grill while whipping up a salad.
—Sandy Kitzmiller, Unityville, Pennsylvania

 1 cup old-fashioned oats
3/4 cup chopped onion
3/4 cup finely chopped sweet red *or* green pepper
1/2 cup shredded zucchini
1/4 cup ketchup
 2 garlic cloves, minced
1/4 teaspoon salt
 1 pound ground turkey
 6 whole wheat hamburger buns, split and toasted

Coat grill rack with nonstick cooking spray before starting the grill. In a bowl, combine the first seven ingredients. Add turkey and mix well. Shape into six 1/2-in.-thick patties.

Grill, covered, over indirect medium heat for 6 minutes on each side or until a meat thermometer reads 165°. Serve on buns. **Yield:** 6 burgers.

■ ■ ■

Carry-Along Hot Dogs

These versatile sandwiches can be made over the grill or in the oven, so they're great any time of year. We especially like them when camping.
—Lorraine Priebe, Noonan, North Dakota

1/3 cup ketchup
 2 tablespoons sweet pickle relish
 1 tablespoon finely chopped onion
 1 teaspoon prepared mustard
 8 slices American cheese
 8 hot dog buns, split
 8 hot dogs

In a small bowl, combine the first four ingredients. Place a slice of cheese on the bottom half of each bun. Slice hot dogs in half lengthwise; place two halves on each bun. Spoon 1 tablespoon of sauce over each hot dog. Replace top of bun and wrap each sandwich in foil.

Grill, uncovered, over medium heat, turning often, for 10-15 minutes. **Yield:** 8 servings.

Green Chili Chicken Sandwiches

(Pictured below)

I enjoyed a sandwich similar to this in a restaurant and decided to try making it at home. The spicy chicken is a quick-and-easy alternative to hamburgers.
—Paula Morigeau, Hot Springs, Montana

- 4 boneless skinless chicken breast halves (1-1/4 pounds)
- 2/3 cup soy sauce
- 1/4 cup cider vinegar
- 2 tablespoons sugar
- 2 teaspoons vegetable oil
- 1 can (4 ounces) whole green chilies, drained and sliced lengthwise
- 4 slices Pepper Jack or Monterey Jack cheese
- 4 kaiser or sandwich rolls, split

Pound chicken to flatten; place in a large re-sealable plastic bag. In a bowl, combine the soy sauce, vinegar, sugar and oil; mix well. Set aside 1/4 cup for basting. Pour the remaining marinade over chicken; seal bag and turn to coat. Refrigerate for 30 minutes.

Drain and discard marinade. Grill chicken, uncovered, over medium heat for 3 minutes. Turn and baste with reserved marinade; grill 3 minutes longer or until juices run clear. Top each with a green chili and cheese slice; cover and grill for 2 minutes or until cheese is melted. Serve on rolls. **Yield:** 4 servings.

■ ■ ■

Pesto-Mozzarella Turkey Burgers

(Pictured at right)

Here's a great way to eat lighter without giving up flavor. These turkey burgers are stuffed with a tasty pesto sauce that spices up our barbecues.
—Jacqueline Marie
Morris Bentonville, Arkansas

Bacon-Wrapped Beef Patties

My family loves these spruced-up hamburgers all year long. Bacon flavors the meat and adds a tasty twist. These pleasing patties can also be enjoyed off the bun.
—Jody Bahler, Wolcott, Indiana

  1 cup (4 ounces) shredded cheddar cheese
2/3 cup chopped onion
1/4 cup ketchup
  2 eggs, lightly beaten
  3 tablespoons Worcestershire sauce
  2 tablespoons grated Parmesan cheese
  1 teaspoon seasoned salt
1/4 teaspoon pepper
  2 pounds ground beef
10 bacon strips
10 hamburger buns, split

In a bowl, combine the first eight ingredients. Crumble beef over mixture and mix well. Shape into ten 3/4-in.-thick patties. Wrap each patty with a bacon strip; secure with toothpicks.

Grill patties, uncovered, over medium heat for 5-6 minutes on each side or until juices run clear and a meat thermometer reads 160°. Remove toothpicks. Serve hamburgers on buns. **Yield:** 10 servings.

Test for Doneness

Cook beef, pork and lamb burgers to 160°; cook chicken or turkey burgers to 165°.

To test for doneness, use tongs to hold burger while inserting instant-read thermometer horizontally from a side. Make sure thermometer is far enough in to read temperature in center.

1-1/2 pounds ground turkey
    1 tablespoon steak sauce
    2 garlic cloves, minced
  3/4 teaspoon salt
  1/2 teaspoon pepper
1-1/2 cups (6 ounces) shredded part-skim mozzarella cheese
    5 tablespoons prepared pesto sauce
    8 slices marble rye bread *or* 4 Italian rolls, split
Lettuce leaves

In a bowl, combine the turkey, steak sauce, garlic, salt and pepper; mix well. Shape into eight thin oval patties. Combine mozzarella and pesto. Spoon about 1/4 cup in the center of four patties. Top with remaining patties; press edges firmly to seal.

Grill, covered, over medium heat for 5 minutes on each side or until a meat thermometer reads 165°. Serve on bread with lettuce. **Yield:** 4 servings.

Teriyaki Burgers

(Pictured above)

Water chestnuts add crunch to these moist patties. Top the burgers with additional teriyaki sauce for a flavorful alternative to ketchup.
—Barb Schutz, Pandora, Ohio

- 1 can (8 ounces) water chestnuts, drained and chopped
- 1/3 cup teriyaki sauce
- 2 tablespoons chopped green onions
- Salt and pepper to taste
- 1-1/2 pounds ground beef
- 7 hamburger buns, split
- 14 tomato slices
- 7 lettuce leaves

In a large bowl, combine the water chestnuts, teriyaki sauce, onions, salt and pepper. Crumble beef over mixture and mix just until combined. Shape into seven 1/2-in.-thick patties.

Grill, covered, over indirect medium heat for 6-8 minutes on each side or until meat is no longer pink. Serve on buns with tomato and lettuce. **Yield:** 7 burgers.

Giant Stuffed Picnic Burger

(Pictured below)

Guests will be delighted when they sink their teeth into juicy wedges of this full-flavored burger. The moist filling is chock-full of mushrooms, onion and parsley. It's a great alternative to regular burgers.
—Helen Hudson, Brockville, Ontario

- 2 pounds ground beef
- 1 teaspoon salt
- 1 teaspoon Worcestershire sauce
- 3/4 cup crushed seasoned stuffing mix
- 1 can (4 ounces) mushroom stems and pieces, drained
- 1/4 cup beef broth
- 1/4 cup minced fresh parsley
- 1/4 cup sliced green onions
- 1 egg, beaten
- 1 tablespoon butter, melted
- 1 teaspoon lemon juice

Combine beef, salt and Worcestershire sauce. Divide in half; pat each half into an 8-in. circle on waxed paper. Combine the remaining ingredients; spoon over one patty to within 1 in.

of the edge. Top with second patty; press edges to seal.

Grill, covered, over medium heat for 12-13 minutes on each side or until the juices run clear. Cut into wedges. **Yield:** 6 servings.

Editor's Note: Stuffed burger may be placed directly on the grill or in a well-greased wire grill basket.

Oriental Chicken Grill

(Pictured at right)

Since my husband and I are empty nesters, this recipe is great for just the two of us, although it could be increased. We both love these tasty sandwiches—especially my husband, who "lives to eat" rather than "eats to live!"
—Rosemary Splittgerber, Mesa, Arizona

    1/2 cup orange juice
      2 tablespoons honey
      2 tablespoons soy sauce
      1 teaspoon lemon-pepper seasoning
      1 teaspoon ground ginger
    1/2 teaspoon garlic powder
      2 boneless skinless chicken breast
         halves
      2 hamburger buns, split
Lettuce leaves and tomato slices, optional

In a small bowl, combine the first six ingredients; mix well. Set aside 1/4 cup for basting chicken; cover and refrigerate. Pound chicken breasts to 3/8-in. thickness. Place in a resealable plastic bag or glass bowl; pour remaining marinade over chicken. Close bag or cover and refrigerate overnight.

Drain, discarding marinade. Grill chicken, uncovered, over medium heat for 6-8 minutes per side or until juices run clear. Baste several times with reserved marinade while grilling. Serve on buns with lettuce and tomato if desired. **Yield:** 2 servings.

Freezing Hamburger Patties

To freeze individual servings of uncooked hamburgers, place patties on waxed paper-lined baking sheets, making sure pieces are not touching one another. Freeze, uncovered, until firm.

Wrap frozen patties in freezer paper or heavy-duty foil or transfer to freezer bags, removing as much air as possible. Label each package and include the date. Properly packaged, hamburgers can be stored in the freezer for up to 3 months.

Grilled Fish Sandwiches

(Pictured below)

I season fish fillets with lime juice and lemon-pepper before charbroiling them on the grill. A simple mayonnaise and honey-mustard sauce puts the sandwiches a step ahead of the rest.
—Violet Beard, Marshall, Illinois

 4 cod fillets (4 ounces *each*)
 1 tablespoon lime juice
 1/2 teaspoon lemon-pepper seasoning
 1/4 cup mayonnaise
 2 teaspoons Dijon mustard
 1 teaspoon honey
 4 hamburger buns, split
 4 lettuce leaves
 4 tomato slices

Brush both sides of fillets with lime juice; sprinkle with lemon-pepper. Coat grill rack with nonstick cooking spray before starting the grill. Grill fillets, covered, over medium heat for 5-6 minutes on each side or until fish flakes easily with a fork.

In a small bowl, combine the mayonnaise, mustard and honey. Spread over the bottom of each bun. Top with a fillet, lettuce and tomato; replace bun tops. **Yield:** 4 servings.

■ ■ ■

Hickory-Smoked Cheeseburgers

Every time I make this recipe, my guests compliment me on how great the burgers taste. The secret is a little bit of Liquid Smoke and a few sprinkles of seasonings.
—Michelle Miller, Abbeville, South Carolina

 3 eggs, beaten
 2 tablespoons Liquid Smoke
 1 medium onion, finely chopped
 1/2 cup crushed saltines (about 15 crackers)
 1 teaspoon salt
 1/2 teaspoon seasoned salt
 1/2 teaspoon seasoning blend
 1/2 teaspoon pepper
 3 pounds ground beef
 12 slices process American cheese
 12 sesame seed hamburger buns, split
Mayonnaise, lettuce leaves, tomato slices and pickle slices

In a large bowl, combine the first eight ingredients. Crumble beef over mixture; mix well. Shape into 12 patties. Grill, covered, over medium heat for 5 minutes on each side or until a meat thermometer reads 160°. Top each burger with a cheese slice. Grill 1-2 minutes longer or until the cheese begins to melt. Serve on buns with mayonnaise, lettuce, tomato and pickles. **Yield:** 12 servings.

Editor's Note: This recipe was tested with Morton's Nature's Seasons Seasoning Blend.

Pork Burgers Deluxe

I found this recipe in a book I got for my wedding. The flavor of the burgers is fantastic. Ground pork is a nice change from beef, and the pineapple slice on top is special.
—Peggy Bellar, Howard, Kansas

- 1/3 **cup white vinegar**
- 1/4 **cup packed brown sugar**
- 1 **small onion, chopped**
- 2 **tablespoons soy sauce**
- 1 **teaspoon salt**
- 1 **teaspoon garlic salt**
- 2 **pounds ground pork**
- 1 **can (20 ounces) pineapple slices, drained**
- 10 **bacon strips**
- 10 **hamburger buns, split**

Combine the first six ingredients; add pork and mix well. Shape into 10 patties. Top each with a pineapple slice; wrap with a bacon strip and secure with a toothpick.

Grill over medium-hot heat for 15-20 minutes or until meat juices run clear, turning once. Serve on buns. **Yield:** 10 servings.

Italian Grilled Cheese

(Pictured above)

Provolone cheese, tomato slices and basil leaves make up the satisfying filling for these flame-broiled sandwiches. Lightly brushed with Italian salad dressing, they're sure to become family favorites.
—Melody Biddinger, Costa Mesa, California

- 8 **fresh basil leaves**
- 8 **thin tomato slices**
- 4 **slices provolone cheese**
- 4 **slices Italian bread (1/4 inch thick)**
- 2 **tablespoons prepared Italian salad dressing**

Layer the basil, tomato and cheese on two slices of bread. Top with remaining bread. Brush outsides of sandwiches with salad dressing. Grill, uncovered, over medium heat for 3-4 minutes on each side. **Yield:** 2 servings.

Spice up your burgers with creative add-ins! For juicier burgers loaded with extra flavor, mix in 2 to 3 tablespoons of beef broth, vegetable juice or other seasoned liquid to a pound of ground meat.

Give leftover veggies a second chance by mincing and mixing into a meat mixture.

Or, replace a quarter pound of meat with 1 cup of grated potatoes or carrots that have been lightly sauteed to add nutrition or to stretch your ground meat.

Fold in 1 stiffly beaten egg white for each pound of meat after seasoning your burger mixture. Cooked burgers will turn out light and juicy this way.

Burger Topping Bar

When serving a burger bar at your barbecue, set out a large platter loaded with an assortment of condiments and toppings.

Traditional additions include lettuce (leaves or shredded), shredded and sliced cheese, dill pickles, pickle relish and tomato and onion slices.

Ketchup and mustard are reliable standbys, but don't forget mayonnaise, butter and even sour cream. If folks want to add a little zip to their burgers, also offer salsa, pickled jalapeno slices and guacamole.

Looking for a few hot additions? Consider sauteed mushrooms, warmed process cheese sauce (Mexican or plain) or a can of heated chili, with or without beans.

There's no limit to what you can use to top hot-off-the-grill burgers!

The Perfect Hamburger

(Pictured at right)

Chili sauce and horseradish add zip to these hamburgers and make them a nice change from ordinary burgers. We think they're perfect and make them often for family and friends, who agree.
—Shirley Kidd, New London, Minnesota

- 1 egg, lightly beaten
- 2 tablespoons chili sauce
- 1 teaspoon dried minced onion
- 1 teaspoon prepared horseradish
- 1 teaspoon Worcestershire sauce
- 1/2 teaspoon salt
- Pinch pepper
- 1 pound lean ground beef
- 4 hamburger buns, split
- Optional toppings: sliced tomato, onion, pickles and condiments

In a large bowl, combine the first seven ingredients. Add beef and mix well. Shape into four 3/4-in.-thick patties. Grill, uncovered, over medium-hot heat for 5-6 minutes on each side or until meat is no longer pink. Serve on buns with toppings of your choice. **Yield:** 4 servings.

■ ■ ■

Brats with Onions

After years of eating plain old brats, I came up with this delicious version slathered in zippy onions. Parboiling them ensures they'll be cooked thoroughly after grilling.
—Gunnard Stark, Englewood, Florida

- 3 cans (12 ounces *each*) beer *or* 4-1/2 cups water
- 3 large onions, thinly sliced and separated into rings
- 6 garlic cloves, minced
- 1 tablespoon hot pepper sauce
- 2 to 3 teaspoons celery salt
- 2 to 3 teaspoons pepper
- 1 teaspoon chili powder
- 15 fresh bratwurst links (3-1/2 to 4 pounds)
- 5 hot dog buns *or* brat buns, split

In a large saucepan or Dutch oven, combine the first seven ingredients. Bring to a boil. Add the bratwurst. Reduce heat; simmer, uncovered, for 8-10 minutes or until the bratwurst is no longer pink. Drain, reserving onions.

Grill bratwurst, covered, over medium heat for 7-8 minutes or until browned. Serve on buns with reserved onions. **Yield:** 15 servings.

Tummy Dogs

(Pictured above)

Looking for a fun and flavorful way to jazz up hot dogs? Try these bacon-wrapped versions with zippy Dijon mustard. They don't take long to fix. And your tummy will thank you.
—*Myra Innes, Auburn, Kansas*

- 8 bacon strips
- 8 hot dogs
- 4 ounces Monterey Jack cheese, cut into strips
- 1/4 cup butter, softened
- 1/4 cup Dijon mustard
- 8 hot dog buns
- 1 small onion, thinly sliced, optional
- 1 can (4 ounces) diced green chilies, optional

Partially cook bacon; drain on paper towels. Cut a 1/4-in. lengthwise slit in each hot dog; place cheese in each slit. Starting at one end, wrap bacon in a spiral around hot dog; se- cure with toothpicks. Split buns just halfway. Combine butter and mustard; spread inside buns. Set aside.

On a covered grill over medium heat, cook hot dogs with cheese side down for 2 minutes. Turn and grill 3-4 minutes longer or until bacon is crisp and cheese is melted. Place buns on grill with cut side down; grill until lightly toasted. Remove toothpicks from the hot dogs; serve in buns with onion and chilies if desired. **Yield:** 8 sandwiches.

■ ■ ■

Spicy Turkey Burgers

(Pictured below)

The hot pepper sauce comes through nicely to add spark to these moist turkey burgers. This is a good low-fat burger without the boring taste of typical low-fat foods.
—*Mavis Diment, Marcus, Iowa*

- 1/2 cup chopped onion
- 2 tablespoons plain yogurt
- 1 tablespoon snipped fresh dill *or* 1 teaspoon dill weed

1-1/2 teaspoons hot pepper sauce
  1/2 teaspoon salt
    1 garlic clove, minced
    1 pound lean ground turkey
    4 kaiser rolls, split
    4 lettuce leaves
    4 tomato slices

In a large bowl, combine the onion, yogurt, dill, hot pepper sauce, salt and garlic. Crumble turkey over mixture; mix well.

Shape into four patties, each about 3/4 in. thick. Grill, uncovered, over medium-hot heat for 6-8 minutes on each side or until no longer pink. Serve on rolls with lettuce and tomato. **Yield:** 4 servings.

■ ■ ■

Grilled Beef Tenderloin Sandwiches

(Pictured above right)

Sweet-sour onions and mushrooms are perfect over the tender beef and lip-smacking garlic mayonnaise.
—Ruth Lee, Troy, Ontario

    1 tablespoon brown sugar
    2 garlic cloves, minced
  1/2 teaspoon coarsely ground pepper
  1/4 teaspoon salt
    1 beef tenderloin (1 pound)
    1 whole garlic bulb
  1/2 teaspoon vegetable oil
  1/4 cup *each* mayonnaise and plain yogurt
ONION TOPPING:
    1 tablespoon olive oil
    1 large sweet onion, thinly sliced
  1/2 pound sliced fresh mushrooms
    2 tablespoons balsamic vinegar
1-1/2 teaspoons sugar
  1/8 teaspoon salt
  1/8 teaspoon pepper

    4 slices French bread (3/4 inch thick)
    1 cup fresh arugula

Combine the first four ingredients; rub over meat. Refrigerate for 2 hours. Remove papery outer skin from garlic (do not peel or separate cloves). Cut top off of garlic. Brush with vegetable oil. Wrap bulb in heavy-duty foil. Bake at 425° for 30-35 minutes or until softened. Cool 10 minutes. Squeeze garlic into food processor; add mayonnaise and yogurt. Process until smooth and refrigerate.

In a large nonstick skillet, heat olive oil and saute onion for 5 minutes. Reduce heat; cook and stir for 10-12 minutes or until onion is golden. Add mushrooms; cook and stir until tender. Add next four ingredients; cook until reduced slightly.

Coat grill rack with nonstick cooking spray before starting the grill. Grill beef, covered, over medium heat for 5-6 minutes on each side or until meat reaches desired doneness (for medium-rare, a meat thermometer should read 145°; medium, 160°; well-done, 170°). Let stand for 10 minutes before cutting into 4 slices.

Serve warm on bread with garlic mayonnaise, arugula and onion mixture. **Yield:** 4 servings.

Fajita Pitas

(Pictured above)

I was late coming home one evening and forgot to pick up tortillas for the fajitas we planned for dinner. So we used pita bread that I had in the freezer instead.
—Diana Jones, Springtown, Texas

- 6 boneless skinless chicken breast halves
- 1 large onion, sliced
- 1 large green pepper, thinly sliced
- 1 tablespoon vegetable oil
- 2 cups (8 ounces) shredded Mexican cheese blend *or* cheddar cheese
- 8 pita breads, halved

SAUCE:
- 1 medium onion, finely chopped
- 1 medium tomato, finely chopped
- 1/2 jalapeno pepper, finely chopped
- 1 tablespoon minced fresh cilantro
- 1 tablespoon vegetable oil

Guacamole and sour cream, optional

Grill chicken, covered, over medium heat for 16-20 minutes or until juices run clear, turning occasionally. Cut into strips.

In a skillet, saute onion and green pepper in oil. Add chicken and cheese. Stuff into pita halves; place on an ungreased baking sheet. Bake at 325° for 10 minutes or until cheese is melted.

Meanwhile, for sauce, combine the onion, tomato, jalapeno, cilantro and oil in a bowl; mix well. Serve sauce, guacamole and sour cream if desired with pitas. **Yield:** 8 servings.

Editor's Note: When cutting or seeding hot peppers, use rubber or plastic gloves to protect your hands. Avoid touching your face.

■ ■ ■

Tortilla Burgers

With pork instead of ground beef and tortillas in place of buns, these Southwestern-style burgers stand out from all others.
—Katie Koziolek, Hartland, Minnesota

- 1 teaspoon ground cumin
- 1/2 teaspoon dried oregano
- 1/2 teaspoon crushed red pepper flakes
- 1/4 teaspoon seasoned salt
- 1 pound ground pork
- 4 flour *or* corn tortillas (6 inches), warmed

Salsa, sour cream and shredded cheese, optional

In a bowl, combine the first four ingredients. Crumble pork over seasonings and mix well. Shape into four oval patties. Grill, covered, over medium heat for 6-7 minutes on each side or until meat is no longer pink. Serve on tortillas with salsa, sour cream and cheese if desired. **Yield:** 4 servings.

Grilled Sub Sandwich

(Pictured below right)

After a long hard day at band camp, my daughter comes home with a huge appetite. This sandwich satisfies my hungry marcher! It's also easy to prepare.
—Char Shanahan, Schererville, Indiana

- 1 large green pepper, thinly sliced
- 1 small onion, thinly sliced and separated into rings
- 1/2 teaspoon olive oil
- 1 loaf (1 pound) unsliced Italian bread
- 1/3 cup prepared Italian salad dressing *divided*
- 2 ounces sliced deli turkey
- 4 slices Swiss cheese
- 2 ounces sliced deli ham
- 3 slices cheddar cheese
- 2 ounces sliced deli pastrami
- 1/2 cup sliced dill pickles
- 1 large tomato, thinly sliced

Additional olive oil

In a bowl, toss green pepper and onion with oil. Place on a double thickness of heavy-duty foil (about 12 in. square). Fold foil around vegetables and seal tightly. Grill, covered, over medium-hot heat for 12-15 minutes or until tender; set aside.

Cut loaf in half horizontally; remove bread from top piece, leaving a 1/2-in. shell. Brush cut sides of loaf with salad dressing; place cut side down on the grill. Grill, uncovered, over medium heat for 3-5 minutes or until golden brown.

Place bottom of loaf on a double thickness of heavy-duty foil (about 18 in. x 12 in.). Layer with turkey, two Swiss cheese slices, ham, cheddar cheese, pastrami and remaining Swiss cheese. Top with green pepper mixture, pick-les and tomato.

Drizzle remaining dressing over cut side of bread top; place over filling. Brush bread with additional oil. Fold foil around sandwich and seal tightly. Grill, covered, over medium heat for 4-8 minutes or until cheese is melted. Cut into slices with a serrated knife. **Yield: 4 servings.**

When grilling lots of burgers, jump-start them in the oven. Place formed patties on shallow baking pans and bake at 350° until partway done. Then move them to the grill to finish cooking.

1 tablespoon honey
4 onion rolls, split
4 lettuce leaves
4 slices tomato
4 ounces fresh mozzarella cheese, cut
  into 1/4-inch slices

In a resealable plastic bag, combine 1/4 cup oil and 2 tablespoons vinegar; add onion slices. Seal bag and turn to coat; marinate for 30 minutes. Meanwhile, in a small bowl, combine the garlic, basil and remaining oil. Brush over both sides of mushroom caps; set aside.

In a small saucepan, bring honey and remaining vinegar to a boil; cook for 5 minutes or until thickened. Set aside.

Drain and discard marinade from onions. Coat grill rack with nonstick cooking spray before starting the grill. Grill onions and mushrooms over medium heat for 10-12 minutes or until tender, turning frequently. Serve on rolls with lettuce, tomato and mozzarella. Drizzle with reserved balsamic-honey sauce. **Yield:** 4 servings.

■ ■ ■

Portobello Mushroom Burgers

(Pictured above)

As a healthy alternative to traditional hamburgers, consider making these portobello "patties" from our Test Kitchen staff. With just fantastic flavor, folks won't miss the meat!

1/4 cup plus 3 tablespoons olive oil,
    divided
  6 tablespoons balsamic vinegar,
    divided
  4 slices onion (1/4 inch thick)
  1 teaspoon minced garlic
1/2 teaspoon dried basil
  4 portobello mushroom caps

Reuben Burgers

For true Reuben flavor, put the ketchup away and top things off with Thousand Island salad dressing.
—Jeanne Fenstermaker, Kendallville, Indiana

  2 pounds ground pork
  2 teaspoons salt
  1 teaspoon pepper
  1 garlic clove, minced
1/2 cup sauerkraut, drained
  8 slices Swiss cheese
  8 hamburger buns, split and toasted

In a bowl, combine pork, salt, pepper and garlic; mix well. Shape into 16 patties, about 3/8 in. thick. Spoon 1 tablespoon sauerkraut in the center of eight patties; top each with a second patty and press edges to seal.

Grill, uncovered, over medium heat for 6-8 minutes on each side or until juices run clear. Top with cheese. Serve on buns. **Yield:** 8 servings.

■ ■ ■

Ground Beef Gyros

(Pictured at right)

If your family likes gyros as much as mine, they'll love this easy version that's made with ground beef instead of lamb. I found the recipe in a newspaper and adapted it to fit our tastes. They're very much like the ones served at a local restaurant. A cucumber yogurt sauce adds an authentic finishing touch.
—Ruth Stahl, Shepherd, Montana

  1 **carton (8 ounces) plain yogurt**
1/3 **cup chopped seeded cucumber**
  2 **tablespoons finely chopped onion**
  1 **garlic clove, minced**
  1 **teaspoon sugar**
FILLING:
  1 **pound ground beef**
1-1/2 **teaspoons dried oregano**
  1 **teaspoon garlic powder**
  1 **teaspoon onion powder**
  1 **teaspoon salt**
3/4 **teaspoon pepper**
  4 **pita breads, halved, warmed**
  3 **cups shredded lettuce**
  1 **large tomato, chopped**
  1 **small onion, sliced**

In a bowl, combine the first five ingredients. Cover and refrigerate. In a bowl, combine beef and seasonings; mix well. Shape into four patties. Grill, covered, over medium-hot heat for 10-12 minutes, turning once. Cut patties into thin slices; stuff into pita halves. Add lettuce, tomato and onion. Serve with the yogurt sauce. **Yield:** 4 servings.

When purchasing

ground beef, remember that the fat content factors into how flavorful the end product will be. The leaner cuts contain less fat and will have a drier texture when cooked.

Ground sirloin and ground round are very lean cuts that work well in both casseroles and low-fat recipes.

Ground chuck has a good balance of fat and lean, making it an ideal choice for hamburgers, meat loaves and meatballs.

Ground beef (a combination of several cuts) has a high fat content and is best used for recipes in which you drain the fat from the meat.

Chip 'n' Dip Burgers

(Pictured above)

French onion dip and potato chips enhance these special hamburgers. They're so delicious, no other fixings are needed!
—Diane Hixon, Niceville, Florida

1-1/2 cups crushed potato chips, *divided*
1-1/2 cups French onion dip, *divided*
1/4 cup dill pickle relish
1-1/2 pounds ground beef
6 hamburger buns, toasted

In a bowl, combine half of the potato chips and half of the dip; add relish. Crumble beef over the mixture and mix well. Shape into six patties. Grill, covered, over medium heat for 6 minutes on each side or until meat is no longer pink. Serve on buns; top with remaining chips and dip. **Yield:** 6 servings.

Hawaiian Turkey Burgers

(Pictured at right)

My husband and I love to grill, so hamburgers are often on the menu. This recipe uses ground turkey instead of beef. Dressed with pineapple slices, the burgers are moist and juicy.
—Babette Watterson, Atglen, Pennsylvania

1 can (8 ounces) sliced pineapple
1/2 cup dry bread crumbs
1/2 cup sliced green onions
1/2 cup chopped sweet red pepper
1 tablespoon soy sauce
1/4 teaspoon salt
1 pound lean ground turkey
1/4 cup teriyaki sauce
4 sesame hamburger buns

Coat grill rack with nonstick cooking spray before starting the grill. Drain pineapple, reserving 1/4 cup juice (discard remaining juice or save for another use); set pineapple aside. In a bowl, combine the bread crumbs, onions, red pepper, soy sauce, salt and reserved pineapple juice. Crumble turkey over mixture and mix well. Shape into four patties.

Grill, covered, over medium heat for 3 minutes on each side. Brush with teriyaki sauce. Grill 4-6 minutes longer on each side or until meat is no longer pink and a meat thermometer reads 165°. Grill pineapple slices for 2 minutes on each side, basting occasionally with teriyaki sauce. Warm buns on grill; top each with a burger and pineapple slice. **Yield:** 4 servings.

Hamburgers are one of the easiest entrees to prepare. And with a few timeless tips, your burgers will turn out tasty every time!

To keep hamburgers moist, first combine the filling ingredients, then add the meat and mix just until combined. Overmixing can cause the burgers to be dense and heavy.

If you don't like getting your hands messy when mixing the meat mixture, put the ingredients in a large resealable plastic bag, then mix. Or if you do use your hands, first dampen them with water and nothing will stick to your fingers.

For uniform-shaped hamburger patties, place the meat mixture on a large sheet of waxed paper. Roll into a log the diameter you want your patties. Wrap log in plastic wrap; freeze for about 1 hour. Cut the log into slices. A large ice cream scoop is also an easy way to make hamburger patties of similar sizes.

The more fat there is in the ground meat, the more the patties will shrink during cooking. So if you're making burgers out of regular ground beef, shape the patties to be slightly larger than the bun. (Burgers made from ground sirloin will shrink the least.)

Don't use a metal spatula to flatten the burgers while cooking...you'll squeeze out all of the succulent juices.

over mixture and mix well. Shape into eight 5-in. patties. Top each patty with 2 tablespoons cheddar cheese; fold in half and press edges to seal, forming a half-moon.

Coat grill rack with nonstick cooking spray before starting the grill. Grill burgers, uncovered, over medium heat for 7-9 minutes on each side or until meat is no longer pink and a meat thermometer reads 160°. Serve on tortillas with lettuce, tomato, salsa and remaining chilies. **Yield:** 8 servings.

◼◼◼

Decked-Out Burgers

Guests will enjoy this burger's topping of bacon, cheese, mushrooms and mayonnaise.
—Karen Bourne, Magrath, Alberta

  1 **cup (4 ounces) shredded cheddar cheese**
  1 **jar (4-1/2 ounces) sliced mushrooms, drained**
1/3 **cup mayonnaise**
  6 **bacon strips, cooked and crumbled**
1/4 **cup finely chopped onion**
  1 **teaspoon salt**
1/2 **teaspoon pepper**
1/4 **teaspoon garlic powder**
1/8 **teaspoon hot pepper sauce**
1-1/2 **pounds lean ground beef**
  6 **hamburger buns, split**
Lettuce leaves and tomato slices, optional

In a bowl, combine cheese, mushrooms, mayonnaise and bacon; cover and refrigerate. In another bowl, combine onion, salt, pepper, garlic powder and hot pepper sauce; add beef and mix well. Shape into six 1/2-in.-thick patties.

Grill, covered, over medium-hot heat for 4-5 minutes on each side. Spoon cheese mixture on top of each burger. Grill 1-2 minutes longer or until the cheese begins to melt. Serve on buns with lettuce and tomato if desired. **Yield:** 6 servings.

Soft Taco Burgers

(Pictured above)

I love to grill these sandwiches for quick summer meals or impromptu get-togethers around the pool. They're a tasty Southwestern twist to traditional burgers.
—Joan Hallford, North Richland Hills, Texas

  1 **cup refried beans**
  1 **can (4 ounces) chopped green chilies, *divided***
1/4 **cup chopped onion**
1/4 **teaspoon salt**
1-1/2 **pounds lean ground beef**
  1 **cup (4 ounces) shredded cheddar cheese**
  8 **flour tortillas (6 inches), warmed**
  1 **cup chopped lettuce**
  1 **medium tomato, chopped**
1/2 **cup salsa**

In a bowl, combine the beans, 2 tablespoons green chilies, onion and salt. Crumble the beef

Herb Burgers

(Pictured above)

*These juicy burgers have lots of flavor!
My dear Uncle Mickey shared the recipe
with me years ago.*
—Brenda Sorrow, Kannapolis, North Carolina

1 egg, lightly beaten
1 medium onion, chopped
2 teaspoons ketchup
2 garlic cloves, minced
1 teaspoon salt
1 teaspoon Worcestershire sauce
1/2 teaspoon pepper
1/4 teaspoon dried oregano
1/4 teaspoon dried parsley flakes
1/4 teaspoon rubbed sage
1/8 to 1/4 teaspoon hot pepper sauce
2 pounds ground beef
8 hamburger buns, split
Mayonnaise, lettuce leaves, and sliced
   tomatoes and red onion

In a bowl, combine the first 11 ingredients.
Crumble beef over mixture and mix well.
Shape into eight patties. Grill, uncovered, over
medium heat for 5-6 minutes on each side or
until meat is no longer pink. Serve on buns
with mayonnaise, lettuce, tomatoes and
onion. **Yield:** 8 servings.

Blues Burgers

(Pictured above)

If you like blue cheese, you'll love the flavorful surprise inside these moist hamburgers.
—Dee Dee Mitchell, Longmont, Colorado

1/2 **pound fresh mushrooms, sliced**
2 **tablespoons butter**
1/2 **teaspoon ground cumin**
1/2 **teaspoon paprika**
1/4 **teaspoon chili powder**
1/4 **teaspoon salt**
1/4 **teaspoon pepper**
Pinch cayenne pepper
1-1/2 **pounds lean ground beef**
2 **ounces crumbled blue cheese**
2/3 **cup barbecue sauce**
4 **onion rolls *or* hamburger buns, split**

In a skillet, saute mushrooms in butter for 2-3 minutes or until tender. Set aside and keep warm. In a bowl, combine the next six ingredients; add beef and mix well. Shape into eight thin patties. Sprinkle half of the patties with blue cheese. Place remaining patties on top and press edges firmly to seal. Grill, uncovered, over medium-hot heat for 3 minutes on each side. Brush with barbecue sauce.

Grill burgers 10-12 minutes longer or until meat is no longer pink, basting and turning occasionally. Drain the mushrooms. Serve burgers on rolls topped with mushrooms. **Yield:** 4 servings.

Grilled Bratwurst

Whether you're hosting a picnic at home or at a park, our Test Kitchen home economists suggest cooking the bratwurst on the stovetop first. Then you can quickly brown them on the grill.

8 **uncooked bratwurst links**
3 **cans (12 ounces *each*) beer *or* nonalcoholic beer**
1 **large onion, halved and sliced**
2 **tablespoons fennel seed**
8 **bratwurst sandwich buns, split**

Place the bratwurst in a large saucepan or Dutch oven; add the beer, onion and fennel. Bring to a boil. Reduce heat; cover and simmer for 8-10 minutes or until meat is no longer pink. Drain and discard beer mixture.

Grill bratwurst, covered, over indirect medium heat for 7-8 minutes or until browned. Serve on buns. **Yield:** 8 servings.

■ ■ ■

Greek Pork Wraps

(Pictured at right)

If you like gyros, you'll love these strips of grilled pork wrapped in tortillas. It's become a popular summer dish in my home ever since a co-worker gave me the idea for the creamy cucumber dressing.
—Christine London, Kansas City, Missouri

1/4 **cup lemon juice**
2 **tablespoons olive oil**
1 **tablespoon prepared mustard**
1-3/4 **teaspoons minced garlic, *divided***
1 **teaspoon dried oregano**
1 **pork tenderloin (1 pound)**
1 **cup chopped peeled cucumber**
1 **cup plain yogurt**
1/4 **teaspoon salt**
1/4 **teaspoon dill weed**

8 **flour tortillas (6 inches)**
1/2 **cup chopped green onions**

In a large resealable plastic bag, combine the lemon juice, oil, mustard, 1-1/4 teaspoons garlic and oregano; add the pork. Seal bag and turn to coat; refrigerate for 2 hours.

In a bowl, combine cucumber, yogurt, salt, dill and remaining garlic; cover and refrigerate until serving.

Drain and discard marinade. Coat grill rack with nonstick cooking spray before starting the grill for indirect medium-hot heat. Grill tenderloin, uncovered, over direct-heated area for 5 minutes, turning once. Move to indirect-heated area; cover and cook 10-15 minutes longer or until a meat thermometer reads 160°. Let stand for 5 minutes.

Meanwhile, wrap tortillas in foil; place on grill for 2-3 minutes or until warmed, turning once. Slice tenderloin into strips; place on tortillas. Top each with 3 tablespoons yogurt sauce and 1 tablespoon green onions. **Yield:** 4 servings.

Cajun Burgers

(Pictured above)

I found the original recipe for these burgers in a cookbook, then added and subtracted ingredients until they suited my family's fondness for spicy food.
—Julie Culbertson, Bensalem, Pennsylvania

CAJUN SEASONING BLEND:
  3 tablespoons ground cumin
  3 tablespoons dried oregano
  1 tablespoon garlic powder
  1 tablespoon paprika
  2 teaspoons salt
  1 teaspoon cayenne pepper

BURGERS:
  1/4 cup finely chopped onion
  1 teaspoon salt
  1 teaspoon Cajun Seasoning Blend (recipe above)
  1/2 to 1 teaspoon hot pepper sauce
  1/2 teaspoon dried thyme
  1/4 teaspoon dried basil
  1 garlic clove, minced
  1 pound ground beef

4 hamburger buns, split
Sauteed onions, optional

Combine all seasoning blend ingredients in a small bowl or resealable plastic bag; mix well. In a bowl, combine the first seven burger ingredients; add beef and mix well. Shape into four patties. Grill over medium-hot heat for 4-5 minutes per side or until meat is no longer pink. Serve on buns; top with sauteed onions if desired. Store remaining seasoning blend in an airtight container. **Yield:** 4 servings.

Editor's Note: Purchased Cajun seasoning may be substituted for the homemade blend.

■ ■ ■

Marinated Chicken Sandwiches

Every bite of this grilled chicken is packed with flavor. The sweet brown sugar combines well with zesty mustard and ginger. Top the sandwich with any kind of cheese.
—Ruth Lee, Troy, Ontario

1/2 cup soy sauce
1/4 cup packed brown sugar
1/4 cup ketchup
1 tablespoon vegetable oil
1 tablespoon molasses
1 teaspoon garlic powder
1 teaspoon minced fresh gingerroot
1 teaspoon prepared mustard
6 boneless skinless chicken breast halves (6 ounces *each*)
3 tablespoons mayonnaise
6 kaiser rolls, split and toasted
6 lettuce leaves
6 slices (1/2 ounce *each*) Swiss cheese

In a large resealable plastic bag, combine the first eight ingredients; add the chicken. Seal bag and turn to coat; refrigerate for at least 1 hour.

Coat grill rack with nonstick cooking spray before starting the grill. Drain and discard marinade. Grill chicken, covered, over medium heat for 4-6 minutes on each side or until juices run clear. Spread mayonnaise over bottom of rolls; top with chicken, lettuce and cheese. Replace roll tops. **Yield:** 6 servings.

■ ■ ■

Provolone Pepper Burgers

I'm known around the neighborhood as the "grill sergeant." I'm often seen making these tasty burgers on my built-in patio gas grill.
—Nick Mescia, Surprise, Arizona

1/3 cup finely cubed provolone cheese
1/4 cup diced roasted red peppers
1/4 cup finely chopped onion
Salt and pepper to taste
1 pound ground beef
4 hamburger buns, split

In a bowl, combine the cheese, red peppers, onion, salt and pepper. Add beef and mix well. Shape into four patties. Grill, covered, over medium-hot heat for 4-5 minutes on each side or until meat is no longer pink. Serve on buns. **Yield:** 4 servings.

Shaping Hamburger Patties

Use a 1/2-cup measuring cup or ice cream scoop to make equal size patties. Gently form each portion into a patty. For moist, light-textured burgers, don't overmix or overhandle the meat mixture.

In a large resealable plastic bag, combine the soy sauce, oil and juice; mix well. Remove 1/2 cup for basting; cover and refrigerate. Add the roast to remaining marinade; turn to coat. Seal and refrigerate for 8 hours or overnight, turning occasionally.

Drain and discard marinade. Grill roast, covered, over indirect heat, basting and turning every 15 minutes, for 1 hour or until meat reaches desired doneness (for medium-rare, a meat thermometer should read 145°; medium, 160°; well-done, 170°). Remove from grill; let stand for 1 hour. Cover and refrigerate overnight. Just before serving, prepare gravy mix according to package directions. Thinly slice roast; add to gravy and heat through. Serve on rolls. **Yield:** 12 servings.

■ ■ ■

Sirloin Sandwiches

(Pictured above)

Mom is always happy to share her cooking, and these tender, delicious beef sandwiches are a real crowd-pleaser. A simple three-ingredient marinade flavors the grilled beef wonderfully.
—Judi Messina, Coeur d'Alene, Idaho

  1 cup soy sauce
1/2 cup vegetable oil
1/2 cup cranberry *or* apple juice
  1 boneless sirloin tip roast
    (3 to 4 pounds)
  1 envelope beef au jus gravy mix
  1 dozen French rolls, split

Special Beef Wraps

(Pictured below right)

These hearty bundles burst with grilled steak, tangy pineapple and crunchy nuts.
—Diane Halferty, Tucson, Arizona

  1 cup white wine vinegar
1/4 cup soy sauce
  2 tablespoons lime juice
  2 tablespoons vegetable oil
  1 tablespoon honey
  1 beef flank steak (1-1/2 pounds)
  2 cups torn mixed salad greens
1/2 cup sliced green onions
  1 cup water
3/4 cup pineapple tidbits, drained
  1 cup honey-roasted peanuts,
    coarsely chopped
  8 flour tortillas (8 inches)

In a 2-cup measuring cup, combine the vinegar, soy sauce, lime juice, oil and honey. Pour 1-1/4 cups into a large resealable plastic bag; add steak. Seal bag and turn to coat. Refrigerate for 1-2 hours. In a bowl, combine the salad greens, green onions and remaining marinade. Cover and refrigerate.

In a skillet, bring water to a boil. Add onion tops; boil for 30-60 seconds. Drain and immediately place in ice water. Drain and pat dry; set aside.

Drain and discard marinade from steak. Grill, uncovered, over medium heat, or broil 4-6 in. from the heat for 7-10 minutes on each side or until meat reaches desired doneness (for medium-rare, a meat thermometer should read 145°; medium, 160°; well-done, 170°). Let stand for 10 minutes; thinly slice across the grain. Layer beef, lettuce mixture, pineapple and nuts on each tortilla. Fold one end over filling, then fold in sides. **Yield:** 8 servings.

When shopping for ground meat, purchase the amount you need. One pound of ground meat serves 3 to 4 people. Purchase any ground meat before the "sell by" date on the package.

Seasoned Turkey Burgers

(Pictured above)

These moist burgers are great alone, but my family likes them best with lettuce, onion, tomato and a dab of mayonnaise on a whole wheat bun.
—*Vicki Engelhardt, Grand Rapids, Michigan*

> 1/2 cup herb-seasoned stuffing croutons
> 1 pound ground turkey breast
> 1 small onion, finely chopped
> 5 hamburger buns, split
> Lettuce leaves, onion, tomato slices and mayonnaise, optional

Crush or process stuffing croutons into fine crumbs. In a bowl, combine crumbs, turkey and onion. Shape into four patties. Grill over medium-hot heat for 8-10 minutes, turning once. Serve on buns with lettuce, onion, tomato and mayonnaise if desired. **Yield:** 5 servings.

·Beef·

Die-hard barbecue fans agree a beef chapter is the meat and potatoes of a grilling book. From Herbed Beef Tenderloin, Marinated Flank Steak and Meatball Shish Kabobs to Tangy Sirloin Strips, Barbecued Beef Brisket and Grilled Cheeseburger Pizza, our mouth-watering recipes are a cut above the rest!

Herbed Beef Tenderloin

(Pictured at left)

Cooking on the grill has always been one of my favorite hobbies.
This recipe is a popular choice for my family's Sunday suppers or our special birthday dinners.
I like to serve the tenderloin with baked potatoes and homegrown vegetables.
—Paul Verner, Wooster, Ohio

1 beef tenderloin (4 to 5 pounds)
2 garlic cloves, minced
2 green onions, finely chopped
1 tablespoon Dijon mustard
1 tablespoon red wine vinegar *or* balsamic vinegar
1/2 cup olive oil
1 tablespoon *each* dried basil, thyme and rosemary, crushed
1 teaspoon salt
1 teaspoon pepper

Place tenderloin in a resealable plastic bag. Combine remaining ingredients; pour over meat. Seal bag; refrigerate overnight, turning occasionally. Drain and discard the marinade.

Grill beef, uncovered, over medium-hot heat for 20 minutes, turning frequently. Cover and continue to grill for 10-20 minutes or until meat reaches desired doneness (for medium-rare, a meat thermometer should read 145°; medium, 160°; well-done, 170°). Let stand 10 minutes before slicing. **Yield:** 8-10 servings.

Beef Grilling Chart

When cooking beef, a meat thermometer should read 145° for medium-rare, 160° for medium and 170° for well-done. Ground beef should be 160°. For direct grilling, turn meat halfway through grilling time. The cooking times given below are a guideline and are for medium-rare to medium doneness. Check for doneness with a meat thermometer or other appropriate doneness test.

Cut	Weight or Thickness	Heat	Approximate Cooking Time
Rib Eye Steak	1 in.	medium/direct	11 to 14 minutes
	1-1/2 in.	medium/direct	17 to 22 minutes
T-bone, Porterhouse or Top Loin Steak-boneless (Strip)	3/4 in.	medium/direct	10 to 12 minutes
	1 in.	medium/direct	15 to 18 minutes
	1-1/2 in.	medium/direct	19 to 23 minutes
Tenderloin Steak	1 in.	medium/direct	13 to 15 minutes
	1-1/2 in.	medium/direct	14 to 16 minutes
Top Sirloin Steak boneless	1 in.	medium/direct	17 to 21 minutes
	1-1/2 in.	medium/direct	22 to 26 minutes
	2 in.	medium/direct	28 to 33 minutes
Flank Steak*	1-1/2 to 2 lbs.	medium/direct	12 to 15 minutes
Skirt Steak	1/4 to 1/2 in.	high/direct	6 to 8 minutes
Top Round Steak*	1 in.	medium/direct	16 to 18 minutes
Chuck Shoulder Steak*	1 in.	medium/direct	16 to 20 minutes
Tenderloin Roast	2 to 3 lbs.	medium-hot/indirect	45 to 60 minutes
	4 to 5 lbs.	medium-hot/indirect	1 to 1-1/4 hours
Tri-Tip	1-3/4 to 2 lbs.	medium/indirect	35 to 45 minutes
Ground Beef or Veal Patty	4 oz. and 1/2 in.	medium/indirect	11 to 14 minutes

*These cuts of meat are best when marinated before grilling.

Tender Flank Steak

(Pictured above)

This mildly marinated flank steak is my son's favorite. I usually slice it thinly and serve it with twice-baked potatoes and a green salad to round out the meal. Leftovers are great for French dip sandwiches.
—*Gayle Bucknam, Greenbank, Washington*

1/4 **cup soy sauce**
2 **tablespoons water**
3 **garlic cloves, thinly sliced**
1 **tablespoon brown sugar**
1 **tablespoon vegetable oil**
1/2 **teaspoon ground ginger**
1/2 **teaspoon pepper**
1 **flank steak (1 pound)**

In a large resealable plastic bag, combine the first seven ingredients; mix well. Add steak; seal bag and turn to coat. Cover and refrigerate for 8 hours or overnight, turning occasionally. Drain and discard marinade.

Grill, covered, over medium-hot heat for 6-8 minutes on each side or until meat reaches desired doneness (for medium-rare, a meat thermometer should read 145°; medium, 160°; well-done, 170°). **Yield:** 4 servings.

Peppered Steaks With Salsa

(Pictured below)

We grill all year, and beef is so good cooked outdoors. The simple marinade makes the steaks very juicy. We enjoy them with the refreshing salsa and tortillas.
—Robin Hyde, Lincoln, Nebraska

1/2 cup red wine vinegar
2 tablespoons lime juice
2 tablespoons olive oil
2 teaspoons chili powder
1 garlic clove, minced
1 to 2 teaspoons crushed red pepper flakes
1 teaspoon salt
1/2 teaspoon pepper
4 boneless chuck eye steaks (about 8 ounces *each*)

SALSA:
1 large tomato, seeded and chopped
1 medium ripe avocado, chopped
2 green onions, thinly sliced
1 tablespoon lime juice
1 tablespoon minced fresh cilantro
1 garlic clove, minced
1/4 to 1/2 teaspoon salt
1/4 teaspoon pepper

In a large resealable plastic bag, combine the first eight ingredients; mix well. Remove 1/4 cup for basting; refrigerate. Add steaks to the remaining marinade; seal bag and turn to coat. Cover and refrigerate 8 hours or overnight. Meanwhile, combine salsa ingredients; cover and chill.

Drain steaks, discarding marinade. Grill, covered, over medium heat for 7-8 minutes on each side, basting with reserved marinade, or until meat reaches desired doneness (for medium-rare, a meat thermometer should read 145°; medium, 160°; well-done, 170°). Serve with salsa. **Yield:** 4 servings.

■ ■ ■

Flank Steak with Horseradish Sauce

An overnight marinade performs double duty, gently flavoring and tenderizing this lean cut of beef. The meaty entree from our Test Kitchen staff can be grilled to perfection in minutes.

1 beef flank steak (1 pound)
3 tablespoons lemon juice
2 tablespoons Dijon mustard
2 tablespoons Worcestershire sauce
2 garlic cloves, minced
1/8 teaspoon hot pepper sauce
HORSERADISH SAUCE:
1/4 cup mayonnaise
1/4 cup sour cream
1 tablespoon Dijon mustard

2 green onions, finely chopped
2 teaspoons prepared horseradish

Using a sharp knife, score the surface of the steak with shallow diagonal cuts at 1-in. intervals, making diamond shapes. Repeat on other side. In a large resealable plastic bag, combine the next five ingredients. Add steak. Seal bag and turn to coat; refrigerate for 8 hours or overnight. Combine the sauce ingredients in a small bowl; cover and refrigerate.

Drain and discard marinade. Grill the steak, covered, over medium-hot heat for 7-9 minutes on each side or until meat reaches desired doneness (for medium-rare, a meat thermometer should read 145°; medium, 160°; well-done, 170°). Thinly slice steak across the grain; serve with sauce. **Yield:** 4 servings.

■ ■ ■

Oriental Steak Skewers

(Pictured at right)

I'm always on the lookout for light meals that will satisfy my family, and these stuffed kabobs fit the bill. Served with a creamy mustard sauce, the colorful bundles are special enough for company.
—*Gina Hatchell, Mickleton, New Jersey*

1 pound boneless beef sirloin
   tip roast
1/3 cup soy sauce
1/4 cup sugar
1/2 teaspoon ground ginger *or* 2
   teaspoons grated fresh gingerroot
1 cup water
4 medium carrots, julienned
1/2 pound fresh green beans
1 large sweet red pepper, julienned
1/2 cup sour cream
2 tablespoons Dijon mustard
1-1/4 teaspoons prepared horseradish

Cut beef widthwise into 16 slices, 1/4 in. thick. In a large resealable plastic bag, combine the soy sauce, sugar and ginger; add the beef. Seal bag and turn to coat; refrigerate for 4 hours.

In a saucepan, bring water and carrots to a boil. Reduce heat; cover and simmer for 3 minutes. Add the beans and red pepper; cover and simmer for 3-5 minutes or until vegetables are crisp-tender. Drain and immediately place vegetables in ice water. Drain and pat dry.

Drain and discard marinade from beef. Arrange three beans, one carrot strip and one pepper strip down the center of each beef slice; roll up. For each kabob, use metal or soaked wooden skewers and thread two bundles on two parallel skewers.

Coat grill rack with nonstick cooking spray before starting the grill. Grill kabobs, covered, over medium heat for 2-3 minutes on each side or until beef reaches desired doneness, turning once. In a bowl, combine the sour cream, mustard and horseradish. Serve with kabobs. **Yield:** 4 servings.

Grilled Cheeseburger Pizza

(Pictured below)

*I combined our daughter's two favorite foods—
pizza and grilled cheeseburgers—
to create this main dish.*
—Tanya Gutierro, Beacon Falls, Connecticut

- 3/4 **pound ground beef**
- 1 **cup ketchup**
- 2 **tablespoons prepared mustard**
- 1 **prebaked Italian bread shell crust (14 ounces)**
- 1 **cup shredded lettuce**
- 1 **medium tomato, thinly sliced**
- 1/8 **teaspoon salt**
- 1/8 **teaspoon pepper**
- 1 **small sweet onion, thinly sliced**
- 1/2 **cup dill pickle slices**
- 1 **cup (4 ounces) shredded cheddar cheese**
- 1 **cup (4 ounces) shredded part-skim mozzarella cheese**

Shape beef into three 1/2-in.-thick patties. Grill, covered, over medium-hot heat for 5 minutes on each side or until meat is no longer pink. Meanwhile, combine ketchup and mustard; spread over the crust to within 1 in. of edge. Sprinkle with lettuce; top with tomato. Sprinkle with salt and pepper. When beef patties are cooked, cut into 1/2-in. pieces; arrange over tomato slices. Top with onion, pickles and cheeses.

Place pizza on a 16-in. square piece of heavy-duty foil; transfer to grill. Grill, covered, over indirect medium heat for 12-15 minutes or until cheese is melted and crust is lightly browned. Remove from the grill. Let stand for 5-10 minutes before slicing. **Yield:** 4-6 servings.

In a large resealable plastic bag, combine the first nine ingredients; mix well. Add roast and turn to coat. Seal bag; refrigerate for at least 3 hours, turning occasionally. Remove roast. Pour marinade into a small saucepan; bring to a boil. Reduce heat; simmer for 15 minutes.

Meanwhile, grill roast, covered, over indirect heat for 20 minutes, turning occasionally. Add applesauce to marinade; brush over roast. Continue basting and turning the roast several times for 1 to 1-1/2 hours, or until meat reaches desired doneness (for medium-rare, a meat thermometer should read 145°; medium, 160°; well-done, 170°). **Yield:** 6-8 servings.

■ ■ ■

Beef and Pepper Kabobs

I'm always on the lookout for new recipes when traveling. I adapted this recipe from a Turkish cookbook.
—Janet Wood, Windham, New Hampshire

    3 tablespoons lemon juice
    2 tablespoons vegetable oil
    1 large onion, finely chopped
1-1/2 teaspoons dried thyme
  1/2 teaspoon salt
  1/4 teaspoon pepper
    2 pounds sirloin, cut into 1-inch cubes
    1 *each* green, yellow, orange and red
       peppers

In a resealable plastic bag; combine lemon juice, oil, onion, thyme, salt and pepper. Add meat; turn to coat. Seal bag; refrigerate 6 hours or overnight. Drain and discard marinade.

Cut peppers into 1-in. squares and thread onto metal or soaked wooden skewers alternately with meat. Grill over hot heat, turning often, for 12-15 minutes or until the meat reaches desired doneness. **Yield:** 6-8 servings.

Barbecued Chuck Roast

(Pictured above)

Whether I serve this roast for church dinners, company or just family, it is always a hit. To go along with it, my family likes scalloped potatoes, tossed salad and pie. Leftovers make great sandwiches.
—Ardis Gautier, Lamont, Oklahoma

1/3 cup cider vinegar
1/4 cup ketchup
  2 tablespoons vegetable oil
  2 tablespoons soy sauce
  1 tablespoon Worcestershire sauce
  1 teaspoon garlic powder
  1 teaspoon prepared mustard
  1 teaspoon salt
1/4 teaspoon pepper
  1 boneless chuck roast (2-1/2 to 3 pounds)
1/2 cup applesauce

Teriyaki Beef Kabobs

(Pictured above)

My sister-in-law brought this recipe on a family camping trip and we fixed it for an outdoor potluck. It was so delicious that I asked for a copy to take home.
—Lisa Hector, Estevan, Saskatchewan

1/4 **cup vegetable oil**
1/4 **cup orange juice**
1/4 **cup soy sauce**
1 **teaspoon garlic powder**
1 **teaspoon ground ginger**
1-3/4 **pounds beef tenderloin, cut into 1-inch cubes**
3/4 **pound cherry tomatoes**
1/2 **pound fresh whole mushrooms**
2 **large green peppers, cubed**
1 **large red onion, cut into wedges**
Hot cooked rice, optional

In a resealable plastic bag, combine the first five ingredients and mix well. Reserve 1/2 cup for basting and refrigerate. Add beef to remaining marinade; turn to coat. Seal bag; refrigerate for 1 hour, turning occasionally. Drain and discard the marinade.

On metal or soaked wooden skewers, alternate beef, tomatoes, mushrooms, green peppers and onions. Grill, uncovered, over medium heat for 3 minutes on each side. Baste with reserved marinade. Continue turning and basting for 8-10 minutes or until meat reaches desired doneness. Serve meat and vegetables over rice if desired. **Yield:** 6-8 servings.

Peppery London Broil

I was bored making the usual London broil, so I got a little creative and sparked up the flavor.
—Dan Wright, San Jose, California

- 1 **beef flank steak (about 3/4 pound)**
- 1 **garlic clove, minced**
- 1/2 **teaspoon seasoned salt**
- 1/8 **teaspoon crushed red pepper**
- 1/4 **cup Worcestershire sauce**

With a fork, poke holes in both sides of meat. Combine garlic, seasoned salt and red pepper; rub over both sides of meat. Place the steak in a gallon-size plastic bag. Add Worcestershire sauce and close bag. Refrigerate for at least 4 hours, turning once.

Remove meat; discard marinade. Grill over hot heat for 4-5 minutes on each side or until meat reaches desired doneness (for medium-rare, a meat thermometer should read 145°; medium, 160°; well-done, 170°). **Yield:** 2 servings.

Marinated Rib Eyes

(Pictured at right)

We have these tempting steaks weekly. If neighbors happen to drop by when I'm preparing steaks, I cut the meat into cubes and grill it on skewers with onions and mushrooms as appetizers.
—Rosalie Usry, Flaxton, North Dakota

- 1/3 **cup hot water**
- 3 **tablespoons finely chopped onion**
- 2 **tablespoons red wine vinegar**
- 2 **tablespoons olive oil**
- 2 **tablespoons soy sauce**
- 1 **teaspoon beef bouillon granules**
- 1 **garlic clove, minced**
- 1/2 **teaspoon paprika**
- 1/2 **teaspoon coarsely ground pepper**
- 2 **beef rib eye steaks (about 1 inch thick and 12 ounces *each*)**

In a bowl, combine the first nine ingredients. Remove 1/2 cup marinade and refrigerate. Pierce steaks several times on both sides with a fork; place in a large resealable plastic bag. Pour remaining marinade over steaks; turn to coat. Seal bag and refrigerate overnight. Remove steaks, discarding marinade.

Grill, uncovered, over medium-hot heat for 4-8 minutes on each side or until meat reaches desired donness (for medium-rare, a meat thermometer should read 145°; medium, 160°; well-done, 170°). Warm reserved marinade; serve with steaks. **Yield:** 2 servings.

1/2 teaspoon ground ginger
1/8 teaspoon pepper

Trim fat from steak and slice lengthwise into 1/2-in. strips; place in a large resealable plastic bag. Combine all remaining ingredients; pour over meat and turn gently. Seal bag and refrigerate for 2-3 hours. Drain, discarding marinade.

Loosely thread meat strips onto skewers. Grill over medium-hot heat, turning often, for 7-10 minutes or until meat reaches desired doneness. Remove from skewers and serve. **Yield:** 6 servings.

■ ■ ■

Paprika Chili Steak

Marinade seasoned with chili powder and paprika gives grilled flank steak a robust flavor. This treasured recipe comes from a German neighbor.
—DiAnn Mallehan, Grand Rapids, Michigan

  1 medium onion, chopped
1/2 cup ketchup
1/4 cup cider vinegar
  1 tablespoon paprika
  1 tablespoon canola oil
  2 teaspoons chili powder
  1 teaspoon salt
1/8 teaspoon pepper
1-1/2 pounds beef flank steak

In a large resealable plastic bag, combine the first eight ingredients; add steak. Seal bag and turn to coat; refrigerate for 3 hours or overnight, turning occasionally.

Coat grill rack with nonstick cooking spray before starting grill. Drain; discard marinade. Grill steak, covered, over medium-hot heat for 6-8 minutes on each side or until meat reaches desired doneness (for medium-rare, a meat thermometer should read 145°; medium, 160°; well-done, 170°). **Yield:** 6 servings.

Teriyaki Finger Steaks

(Pictured above)

When these flavorful skewered steaks are sizzling on the grill, the aroma makes everyone around stop what they're doing and come to see what's cooking. The tasty marinade is easy to make, and these little steaks are quick to cook and fun to eat.
—Jeri Dobrowski, Beach, North Dakota

  2 pounds boneless sirloin steak
1/2 cup soy sauce
1/4 cup white vinegar
  2 tablespoons brown sugar
  2 tablespoons minced onion
  1 tablespoon vegetable oil
  1 garlic clove, minced

Chili Flank Steak

(Pictured below)

My husband loves this juicy steak and its tasty sauce. I like that I can have it ready to marinate in no time.
—Karma Henry, Glasgow, Kentucky

- 2/3 **cup packed brown sugar**
- 2/3 **cup V8 juice**
- 2/3 **cup soy sauce**
- 1/2 **cup olive oil**
- 4 **garlic cloves, chopped**
- 2 **tablespoons chili powder**
- 1/4 **teaspoon ground cumin**
- 1 **beef flank steak (about 1-1/2 pounds)**

In a large bowl, combine first seven ingredients; mix well. Pour half the marinade into a large resealable bag; add steak. Seal bag and turn to coat; refrigerate for 8 hours or overnight, turning occasionally. Cover and refrigerate remaining marinade.

Drain and discard marinade from steak. Grill steak, covered, over medium-hot heat for 6-10 minutes on each side or until meat reaches desired doneness (for medium-rare, a meat thermometer should read 145°; medium, 160°; well-done, 170°). Serve with reserved marinade. **Yield:** 4-6 servings.

Grilled Steak Pinwheels

(Pictured below)

I've been serving this recipe to family and friends for over 20 years and very seldom do I have leftovers. We try to keep the house cool, so we grill out often. I get most of the herbs in this recipe from my son's garden.
—Mary Hills, Scottsdale, Arizona

- 2 flank steaks (1 pound *each*), trimmed
- 1/2 pound sliced bacon, cooked and crumbled
- 1 cup finely chopped fresh mushrooms
- 1 cup finely chopped green onions
- 1/4 cup finely chopped fresh basil *or* 4 teaspoons dried basil
- 2 tablespoons minced fresh chives

Pound flank steaks on each side. Combine bacon, mushrooms, onions, basil and chives; spread evenly over steaks. Roll the meat up and secure with skewers or wooden picks. Cut each roll into 1/2- to 3/4-in. slices and secure with a wooden pick or skewer.

Grill over hot heat for 4-6 minutes per side or until meat reaches desired doneness (for medium-rare, a meat thermometer should read 145°, medium, 160°, well-done, 170°). Remove picks before serving. **Yield:** 6-8 servings.

■ ■ ■

Onion-Smothered Sirloins

(Pictured at right)

For spicier steaks, you can increase the pepper flakes and cumin in this recipe.
—Tina Michalicka, Hudson, Florida

- 1 teaspoon garlic powder
- 3/4 teaspoon salt, *divided*
- 1/2 teaspoon ground cumin
- 1/2 teaspoon dried oregano
- 1/4 teaspoon crushed red pepper flakes
- 4 boneless beef sirloin steaks (about 8 ounces *each* and 1 inch thick)
- 2 large sweet onions, cut into 1/2-inch slices and separated into rings
- 1/4 cup olive oil
- 1/4 teaspoon pepper
- 1 medium lime, cut into quarters

In a bowl, combine the garlic powder, 1/2 teaspoon salt, cumin, oregano and pepper flakes. Rub over the steaks; set aside. Place onions in a disposable foil pan; add oil and toss to coat. Grill, covered, over medium heat for 30-40 minutes or until golden brown, stirring occasionally. Season onions with pepper, remaining salt and a squeeze of lime.

Grill steaks, uncovered, over medium heat for 7-10 minutes on each side or until meat reaches desired doneness (for medium-rare, a meat thermometer should read 145°; medium, 160°; well-done, 170°). Squeeze remaining lime over the steaks; top with onions. **Yield:** 4 servings.

Honey-Mustard Beef Kabobs

Here's an easy entree that's sure to get mustard lovers all fired up. I rely on the tangy condiment to season these beefy skewers.
—Suzanne McKinley, Lyons, Georgia

- 1/2 **cup Dijon mustard**
- 1/4 **cup honey**
-   1 **teaspoon Worcestershire sauce**
- 1/4 **teaspoon salt**
- 1/8 **teaspoon pepper**
- 3/4 **pound boneless beef sirloin steak, cut into 1-inch cubes**

In a bowl, combine the mustard, honey, Worcestershire sauce, salt and pepper. Pour half of the sauce into a large resealable plastic bag; add beef cubes and toss to coat. Set remaining sauce aside.

Thread beef onto metal or soaked wooden skewers. Discard marinade from beef. Grill, covered, over medium heat for 8-10 minutes or until meat reaches desired doneness, turning once. Serve with reserved sauce. **Yield:** 3 servings.

Kabobs

are not only easy to assemble and grill to perfection in mere minutes, they're just plain fun because of the countless delicious food combinations.

Meat selections include beef, pork tenderloin, chicken breasts, kielbasa, lamb, shrimp, scallops, tuna, swordfish and salmon.

For a wholesome meal, include vegetables like pearl onions, cherry tomatoes, mushrooms, eggplant, zucchini, squash, baby potatoes, carrots and peppers.

Or add a little sweetness with fruits such as pineapple, strawberries or mango.

Which Steak to Take

Tenderloin

Considered the queen of steaks, this boneless loin cut is commonly called filet mignon. It's the most tender of steaks and boasts fine marbling. Although lean, its mild buttery flavor has made it popular.

Choice-grade tenderloin steaks are the most expensive steak, but there is no waste on edge fat or bone.

Serving size and cost: Their small size makes tenderloin ideal for individual servings. Choose filets that are around 1-1/2 to 2 inches thick. Choice-grade tenderloin steaks are about $15 or more a pound.

Grilling tip: Since tenderloins have little fat, they're best grilled medium-rare to medium.

Sirloin Steak

When shopping for sirloin, choose those labeled top sirloin, indicating that it is cut from the loin. Other steaks labeled as sirloin, such as petite sirloin or sirloin tip steak, are less tender and best when marinated before grilling. Lightly marbled sirloin steaks are lean and have a good chew, but are less moist than heavily marbled steaks.

Serving size and cost: Usually sold boneless from 1 to 2 inches thick, sirloins are intended to serve three to six people. As the least expensive of the tender steaks, sirloins are a great choice for families.

Grilling tip: When grilling a thick sirloin, a two-level fire assures steaks cooked past medium will remain moist.

Rib Eye Steaks

Known in some parts of the country as Delmonico steak, these bone-in or boneless steaks are cut from the rib section. Rib eyes are juicy, rich and very tender.

Serving size and cost: Boneless rib eyes are typically 3/4 to 1 inch thick, while bone-in versions are about 1-1/2 inches. Thinner rib eyes serve one, while thicker steaks feed two. Rib eyes are the second most costly steak behind the tenderloin.

Grilling tip: These heavily marbled steaks are prone to flare-ups on the grill; medium heat and a watchful eye is the key to a well-grilled rib eye. Rib eye steaks can withstand longer grilling and can be cooked medium to well-done.

Porterhouse and T-Bone Steaks

With their characteristic "T"-shaped bone, these cuts are actually two steaks in one. The longer narrow section is top loin steak and the smaller is tenderloin. The porterhouse, often called the "king" of steaks because of its size, has a larger rounder tenderloin section than the T-bone.

Serving size and cost: These steaks may be found from 3/4 to 2 inches thick, with 3/4-inch T-bones being a generous individual serving. Porterhouses around 2 inches thick are intended to serve two to three people. And cost…they're middle-of-the-road.

Grilling tip: Grill thick porterhouse steaks over a two-level fire—a hot zone for searing, and a medium-heat zone for the remainder of the cooking. Porterhouse and T-bone steaks can be grilled from medium-rare to well-done.

Top Loin Steak

Strip, New York strip, Kansas City strip and club steak… this hearty steak goes by many names. No matter what it's called, you can't miss with this flavorful well-marbled steak and its firm chewy texture. Cut from the loin, it's available bone-in or boneless.

Serving size and cost: Top loin steaks may be cut from 3/4 to 2 inches thick; the thinner 3/4 to 1-inch cuts are better suited for single servings. While their price per pound may be more expensive than a porterhouse or T-bone, boneless strips are a better value since you aren't paying for the bone.

Grilling tip: Because they're fairly lean, strip steaks are great grilled medium-rare to medium.

Flank Steak

Its characteristic horizontal grain easily identifies this steak. Though most think of flank steak as a marinating steak, choice-grade flank grills well when seasoned. Flank steak has a rich beefy flavor and a moderate chew.

Serving size and cost: Flank steaks are 1 to 1-1/2 pounds and serve four to six people. Flank steaks are fairly economical; they cost a little more than sirloin steak.

Grilling tip: The key to tender moist flank steak is grilling to medium-rare or medium, and thinly slicing 1/4-inch thick across the grain.

Beef cuts: ©Cattlemen's Beef Board and National Cattlemen's Beef Assoc.

Sesame Steaks

(Pictured below)

There's enough flavor in these steaks to allow the side dish to be simple. So consider serving them with baked potatoes, rice pilaf or a vegetable and salad. The meal has always gone over big when I've fixed it for my husband and friends.
—*Elaine Anderson, Aliquippa, Pennsylvania*

1/2 **cup soy sauce**
2 **tablespoons brown sugar**
2 **tablespoons vegetable oil**
2 **tablespoons sesame seeds**
2 **teaspoons onion powder**
2 **teaspoons lemon juice**
1/4 **teaspoon ground ginger**
4 **T-bone steaks (about 1 inch thick)**

In a large resealable plastic bag, combine the first seven ingredients; mix well. Add steaks and turn to coat. Seal bag and refrigerate for at least 4 hours. Drain and discard marinade.

Grill steaks, uncovered, over medium heat for 5-7 minutes on each side or until the meat reaches desired doneness (for medium-rare, a meat thermometer should read 145°; medium, 160°; well-done, 170°). **Yield:** 4 servings.

Yankee-Doodle Sirloin Roast

(Pictured above)

In the spirit of July Fourth, my sister and I planned a theme menu for our families that included this grilled roast. Marinating the meat overnight really boosts the flavor. This entree kept us out of the kitchen and was a nice change from the usual burgers and hot dogs.
—Laurie Neverman, Green Bay, Wisconsin

1/2 cup beef broth
1/2 cup teriyaki *or* soy sauce
1/4 cup vegetable oil
  2 tablespoons brown sugar
  2 tablespoons finely chopped onion
  3 garlic cloves, minced
  1 teaspoon Worcestershire sauce
1/2 teaspoon hot pepper sauce
  1 boneless beef sirloin tip roast
    (about 4 pounds)

In a large resealable plastic bag, combine the first eight ingredients; add roast. Seal bag and turn to coat; refrigerate overnight.

Drain and discard marinade. Grill roast, covered, over indirect medium heat for 2 to 2-1/2 hours or until meat reaches desired doneness (for medium-rare, a meat thermometer should read 145°; medium, 160°; well-done, 170°). Or place roast on a rack in a shallow roasting pan. Bake, uncovered, at 350° for 2 to 2-1/2 hours. Let stand for 10-15 minutes before slicing. **Yield:** 12-14 servings.

■ ■ ■

Garlic-Pepper Tenderloin Steaks

I give a little kick to these grilled tenderloin steaks with a zippy dry rub that combines paprika, thyme, ground mustard, chili powder and cayenne pepper. The steaks can also be broiled when the weather isn't right for grilling.
—Vicki Atkinson, Kamas, Utah

1-1/2	teaspoons minced garlic
1	teaspoon ground mustard
1	teaspoon paprika
1	teaspoon chili powder
1	teaspoon pepper
1/2	teaspoon salt
1/2	teaspoon dried thyme
1/4 to 1/2	teaspoon cayenne pepper
4	beef tenderloin steaks (4 ounces *each*)
2	teaspoons olive oil

In a small bowl, combine the first eight ingredients. Brush steaks with oil; rub in seasoning mixture. Cover and refrigerate for at least 1 hour.

Coat the grill rack with nonstick cooking spray before starting the grill. Grill the steaks, uncovered, over medium heat for 7-10 minutes on each side or until the meat reaches desired doneness (for medium-rare, a meat thermometer should read 145°; medium, 160°; well-done, 170°). **Yield:** 4 servings.

Grate Grill Marks

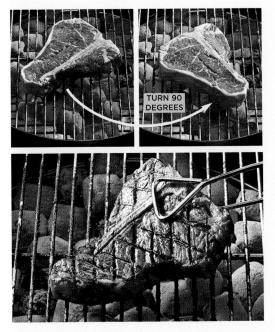

TURN 90 DEGREES

It's easy to get professional-looking diamond-shaped grill marks on your foods. The trick is to sear food just long enough to get good lines, then to rotate it 90 degrees without flipping it and continue searing until you've got the second set of lines. Generally, only one side is rotated to get the diamond grill marks; too much time over high heat will dry out the meat. Once the food is nicely marked, move it to the cooler area of the grill to finish cooking.

A few tips to keep in mind:
- A clean, hot grate produces the best grill marks.
- Put the most attractive side of the food down on the grill first and give it the diamond-shaped grill marks (if cooking poultry, start with the skin side down). This is the side that will be seen when you bring the food to the table, so you want it to look nice.
- Don't try to rush it; when the meat is properly seared, it will release naturally from the grate. If you pry meat off the grill before it's ready, you could tear the surface.

Basil-Stuffed Steak

(Pictured below)

Grilling is an easy way to add variety to our meals. My mom and grandma taught me how to cook when I was young. I've entered several cooking competitions and have won some awards.
—*Linda Gronewaller, Hutchinson, Kansas*

    1   boneless sirloin steak (2 to
        2-1/2 pounds and about 1-1/2
        inches thick)
  1/2   teaspoon salt
  1/4   teaspoon pepper
  1/4   teaspoon dried parsley flakes
1-1/2   cups lightly packed fresh basil
  1/4   cup finely chopped onion
    4   garlic cloves, minced
1-1/2   teaspoons minced fresh rosemary
        or 1/2 teaspoon dried rosemary,
        crushed
  1/8   teaspoon minced fresh thyme *or*
        pinch dried thyme
    1   teaspoon olive oil

With a sharp knife, make five lengthwise cuts three-fourths of the way through the steak. Combine salt, pepper and parsley; rub over steak. Coarsely chop the basil; add onion, garlic, rosemary and thyme.

Stuff into pockets in steak; using heavy-duty string, tie the steak at 2-in. intervals, closing the pockets. Drizzle with oil. Grill, covered, over indirect medium heat for 35-45 minutes or until the meat reaches desired doneness (for medium-rare, a meat thermometer should read 145°; medium, 160°; well-done, 170°). Cover and let stand for 5-10 minutes. Remove string before slicing. **Yield:** 6-8 servings.

■ ■ ■

Barbecued Beef Brisket

(Pictured at right)

A guest at the RV park and marina my husband and I used to run gave me this flavorful brisket recipe. It's become the star of countless meal gatherings.
—*Bettye Miller, Blanchard, Oklahoma*

  1/2   cup packed brown sugar
  1/2   cup ketchup
  1/4   cup water
  1/4   cup cider vinegar
    6   tablespoons vegetable oil, *divided*
    3   tablespoons dark corn syrup
    2   tablespoons prepared mustard
    1   tablespoon prepared horseradish
    1   garlic clove, minced
    1   fresh beef brisket (2 to 2-1/2
        pounds), trimmed

In a saucepan, combine the brown sugar, ketchup, water, vinegar, 4 tablespoons oil, corn syrup, mustard, horseradish and garlic. Cook and stir over medium heat until sugar is dissolved, about 3 minutes. Pour mixture into

a disposable aluminum pan; set aside.

In a large skillet, brown brisket on both sides in remaining oil. Place brisket in pan; turn to coat with sauce. Cover pan tightly with foil.

Grill, covered, over indirect medium heat for 1 hour. Add 10 briquettes to coals. Cover and cook about 1-1/4 hours longer, adding more briquettes if needed, or until meat reaches desired doneness (for medium-rare, a meat thermometer should read 145°; medium, 160°; well-done, 170°). Slice beef; serve with pan drippings. **Yield:** 6-8 servings.

Editor's Note: This is a fresh brisket, not corned beef.

Beef Doneness Guide

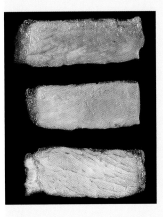

Medium-rare: internal temperature 145°

Medium: internal temperature 160°

Well-done: internal temperature 170°

In a bowl, combine the first six ingredients. Add beef and mix well. Shape into two loaves; place each loaf in a disposable 8-in. x 4-in. x 2-in. loaf pan. Cover with foil. Grill, covered, over indirect medium heat for 30 minutes or until the meat is no longer pink and a meat thermometer reads 160°.

Meanwhile, in a saucepan, combine the sauce ingredients. Cook and stir over low heat until sugar is dissolved. Spoon over meat loaves before serving. **Yield:** 2 loaves (3 servings each).

■ ■ ■

Cool Kitchen Meat Loaf

(Pictured above)

Juicy slices of this savory meat loaf are wonderful served with a homemade sweet-and-sour sauce.
—Susan Taul, Birmingham, Alabama

- 1 **cup soft bread crumbs**
- 1 **medium onion, chopped**
- 1/2 **cup tomato sauce**
- 1 **egg**
- 1-1/2 **teaspoons salt**
- 1/4 **teaspoon pepper**
- 1-1/2 **pounds lean ground beef**

SAUCE:
- 1/2 **cup ketchup**
- 3 **tablespoons brown sugar**
- 3 **tablespoons Worcestershire sauce**
- 2 **tablespoons cider vinegar**
- 2 **tablespoons prepared mustard**

Sirloin Squash Shish Kabobs

When our grill comes out in the spring, this is the first recipe my family asks me to make. You can also use this marinade on six pork chops or a large piece of round steak cut into serving-size pieces.
—Ronda Karbo, Russell, Minnesota

- 1 **cup packed brown sugar**
- 1 **cup soy sauce**
- 1 **teaspoon** *each* **garlic powder, ground mustard and ground ginger**
- 1 **pound boneless beef sirloin steak, cut into 1-inch pieces**
- 1 **medium zucchini, cut into 1/4-inch slices**
- 1 **medium yellow summer squash, cut into 1/4-inch slices**
- 1 **medium sweet red pepper, cut into 1-inch pieces**
- 1 **medium red onion, cut into eight wedges, optional**

In a bowl, combine the brown sugar, soy sauce, garlic powder, mustard and ginger. Place the beef in a large resealable plastic bag; add 1 cup of the marinade. Seal the bag and toss to coat. Place zucchini, yellow squash, red pepper and onion if desired in another re-sealable bag; add remaining marinade and toss to coat. Refrigerate beef and vegetables for at least 4 hours, turning occasionally.

Drain and discard marinade. On eight metal or soaked wooden skewers, alternately thread beef and vegetables. Grill, covered, over medium-hot heat for 10 minutes or until meat reaches desired doneness, turning occasionally. **Yield:** 4 servings.

■ ■ ■

Steaks with Cucumber Sauce

(Pictured below)

Tender steaks, marinated with teriyaki sauce, are accompanied by a creamy cucumber sauce in this recipe.
—Erika Aylward, Clinton, Michigan

4 **boneless beef New York strip steaks (8 to 10 ounces** *each***)**
3/4 **cup teriyaki sauce**
1/2 **cup chopped seeded peeled cucumber**
1/2 **cup sour cream**
1/2 **cup mayonnaise**
  1 **tablespoon minced chives**
1/2 **to 1 teaspoon dill weed**
1/4 **teaspoon salt**

Place steaks in a large resealable plastic bag; add teriyaki sauce. Seal bag and turn to coat; refrigerate overnight. In a bowl, combine the cucumber, sour cream, mayonnaise, chives, dill and salt. Cover and refrigerate.

Drain and discard marinade. Grill steaks, uncovered, over medium-hot heat for 4-5 minutes on each side or until meat reaches desired doneness (for medium-rare, a meat thermometer should read 145°; medium, 160°; well-done, 170°). Serve with cucumber sauce. **Yield:** 4 servings.

Summer Steak Kabobs

(Pictured above)

These meaty skewers not only satisfy my love of outdoor cooking, they feature a mouth-watering marinade, too. It's terrific with chicken and pork, but I prefer it with beef because it tenderizes remarkably well.
—Christi Ross, Guthrie, Texas

1/2 cup vegetable oil
1/4 cup soy sauce
  3 tablespoons honey
  2 tablespoons white vinegar
1/2 teaspoon ground ginger
1/2 teaspoon garlic powder
1-1/2 pounds boneless beef sirloin steak, cut into 1-inch cubes
1/2 pound fresh mushrooms
2 medium onions, cut into wedges
1 medium sweet red pepper, cut into 1-inch chunks
1 medium green pepper, cut into 1-inch chunks
1 medium yellow summer squash, cut into 1/2-inch slices
Hot cooked rice

In a large resealable plastic bag, combine the first six ingredients; add the steak. Seal bag and turn to coat; refrigerate for 8 hours or overnight.

Drain and discard marinade. On 12 metal or soaked wooden skewers, alternately thread steak, mushrooms, onions, peppers and squash. Grill, uncovered, over medium heat for 12-14 minutes or until meat reaches desired doneness, turning occasionally. Serve with rice. **Yield:** 6 servings.

Grilled Flank Steak

(Pictured below right)

Mustard and soy sauce really add flavor to this juicy steak. With a potato dish, green salad and crusty bread, this is my favorite meal.
—*Kristin Roberts, Colorado Springs, Colorado*

- 1/2 **cup soy sauce**
- 1/4 **cup red wine *or* beef broth**
- 2 **green onions, sliced**
- 3 **tablespoons lemon juice**
- 3 **tablespoons vegetable oil**
- 2 **tablespoons Worcestershire sauce**
- 1 **to 2 garlic cloves, minced**
- 1 **beef flank steak (1-1/2 pounds)**
- 2 **tablespoons prepared mustard**

In a large resealable plastic bag, combine the first seven ingredients; mix well. Add beef; seal bag and turn to coat. Refrigerate for several hours or overnight, turning once.

Drain and discard marinade. Brush both sides of meat with mustard. Grill, covered, over medium-hot heat for 5-10 minutes on each side (for medium-rare, a meat thermometer should read 145°; medium, 160°; well-done, 170°). Slice thinly across the grain. **Yield:** 6 servings.

■ ■ ■

Steak on a Stick

I combine molasses, mustard and soy sauce to make these the most robust kabobs you've ever tasted. You'll never miss the oil in this hearty marinade.
—*Jennifer Schwerin, Rockford, Illinois*

- 1 **beef flank steak (1-1/2 pounds)**
- 1/2 **cup soy sauce**
- 1/4 **cup water**

- 2 **tablespoons molasses**
- 2 **teaspoons ground mustard**
- 1 **teaspoon ground ginger**
- 1/2 **teaspoon garlic powder**

Freeze steak for 1-1/2 hours. Cut diagonally into 1/4-in. slices. In a bowl, combine the remaining ingredients. Pour 1/4 cup into a small bowl for basting; cover and refrigerate. Pour remaining marinade into a large resealable plastic bag; add the beef. Seal bag and turn to coat; refrigerate for at least 4 hours.

Drain and discard marinade. Coat grill rack with nonstick cooking spray before starting the grill. Thread beef ribbon-style on 12 metal or soaked wooden skewers. Grill, uncovered, over medium heat for 3-4 minutes on each side or until meat reaches desired doneness, basting frequently with reserved marinade. **Yield:** 6 servings.

Thyme Lemon Sirloins

(Pictured above)

We love to serve steaks when friends drop by…and have found that the tangy lemon herb rub in this recipe really livens up the taste buds.
—*Suzanne Whitaker, Knoxville, Tennessee*

- 2 **teaspoons grated lemon peel**
- 2 **garlic cloves, minced**
- 1 **teaspoon dried thyme**
- 1/4 **teaspoon salt**
- 1/4 **teaspoon pepper**
- 2 **tablespoons butter**
- 1 **tablespoon lemon juice**
- 4 **boneless beef sirloin steaks (about 2 pounds and 1 inch thick)**

In a small bowl, combine the lemon peel, garlic, thyme, salt and pepper. Set aside 1 tablespoon seasoning mixture for steaks. In a small saucepan, melt butter; stir in lemon juice and remaining seasoning mixture. Set aside and keep warm.

Rub steaks with reserved seasoning mixture. Grill steaks, uncovered, over medium heat for 8-12 minutes on each side or until meat reaches desired doneness (for medium-rare, a meat thermometer should read 145°; medium, 160°; well-done, 170°). Serve with reserved butter sauce. **Yield:** 4 servings.

■ ■ ■

Louisiana Barbecue Brisket

Turn to this dish when you need a special entree to feed a crowd. Don't be deterred by the length of this recipe…it has many make-ahead steps. Plus, it grills unattended for hours, so there's no last-minute fuss.
—*Allan Stackhouse, Jennings, Louisiana*

3 tablespoons paprika
2 teaspoons *each* salt, garlic powder
and pepper
1 teaspoon *each* cayenne pepper,
dried oregano and ground mustard
1/2 teaspoon chili powder
1 fresh beef brisket (4 to 6 pounds)
BARBECUE SAUCE:
2 cups ketchup
1 cup packed brown sugar
1 cup unsweetened pineapple juice
2/3 cup light corn syrup
1/2 cup finely chopped onion
1/2 cup apple juice
1/4 cup chili powder
2 to 4 tablespoons hot pepper sauce
4 teaspoons Worcestershire sauce
1 to 4 teaspoons Liquid Smoke,
optional

In a small bowl, combine the seasonings. Rub 2 teaspoons over brisket. (Place remaining seasoning mixture in an airtight container; save for up to 3 months for another use.)

In a bowl, combine the sauce ingredients; stir until brown sugar is dissolved. Pour 2 cups into a large resealable plastic bag; add the brisket. Seal bag and turn to coat; refrigerate for 8 hours or overnight, turning several times. Cover and refrigerate remaining sauce.

Prepare grill for indirect heat, using a drip pan. Drain and discard marinade from brisket; pat dry with paper towels. Place brisket over pan; grill, covered, over indirect low heat for 30-45 minutes on each side or until browned.

Transfer brisket to a heavy-duty disposable roasting pan. Pour 1-1/4 cups of the reserved sauce over the brisket. Cover with a double layer of heavy-duty foil and seal tightly. Grill, covered, over indirect low heat for 3-4 hours or until meat is tender. Serve with remaining sauce. **Yield:** 12-16 servings.

Editor's Note: This is a fresh beef brisket, not corned beef. This recipe is best when the brisket is untrimmed.

■ ■ ■

Mustard-Herb Grilled Tenderloin

Our area is known for beef, and we make this tenderloin recipe often. But the marinade would also be good with grilled pork or chicken.
—*Phyllis Schmalz, Kansas City, Kansas*

2/3 cup olive oil
1/2 cup beef broth
3 tablespoons Dijon mustard
2 tablespoons red wine vinegar
2 tablespoons lemon juice
1/2 teaspoon sugar
2 garlic cloves, minced
1/2 teaspoon salt
1/4 teaspoon *each* dried oregano,
summer savory, tarragon and
thyme
1/8 teaspoon pepper
1 beef tenderloin
(about 1-1/2 pounds)

In a bowl, combine the oil, broth, mustard, vinegar, lemon juice, sugar and seasonings. Pour 3/4 cup into a large resealable plastic bag; add the beef. Seal bag and turn to coat; refrigerate overnight, turning bag once or twice. Cover and refrigerate remaining marinade for basting.

Drain and discard marinade from beef. Grill, covered, over medium heat for 20-25 minutes or until meat reaches desired doneness (for medium-rare, a meat thermometer should read 145°; medium, 160°; well-done, 170°). Turn once and baste with 1/4 cup reserved marinade during the last 5 minutes. Let tenderloin stand for 10 minutes before slicing. Serve with the remaining reserved marinade. **Yield:** 6 servings.

Steak with Citrus Salsa

(Pictured below)

A lime juice marinade really perks up grilled steaks, and the snappy, light citrus salsa is a super change from the usual steak sauce.
—Kathleen Smith, Pittsburgh, Pennsylvania

1/2 cup soy sauce
1/4 cup chopped green onions
   3 tablespoons lime juice
   2 tablespoons brown sugar
1/8 teaspoon hot pepper sauce
   1 garlic clove, minced
1-1/2 pounds boneless sirloin steak
       (about 1 inch thick)

SALSA:
   2 navel oranges, peeled, sectioned
      and chopped
1/4 cup chopped green onions
   2 tablespoons orange juice
   2 tablespoons red wine vinegar
   2 tablespoons chopped lemon
   1 tablespoon chopped lime
   1 tablespoon sugar
   1 tablespoon minced fresh cilantro
   1 teaspoon minced jalapeno pepper
1/2 teaspoon grated lemon peel
1/2 teaspoon grated lime peel
1/8 teaspoon salt

In a large resealable plastic bag, combine the

first six ingredients; add beef. Seal and refrigerate for 2 hours or overnight, turning occasionally. Drain and discard marinade. Grill steak, uncovered, over medium heat for 4-6 minutes on each side or until meat reaches desired doneness (for medium-rare, a meat thermometer should read 145°; medium, 160°; well-done, 170°).

Combine salsa ingredients in a bowl. Cut steak across the grain into thin slices. Serve with salsa. **Yield:** 4-6 servings.

Editor's Note: When cutting or seeding hot peppers, use rubber or plastic gloves to protect your hands. Avoid touching your face.

■ ■ ■

Barbecued Beef Short Ribs

(Pictured at right)

These sweet-spicy barbecue ribs are always a hit. The sauce is also very good on pork ribs.
—Paula Zsiray, Logan, Utah

   1 **cup sugar**
 1/2 **cup packed brown sugar**
   2 **tablespoons salt**
   2 **tablespoons garlic powder**
   2 **tablespoons paprika**
   2 **teaspoons pepper**
 1/4 **teaspoon cayenne pepper**
   7 **pounds beef short ribs, trimmed**
SAUCE:
   1 **small onion, finely chopped**
   2 **teaspoons vegetable oil**
1-1/2 **cups water**
   1 **cup ketchup**
   1 **can (6 ounces) tomato paste**
   2 **tablespoons brown sugar**
Pepper to taste

In a bowl, combine the first seven ingredients; rub over ribs. Place in two large resealable plastic bags; seal and refrigerate overnight.

Line two 15-in. x 10-in. x 1-in. baking pans with foil; grease the foil. Place ribs in prepared pans. Bake, uncovered, at 325° for 2 hours or until meat is tender.

Meanwhile, in a large saucepan, saute onion in oil until tender. Stir in the water, ketchup, tomato paste, brown sugar and pepper. Bring to a boil. Reduce heat; cover and simmer for 1 hour.

Remove ribs from the oven. Grill ribs, covered, over indirect medium heat for 20 minutes, turning and basting frequently with sauce. **Yield:** 14 servings.

For food safety reasons, beef should be defrosted in the refrigerator, never at room temperature. Place the package of beef on a tray or plate to catch any drippings.

Allow 12 to 24 hours to defrost ground beef and steaks (depending on the thickness). Large roasts require 4 to 7 hours per pound to defrost, while smaller roasts can thaw in 3 to 5 hours.

Pineapple Sirloin Skewers

(Pictured below)

I like to add mushrooms to these skewers and serve them with hot cooked rice.
—Karen Hamlin, Marysville, Washington

- 1 can (8 ounces) pineapple chunks
- 6 tablespoons soy sauce
- 2 tablespoons brown sugar
- 2 tablespoons vegetable oil
- 2 teaspoons ground ginger
- 1 teaspoon minced garlic
- 1/2 teaspoon pepper
- 1 pound boneless beef sirloin steak, cut into 1-inch cubes

Drain pineapple, reserving juice. Refrigerate the pineapple. In a small bowl, combine the pineapple juice, soy sauce, brown sugar, oil, ginger, garlic and pepper. Reserve 1/3 cup marinade for basting and 1/3 cup for serving; cover and refrigerate.

Pour the remaining marinade into a large resealable plastic bag; add beef cubes. Seal bag and turn to coat; refrigerate for 8 hours or overnight.

Drain and discard marinade from beef. On metal or soaked wooden skewers, alternately thread beef and pineapple chunks. Grill, uncovered, over medium heat for 5 minutes on each side or broil 4-6 in. from the heat until beef reaches desired doneness, basting frequently with one portion of reserved marinade. Serve with remaining marinade. **Yield:** 4 servings.

■ ■ ■

Meatball Shish Kabobs

Convenience foods make this hearty entree a snap to prepare. Purchased meatballs are easy to thread onto skewers. Basting with bottled barbecue sauce adds fast flavor.
—Shawn Solley, Lawton, Oklahoma

- 1 package (16 ounces) frozen fully cooked meatballs, thawed (about 30 meatballs)
- 2 medium zucchini, cut into 1/2-inch slices
- 2 medium yellow summer squash, cut into 1/2-inch slices
- 12 cherry tomatoes
- 12 pearl onions
- 1 cup barbecue sauce
- Hot cooked rice

On metal or soaked wooden skewers, alternate meatballs, zucchini, summer squash, tomatoes and onions.

Grill, uncovered, over medium heat for 6 minutes, turning once. Baste with barbecue sauce. Grill 8-10 minutes longer or until meatballs are heated through and vegetables are tender, turning and basting frequently. Serve over rice. **Yield:** 5 servings.

■ ■ ■

Marinated Flank Steak

(Pictured at right)

I first grilled this appetizing flank steak for my father on a special occasion. We loved its tangy taste so much that I now make it this way for our family all the time.
—Ann Fox, Austin, Texas

  2/3 **cup olive oil**
  1/4 **cup lemon juice**
    2 **tablespoons red wine vinegar**
    1 **tablespoon Worcestershire sauce**
    1 **tablespoon soy sauce**
    1 **tablespoon Dijon mustard**
    1 **teaspoon dried basil**
  1/2 **teaspoon dried oregano**
  1/4 **teaspoon dried thyme**
    1 **flank steak (about 1-1/2 pounds)**

In a large resealable bag, combine the first nine ingredients; mix well. Add steak and turn to coat. Seal bag and refrigerate for 8 hours or overnight, turning occasionally.

Drain and discard marinade. Grill, covered, over medium-hot heat for 6-10 minutes on each side or until meat reaches desired doneness (for medium-rare, a meat thermometer should read 145°; medium, 160°; well-done, 170°). **Yield:** 4-6 servings.

Success with steaks is certain if you follow these tips:

- Trim steaks to avoid flare-ups, leaving a thin layer of fat if desired to help maintain juiciness.
- Pat dry with paper towels before grilling—a dry steak will brown better than a moist one.
- Avoid grilling at too high a temperature, which will char the outside of the steak before the inside reaches the desired doneness.
- Grill steaks to at least medium-rare, 145°, but don't overcook.

Spicy Filet Mignon

(Pictured above)

I adapted this recipe from a seasoning I saw for blackened catfish. These steaks have a lot of kick so I make a mellow side dish, like potatoes.
—Vera Kobiako, Jupiter, Florida

  2 **tablespoons paprika**
  2 **teaspoons onion salt**
1-1/2 **teaspoons garlic powder**
1-1/2 **teaspoons dried basil**
  1 **to 1-1/2 teaspoons cayenne pepper**
  1 **teaspoon dried thyme**
  6 **beef tenderloin steaks**
    (about 1-1/2 inches thick)

Combine the seasonings; rub over steaks. Grill, covered, over indirect medium heat for 9-11 minutes on each side or until meat reaches desired doneness (for medium-rare, a meat thermometer should read 145°; medium, 160°; well-done, 170°). **Yield:** 6 servings.

Tacos on a Stick

Teens like assembling these creative kabobs almost as much as they like devouring them. The whole family is sure to enjoy these sensational kabobs.
—*Dixie Terry, Goreville, Illinois*

  1 envelope taco seasoning
  1 cup tomato juice
  2 to 4 tablespoons vegetable oil
  2 pounds boneless beef top sirloin, cut into 1-inch cubes
  1 medium green pepper, cut into chunks
  1 medium sweet red pepper, cut into chunks
  1 large onion, cut into wedges
 16 cherry tomatoes

In a large resealable plastic bag, combine the taco seasoning, tomato juice and oil; mix well. Remove 1/2 cup for basting; refrigerate. Add beef to the bag; seal and turn to coat. Refrigerate for at least 5 hours.

Drain and discard marinade from beef. On metal or soaked wooden skewers, alternately thread beef, peppers, onion and tomatoes. Grill, uncovered, over medium heat for 3 minutes on each side. Baste with reserved marinade. Continue turning and basting for 8-10 minutes or until meat reaches desired doneness. **Yield:** 6 servings.

■ ■ ■

Zesty Steak Fajitas

A zesty tomato and jalapeno relish and tender strips of steak make these traditional fajitas extra special.
—*Rebecca Baird, Salt Lake City, Utah*

  2 medium tomatoes, seeded and diced
1/2 cup diced red onion
1/4 cup lime juice
  3 tablespoons minced fresh cilantro
  1 jalapeno pepper, seeded and chopped
  2 teaspoons ground cumin
1/2 teaspoon salt
  1 beef flank steak (about 1-1/2 pounds)
  1 large onion, halved and sliced
  1 tablespoon vegetable oil
  6 flour tortillas (6 inches), warmed

In a bowl, combine the first seven ingredients. Cover and refrigerate. Broil or grill steak over medium-hot heat for 6-8 minutes on each side or until meat reaches desired doneness (for medium-rare, a meat thermometer should read 145°; medium, 160°; well-done, 170°).

Meanwhile, in a skillet, saute onion in oil until crisp-tender. Slice steak into thin strips across the grain; place on tortillas. Top with onion and the reserved tomato relish. **Yield:** 6 servings.

Editor's Note: When cutting or seeding hot peppers, use rubber or plastic gloves to protect your hands. Avoid touching your face.

Purchase beef on or before the package's "sell by" date. Choose meat with a bright, cherry-red color, without any grayish or brown blotches. Once exposed to oxygen, beef will turn from a darker red to bright red.

Choose packages that are cold, tightly wrapped and have no tears or punctures. For vacuum-packaged beef, be sure that the seal has not been broken and that the package is not leaking.

Choose beef roasts and steaks that are firm to the touch, not soft.

Garden Bounty Beef Kabobs

(Pictured at right)

These classic kabobs are a hearty way to use up your garden harvest.
—*Christine Klessig, Amherst Junction, Wisconsin*

- 1/4 cup soy sauce
- 2 tablespoons olive oil
- 1 tablespoon molasses
- 3 garlic cloves, minced
- 1 teaspoon ground ginger
- 1 teaspoon ground mustard
- 1 pound boneless beef sirloin steak, cut into 1-inch cubes
- 1 large sweet onion, cut into 1-inch pieces
- 1 large green *or* sweet red pepper, cut into 1-inch pieces
- 1 medium zucchini, cut into 1-inch slices
- 1 pint cherry tomatoes
- 1/2 pound large fresh mushrooms

DIPPING SAUCE:
- 1 cup (8 ounces) sour cream
- 1/4 cup milk
- 3 tablespoons dry onion soup mix
- 2 tablespoons Dijon mustard
- 1/8 teaspoon pepper

In a large resealable plastic bag, combine the first six ingredients; add the beef. Seal bag and turn to coat; refrigerate for 1 hour.

Coat grill rack with nonstick cooking spray before starting the grill. Drain and discard marinade. On eight metal or soaked wooden skewers, alternately thread beef and vegetables. Grill, covered, over medium heat for 3-4 minutes on each side or until beef reaches desired doneness, turning three times.

In a saucepan, combine the dipping sauce ingredients; mix well. Cook over low heat until heated through. Serve with kabobs. **Yield:** 4 servings.

Marinated Chuck Roast

This marinade makes the toughest cuts of meat tender. I'm frequently asked for the recipe.
—*Marte Schoening, Superior, Montana*

- 2 tablespoons ketchup
- 2 tablespoons red wine vinegar
- 2 teaspoons vegetable oil
- 2 teaspoons soy sauce
- 1 teaspoon Worcestershire sauce
- 1/4 teaspoon prepared mustard
- 1/4 teaspoon garlic powder
- 1/4 teaspoon salt
- 1/4 teaspoon pepper
- 1 boneless beef chuck steak (about 3/4 pound and 3/4 inch thick)

In a resealable plastic bag, combine the ketchup, vinegar, oil, soy sauce, Worcestershire sauce, mustard, garlic powder, salt and pepper; add meat. Seal bag and turn to coat; refrigerate 8 hours or overnight.

Drain and discard the marinade. Grill the steak, covered, over medium heat for 6-8 minutes on each side or until meat reaches desired doneness (for medium-rare, a meat thermometer should read 145°; medium, 160°; well-done 170°). **Yield:** 2 servings.

■ ■ ■

Spinach Steak Pinwheels

(Pictured below)

Bacon and spinach bring plenty of flavor to these sirloin steak spirals. It's an easy dish to make and great to grill at a backyard cookout. I get lots of compliments on it, no matter how many times I serve it.
—Helen Vail, Glenside, Pennsylvania

1-1/2 pounds boneless beef sirloin steak
8 bacon strips, cooked and drained
1 package (10 ounces) frozen chopped spinach, thawed and squeezed dry
1/4 cup grated Parmesan cheese
1/2 teaspoon salt
1/8 teaspoon cayenne pepper

Make diagonal cuts in steak at 1-in. intervals to within 1/2 in. of bottom of meat. Repeat cuts in opposite direction. Pound to 1/2-in. thickness. Place bacon down the center of the meat. In a bowl, combine the spinach, Parmesan cheese, salt and cayenne; spoon over bacon. Roll up and secure with toothpicks. Cut into six slices.

Grill, uncovered, over medium heat for 6 minutes on each side or until meat reaches desired doneness (for medium-rare, a meat thermometer should read 145°; medium, 160°; well-done, 170°). Discard toothpicks. **Yield:** 6 servings.

Grilled Rib Eye Steaks

(Pictured above)

In summer, I love to marinate these steaks overnight, then grill them for family and friends.
—Tim Hanchon, Muncie, Indiana

- 1/2 **cup soy sauce**
- 1/2 **cup sliced green onions**
- 1/4 **cup packed brown sugar**
-   2 **garlic cloves, minced**
- 1/4 **teaspoon ground ginger**
- 1/4 **teaspoon pepper**
- 2-1/2 **pounds beef rib eye steaks**

In a large resealable plastic bag, combine the soy sauce, onions, brown sugar, garlic, ginger and pepper. Add the steaks. Seal bag and turn to coat; refrigerate for 8 hours or overnight.

Drain and discard marinade. Grill steaks, uncovered, over medium-hot heat for 8-10 minutes or until the meat reaches desired doneness (for medium-rare, a meat ther-mometer should read 145°; medium, 160°; well-done, 170°). **Yield:** 2-4 servings and about 1-1/4 pounds leftover steak.

■ ■ ■

Grilled Steak Fajitas

(Pictured at right)

This tasty, marinated main dish is as quick and easy to assemble as tacos.
—Pamela Pogue, Quitman, Texas

-   1 **flank steak (1-1/2 pounds)**
-   1 **large onion, cut into wedges**
-   1 **medium green pepper, julienned**
-   1 **can (4 ounces) chopped green chilies**
- 1/2 **cup lemon juice**
- 1/2 **cup red wine vinegar**
- 1/2 **cup vegetable oil**
-   4 **garlic cloves, minced**
-   1 **tablespoon Worcestershire sauce**
-   1 **teaspoon dried oregano**
- 1/2 **teaspoon salt**
- 1/2 **teaspoon pepper**

12 flour tortillas (6 inches)
1 medium avocado, peeled and
sliced, optional
Sour cream, optional

Place steak in large resealable plastic bag. Place onion and green pepper in another bag. Combine chilies, lemon juice, vinegar, oil, garlic, Worcestershire sauce, oregano, salt and pepper. Pour 1-1/2 cups over meat. Pour remaining marinade over vegetables. Seal bags and refrigerate overnight. Drain meat and vegetables, discarding marinade.

Grill steak, covered, over medium-hot heat for 10 minutes on each side or until meat reaches desired doneness (for medium-rare, a meat thermometer should read 145°; medium, 160°; well-done, 170°).

Meanwhile, cut two pieces of heavy-duty foil into 18-in. x 12-in. rectangles. Wrap tortillas in one piece and vegetables in the other; seal foil tightly. Grill, covered, over indirect heat for 5-7 minutes, turning occasionally. Cut steak into 1/8-in. slices across the grain; place on tortillas. Top with vegetables and roll up. Serve with avocado and sour cream if desired. **Yield:** 6 servings.

Tangy Sirloin Strips

My love of cooking started when I was trying to earn my Girl Scout cooking badge. My family savors the sweet sauce on these bundles. Plus the bacon lends a subtle smokiness and slight crunch that are irresistible.
—Joanne Haldeman, Bainbridge, Pennsylvania

1/4 cup vegetable oil
2 tablespoons Worcestershire sauce
1 garlic clove, minced
1/2 teaspoon onion powder
1/2 teaspoon salt
1/4 teaspoon pepper
1 pound boneless sirloin steak
(1 inch thick)
4 bacon strips
Lemon-pepper seasoning
GLAZE:
1/2 cup barbecue sauce
1/2 cup steak sauce
1/2 cup honey
1 tablespoon molasses

In a large resealable plastic bag, combine the first six ingredients. Cut steak into four wide strips; add to the marinade. Seal bag and turn to coat; refrigerate for 2-3 hours or overnight, turning once.

Drain and discard marinade. Wrap a bacon strip around each steak piece; secure with a toothpick. Sprinkle with lemon-pepper. Coat grill rack with nonstick cooking spray before starting the grill.

Grill steak, covered, over medium-low heat for 10-15 minutes, turning occasionally, until meat reaches desired doneness (for medium-rare, a meat thermometer should read 145°; medium, 160°; well-done, 170°). Combine the glaze ingredients; brush over steak. Grill until glaze is heated. Discard toothpicks. **Yield:** 4 servings.

·Chicken·

Guaranteed good eating from the grill begins with versatile chicken. Satisfy your family and take your pick from Maple-Glazed Chicken Wings, Grilled Chicken Cordon Bleu, Citrus Chicken Kabobs, Southwestern Skewers and more. We even show you the proper technique for preparing popular beer can chicken!

Jalapeno Grilled Chicken

(Pictured at left)

I've had this recipe for years, so it's long been a family favorite. The jalapeno stuffing adds some spice to ordinary grilled chicken.
—Cheryl Kvintus, Altus, Oklahoma

4 to 8 jalapeno peppers, seeded and chopped *or* 1 can (4 ounces) chopped green chilies
2/3 cup lemon juice, *divided*
1/4 cup minced fresh parsley *or* 1 tablespoon dried parsley flakes
6 to 10 garlic cloves, minced
2 teaspoons dried rosemary, crushed
2 teaspoons dried thyme
8 bone-in chicken breast halves
2/3 cup chicken broth
2 teaspoons pepper
1/2 teaspoon grated lemon peel

In a bowl, combine the peppers, 1/3 cup lemon juice, parsley, garlic, rosemary and thyme. Gently stuff pepper mixture under the skin of each chicken breast. Place in a greased 13-in. x 9-in. x 2-in. baking dish. Combine the broth, pepper, lemon peel and remaining lemon juice; pour over chicken. Cover and refrigerate for at least 6 hours.

Drain and discard marinade. Place the chicken skin side up on grill. Grill, covered, over medium heat for 45 minutes or until the juices run clear, turning once. **Yield:** 8 servings.

Editor's Note: When cutting or seeding hot peppers, use rubber or plastic gloves to protect your hands. Avoid touching your face.

Peanut Butter Chicken Skewers

(Pictured above)

This fantastic dish proves peanut butter makes a tasty sauce for chicken.
—Jeanne Bennett, North Richland Hills, Texas

- 1/2 **cup creamy peanut butter**
- 1/2 **cup water**
- 1/4 **cup soy sauce**
- 4 **garlic cloves, minced**
- 3 **tablespoons lemon juice**
- 2 **tablespoons brown sugar**
- 3/4 **teaspoon ground ginger**
- 1/2 **teaspoon crushed red pepper flakes**
- 4 **boneless skinless chicken breast halves (1-1/4 pounds)**
- 2 **cups shredded red cabbage**

Sliced green onion tops

In a saucepan, combine the first eight ingredients; cook and stir over medium-high heat for 5 minutes or until smooth. Reserve half of the sauce. Slice chicken lengthwise into 1-in. strips; thread onto metal or soaked wooden skewers.

Grill, uncovered, over medium-hot heat for 2 minutes; turn and brush with peanut butter sauce. Continue turning and basting for 4-6 minutes or until juices run clear.

Place cabbage on a serving plate; top with chicken. Sprinkle with onion tops. Serve with reserved sauce. **Yield:** 4 servings.

■ ■ ■

Taste-of-Summer Chicken

I rely on bottled Italian salad dressing and pineapple juice for my made-in-minutes chicken marinade.
—Beverly Saunders, Lexington, Virginia

- 3/4 **cup Italian salad dressing**
- 3/4 **cup unsweetened pineapple juice**
- 3/4 **cup white wine** *or* **white grape juice**
- 6 **boneless skinless chicken breast halves (1-1/2 pounds)**

In a large resealable plastic bag, combine the salad dressing, pineapple juice and wine or grape juice. Add the chicken. Seal bag and turn to coat; refrigerate for 8 hours or overnight.

Drain and discard marinade. Grill chicken, covered, over medium heat for 6-7 minutes on each side or until juices run clear. **Yield:** 6 servings.

■ ■ ■

Southern Barbecued Chicken

(Pictured at far right)

Growing up, I traveled the U.S. and abroad as part of a military family. Tasting various cuisines made me adventurous in the kitchen.
—Revonda Stroud, Fort Worth, Texas

- 2 **cups cider vinegar**
- 1 **cup vegetable oil**
- 1 **egg, beaten**
- 2 **tablespoons hot pepper sauce**

Chicken Grilling Chart

Chicken breasts are done at 170°; whole chickens at 180° as measured in the thigh. Kabobs are done when juices run clear. Ground chicken is done at 165°. For direct grilling, turn meat halfway through grilling time. The cooking times given are a guideline. Check for doneness with a meat thermometer or other appropriate doneness test.

Cut	Weight or Thickness	Heat	Approximate Cooking Time
Broiler/Fryer, whole	3 to 4 lbs.	medium/indirect	1-1/4 to 1-3/4 hours
Roaster, whole	5 to 6 lbs.	medium/indirect	1-3/4 to 2-1/4 hours
Meaty bone-in pieces, breast halves, legs, quarters	1-1/4 to 1-1/2 lbs.	medium/direct medium/indirect	35 to 45 minutes 40 to 50 minutes
Bone-in thighs, drumsticks, wings	3 to 7 oz. each	medium-low/direct medium/indirect	15 to 30 minutes 20 to 30 minutes
Breast halves, boneless	6 oz. each	medium/direct	10 to 15 minutes
Kabobs	1-in. cubes	medium/direct	10 to 15 minutes

1 tablespoon garlic powder
1 tablespoon poultry seasoning
2 teaspoons salt
1 teaspoon pepper
1 broiler/fryer chicken
(3 to 4 pounds), cut up

In a saucepan, combine the vinegar, oil, egg and seasonings. Bring to a boil, stirring constantly. Reduce heat; simmer, uncovered, for 10 minutes, stirring often. Cool. Pour 1-2/3 cups of marinade into a large resealable plastic bag; add the chicken.

Seal bag and turn to coat; refrigerate overnight, turning occasionally. Cover and refrigerate remaining marinade for basting.

Prepare grill for indirect heat, using a drip pan. Drain and discard marinade from chicken. Place skin side down over pan. Grill, covered, over indirect medium heat for 20 minutes. Turn; grill 20-30 minutes longer or until juices run clear, basting occasionally with reserved marinade. **Yield:** 4 servings.

Blackened Chicken

(Pictured below)

This spicy standout packs a one-two punch of flavor. The grilled chicken is basted with a peppery white sauce. Plus, there's extra sauce left over for dipping. Served with corn on the cob, it's the perfect picnic food.
—Stephanie Kenney, Falkville, Alabama

1 **tablespoon paprika**
4 **teaspoons sugar,** *divided*
1-1/2 **teaspoons salt,** *divided*
1 **teaspoon garlic powder**
1 **teaspoon dried thyme**
1 **teaspoon lemon-pepper seasoning**
1 **teaspoon cayenne pepper**
1-1/2 **to 2 teaspoons pepper,** *divided*
4 **boneless skinless chicken breast halves**
1-1/3 **cups mayonnaise**
2 **tablespoons water**
2 **tablespoons cider vinegar**

In a small bowl, combine paprika, 1 teaspoon sugar, 1 teaspoon salt, garlic powder, thyme, lemon-pepper, cayenne and 1/2 to 1 teaspoon pepper; sprinkle over both sides of chicken. Set aside. In another bowl, combine mayonnaise, water, vinegar and remaining sugar, salt and pepper; cover and chill 1 cup for serving. Save remaining sauce for basting.

Grill chicken, covered, over indirect medium heat for 4-6 minutes on each side or until juices run clear, basting frequently with remaining sauce. Serve with reserved sauce. **Yield:** 4 servings.

Southwestern Skewers

(Pictured at right)

Juicy chicken, cherry tomatoes, mushrooms and sweet peppers make these skewers filling. But it's the fresh garlic, chili powder, cumin and cayenne pepper that give them their zesty kick.
—Larry Smith, Youngstown, Ohio

  1 **bottle (8 ounces) Italian salad dressing**
10 **garlic cloves, minced**
  1 **teaspoon white pepper**
  1 **teaspoon chili powder**
  1 **teaspoon ground cumin**
  1 **teaspoon paprika**
1/2 **teaspoon cayenne pepper**
  1 **medium green pepper, cut into 1-inch pieces**
  1 **medium sweet red pepper, cut into 1-inch pieces**
  1 **medium onion, cut into 1-inch pieces**
  8 **large fresh mushrooms**
  8 **cherry tomatoes**
  1 **pound boneless skinless chicken breasts, cut into 1-inch cubes**

In a bowl, combine the first seven ingredients; mix well. Pour half into a large resealable plastic bag; add the vegetables. Seal bag and turn to coat. Pour remaining marinade into another large resealable plastic bag; add the chicken. Seal bag and turn to coat. Refrigerate vegetables and chicken for at least 2-3 hours.

Coat grill rack with nonstick cooking spray before starting the grill. Drain chicken, discarding marinade. Drain vegetables, reserving marinade for basting. On eight metal or soaked wooden skewers, alternately thread chicken and vegetables. Grill, covered, over medium heat for 3-4 minutes on each side or until chicken is no longer pink and vegetables are tender, turning three times and basting frequently with reserved marinade. **Yield:** 4 servings.

Barbecue Basics

- Leave the skin on the chicken while grilling to preserve the chicken's natural moisture. The skin can be removed before serving.
- Aromatic woods, such as hickory, mesquite or cherry, can be added to the preheated coals to give the chicken a distinctive flavor.
- Place smaller pieces of chicken around the outer edges, further away from the main heat source, to allow them to cook slower. Do not overcrowd chicken pieces when cooking. Leaving space between them will allow them to brown and cook more evenly.
- Take pieces off the grill as they get done to avoid overcooking while finishing other pieces. White meat and smaller pieces, such as breasts and wings, will get done faster than dark meat pieces, such as legs and thighs.
- To speed grilling or broiling time, partially cook the chicken in the microwave first. Microwave on high approximately 4 to 5 minutes per pound, or 3 to 4 minutes if using cut-up parts. Grill or broil the microwaved pieces of chicken immediately to finish cooking.

In a large bowl, combine the first 11 ingredients. Pour into two large resealable plastic bags; add chicken. Seal bags and turn to coat; refrigerate overnight.

Prepare grill for indirect heat. Drain and discard marinade. Sprinkle chicken with seasoned salt. Grill chicken skin side down, covered, over indirect medium heat for 15 minutes. Turn; grill 15-20 minutes longer or until juices run clear. **Yield:** 12-14 servings.

■ ■ ■

Can-Can Chicken

(Pictured at right)

The flavor of beer-can chicken comes mostly from the seasoning rub applied under the skin. I also spray my chicken with a mixture of 2 cups apple cider and 1 tablespoon of balsamic vinegar. This adds moisture to the crisp skin, but will require an additional 15 to 30 minutes of cooking time.
—Steve Bath, Lincoln, Nebraska

- 1 **tablespoon kosher salt**
- 1 **teaspoon sugar**
- 1 **teaspoon onion powder**
- 1 **teaspoon garlic powder**
- 1 **teaspoon cayenne pepper**
- 1 **teaspoon paprika**
- 1 **teaspoon ground mustard**
- 1 **broiler/fryer chicken (3-1/2 to 4 pounds)**
- 1 **can (12 ounces) beer**

In a bowl, combine the first seven ingredients. Loosen skin from around the chicken breast, thighs and legs. Rub the spice mixture onto and under skin. Tuck wing tips behind the back. Refrigerate for 1 hour.

Pour out half of the beer. Poke additional holes in the top of the can with a can opener. Holding the chicken with legs pointed down, lower chicken over the can so it fills the body

Grilled Thighs And Drumsticks

(Pictured above)

This chicken is juicy, has great barbecue flavor and makes a big batch, so it's perfect for summer picnics and family reunions.
—Brenda Beachy, Belvidere, Tennessee

- 2-1/2 **cups packed brown sugar**
- 2 **cups water**
- 2 **cups cider vinegar**
- 2 **cups ketchup**
- 1 **cup vegetable oil**
- 4 **tablespoons salt**
- 3 **tablespoons prepared mustard**
- 4-1/2 **teaspoons Worcestershire sauce**
- 1 **tablespoon soy sauce**
- 1 **teaspoon pepper**
- 1 **teaspoon Liquid Smoke, optional**
- 10 **pounds chicken thighs and drumsticks**
- 1/2 **teaspoon seasoned salt**

cavity. Place chicken over drip pan; grill, covered, over indirect medium heat for 1-1/4 to 1-1/2 hours or until a meat thermometer inserted into a thigh reads 180°. Remove chicken from grill; cover and let stand for 10 minutes. Remove chicken from can. **Yield:** 6 servings.

When selecting fresh chicken, avoid meat that shows sign of freezing by looking and feeling for ice formations. When buying frozen chicken, select packages that feel rock hard and have no signs of freezer burn.

Refrigerate fresh, raw chicken in its original packaging and use within 1 to 2 days. Or wrap in plastic wrap, then place in a freezer bag. Freeze whole chickens for 1 year and chicken parts for 9 months.

Beer-Can Basics

1 Season the chicken. To do this, carefully loosen the skin around the chicken by placing a hand between the skin and meat. Kitchen scissors are useful to snip the membrane attaching the skin to the middle of the breastbone.

Using fingertips, generously rub the seasoning into the meat. Rub remaining spices into the cavity.

Let the chicken rest several hours in the refrigerator before grilling so the seasoning permeates the meat.

2 Place onto can. Be sure it's a partially filled beverage can or holder. One-half to 3/4 cup is all the liquid needed to keep the chicken moist.

Punch extra holes in the can top to allow moist air to escape evenly from the can. You can also add seasonings to the can. Ones using salt will cause beer to foam.

3 Grill over indirect medium heat until a meat thermometer inserted deep into a thigh reads 180°.

To remove from the grill, carefully slide a wide grilling spatula under the can or holder while firmly grasping the chicken with tongs.

For your safety, allow the chicken and can to cool slightly before attempting to remove the can. Using tongs or insulated gloves, grasp the can or holder, then gently twist the chicken slightly while pulling upward to release from the can.

Tarragon Chicken Bundles

(Pictured above)

Loaded with chicken strips, summer squash, zucchini and tomatoes, this robust entree is always pleasing.
—Michelle Isenhoff, Grand Rapids, Michigan

- 1 **pound boneless skinless chicken breasts, cut into strips**
- 2 **medium carrots, julienned**
- 1 **medium yellow summer squash, julienned**
- 1 **medium zucchini, julienned**
- 1 **cup fresh mushrooms, halved**
- 1 **cup cherry tomatoes, halved**
- 4 **tablespoons butter**
- 2 **teaspoons dried tarragon**
- 1 **teaspoon salt**

Pepper to taste

Divide the chicken strips and vegetables among four pieces of heavy-duty foil. Top each with 1 tablespoon butter, tarragon, salt and pepper. Fold foil over and seal tightly. Grill, covered, over medium heat for 15-20 minutes or until chicken juices run clear and vegetables are tender. **Yield:** 4 servings.

◼◼◼

Moist Lemon Chicken

I originally developed this marinade for seafood, but it's wonderful with chicken, too. It adds mild lemon zing and keeps the meat moist and tender.
—Nancy Schickling, Bedford, Virginia

- 3/4 **cup water**
- 1/4 **cup lemon juice**
- 2 **tablespoons dried minced onion**
- 1 **tablespoon dried parsley flakes**
- 1 **tablespoon Worcestershire sauce**
- 2 **garlic cloves, minced**
- 1 **teaspoon dill seed**
- 1/2 **teaspoon salt**
- 1/2 **teaspoon curry powder**
- 1/2 **teaspoon pepper**

1 broiler/fryer chicken
(3 to 3-1/2 pounds), cut up

In a large resealable plastic bag, combine the first 10 ingredients. Add chicken and turn to coat. Seal and refrigerate for 4-6 hours. Drain, discarding marinade.

Grill the chicken, covered, over indirect low heat for 50-60 minutes or until the juices run clear, turning several times. **Yield:** 4 servings.

■ ■ ■

Chicken on Rainbow Rice

(Pictured below right)

Chicken breasts can make a variety of interesting dishes. Here, I enhance the meat with a lightly seasoned marinade and rice pilaf. It's perfectly portioned for one.
—Bill Hilbrich, St. Cloud, Minnesota

1/4 cup olive oil
2 tablespoons lime *or* lemon juice
1 boneless skinless chicken breast half
1/4 cup *each* chopped onion, sweet red pepper and green pepper
1 tablespoon butter
1 cup cooked long grain rice
1/4 teaspoon salt
Dash pepper

In a small resealable plastic bag, combine the oil and lime juice; add chicken. Seal bag and turn to coat; refrigerate for at least 1 hour.

Drain and discard marinade. Grill chicken, uncovered, over medium heat for 5-7 minutes on each side or until juices run clear. Meanwhile, in a skillet, saute onion and peppers in butter until tender. Stir in the rice, salt and pepper; heat through. Serve with chicken. **Yield:** 1 serving.

Chicken Broccoli Packets

I like this recipe because it's simple to prepare and cleanup is a snap! I just put some chicken and veggies in a foil packet, then pop them on the grill.
—Lynda Simmons, Fayetteville, North Carolina

4 boneless skinless chicken breast halves (1-1/4 pounds)
Seasoned salt
1 package (10 ounces) frozen broccoli spears
1 medium onion, sliced into rings
4 teaspoons lemon juice
4 tablespoons butter

Place each chicken breast in the center of a piece of heavy-duty foil (about 12 in. x 12 in.). Sprinkle with seasoned salt. Top each with 2 broccoli spears, 3-4 onion rings, 1 teaspoon lemon juice and 1 tablespoon butter. Fold foil around chicken; seal tightly.

Grill, covered, over medium-hot heat for 20 minutes or until meat juices run clear. Serve in foil packets if desired. **Yield:** 4 servings.

On a floured surface, roll dough into a 13-in. circle. Transfer to a greased 12-in. pizza pan. Build up edges slightly. Grill, covered, over medium heat for 5 minutes. Remove from grill. Combine chicken and barbecue sauce; spread over the crust. Sprinkle with green pepper and cheese. Grill, covered, 5-10 minutes longer or until crust is golden and cheese is melted. **Yield:** 4 servings.

Garlic Chicken Kabobs

This is a lighter version of a dish my Lebanese mother-in-law taught me to make. I reduced the amount of oil and substituted yogurt for the mayonnaise. Tender and moist, these kabobs are special.
—Sheri Jean Waked, Loveland, Ohio

- 8 garlic cloves, minced
- 1/2 teaspoon salt
- 1/4 cup minced fresh cilantro
- 1 teaspoon ground coriander
- 1/2 cup plain yogurt
- 2 tablespoons lemon juice
- 1-1/2 teaspoons olive oil
- 2 pounds boneless skinless chicken breasts, cut into 1-inch cubes

GARLIC DIPPING SAUCE:
- 4 garlic cloves, minced
- 1/4 teaspoon salt
- 2 tablespoons olive oil
- 1 cup (8 ounces) plain yogurt

Place garlic and salt in a small bowl; crush with the back of a sturdy spoon. Add cilantro and coriander; crush together. Add the yogurt, lemon juice and oil; mix well. Pour into a large resealable plastic bag; add the chicken. Seal bag and turn to coat; refrigerate for 2 hours.

For dipping sauce, place garlic and salt in a small bowl; crush with the back of a sturdy spoon. Mix in oil. Stir in yogurt. Cover and refrigerate until serving.

Pizza on the Grill

(Pictured above)

Pizza is such a favorite, I make it once a week. The barbecue flavor in this recipe is delicious.
—Lisa Boettcher, Columbus, Wisconsin

- 1 package (1/4 ounce) active dry yeast
- 1 cup warm water (110° to 115°)
- 2 tablespoons vegetable oil
- 2 teaspoons sugar
- 1 teaspoon baking soda
- 1 teaspoon salt
- 2-3/4 to 3 cups all-purpose flour
- 2 cups cubed cooked chicken
- 1/2 to 3/4 cup barbecue sauce
- 1/2 cup julienned green pepper
- 2 cups (8 ounces) shredded Monterey Jack cheese

In a mixing bowl, dissolve yeast in water. Add the oil, sugar, baking soda, salt and 2 cups flour. Stir in enough remaining flour to form a soft dough. Turn onto a floured surface; knead until smooth and elastic, about 6-8 minutes. Cover and let rest for 10 minutes.

Coat grill rack with nonstick cooking spray before starting the grill. Drain and discard marinade. Thread chicken on eight metal or soaked wooden skewers. Grill kabobs, covered, over medium heat for 3-4 minutes on each side or until juices run clear, turning once. Serve with dipping sauce. **Yield:** 8 servings.

■ ■ ■

Citrus Chicken Kabobs

(Pictured below)

I've been experimenting with lighter meals. My family loves how fresh these appealing glazed kabobs taste.
—Suzi Sisson, San Diego, California

1 **pound fresh broccoli, broken into florets**
2 **large navel oranges**
1 **pound boneless skinless chicken breasts, cut into 1-inch cubes**
4 **plum tomatoes, quartered**
1 **large onion, cut into wedges**
GLAZE:
1/4 **cup barbecue sauce**
2 **tablespoons lemon juice**
2 **tablespoons soy sauce**
2 **tablespoons honey**

Place 1 in. of water in a large saucepan; add broccoli. Bring to a boil. Reduce heat; cover and simmer for 3-4 minutes or until crisp-tender. Drain. Cut each orange into eight wedges. On eight metal or soaked wooden skewers, alternately thread chicken, vegetables and oranges. In a small bowl, combine the glaze ingredients.

Coat grill rack with nonstick cooking spray before starting the grill. Grill kabobs, uncovered, over medium heat for 5-7 minutes on each side or until chicken juices run clear, turning once. Brush frequently with glaze. **Yield:** 4 servings.

Marinated Rosemary Chicken

(Pictured above)

This moist chicken is partially cooked in the microwave just before grilling to speed up cooking. The rosemary marinade enhances the meat flavor…and there's enough sauce to set aside for basting.
—Wendy Molzahn, Beaumont, Alberta

1/3 cup soy sauce
1/4 cup lemon juice
  2 tablespoons olive oil
  4 garlic cloves, minced
  4 tablespoons minced fresh rosemary
    or 4 teaspoons dried rosemary, crushed
  1 broiler/fryer chicken (3 pounds), cut up and skin removed

In a measuring cup, combine the soy sauce, lemon juice, oil, garlic and rosemary. Pour 1/2 cup into a large resealable plastic bag; add chicken. Seal bag and turn to coat; refrigerate for 8 hours or overnight. Cover and refrigerate remaining marinade for basting.

Coat grill rack with nonstick cooking spray before starting the grill. Prepare grill for indirect heat. Drain and discard marinade from chicken.

Place chicken in an ungreased 13-in. x 9-in. x 2-in. microwave-safe dish. Cover loosely and microwave on high for 6 minutes, rotating once.

Immediately grill chicken, covered, over indirect medium heat for 5 minutes. Turn; grill 8-10 minutes longer or until juices run clear, basting occasionally with reserved marinade. **Yield:** 6 servings.

Editor's Note: This recipe was tested in a 1,100-watt microwave.

Maple-Glazed Chicken Wings

(Pictured below right)

Some wonderful maple syrup I brought back from my last trip to Vermont inspired this recipe.
—Janice Henck, Clarkston, Georgia

- 2 to 3 pounds whole chicken wings
- 1 cup maple syrup
- 2/3 cup chili sauce
- 1/2 cup finely chopped onion
- 2 tablespoons Dijon mustard
- 2 teaspoons Worcestershire sauce
- 1/4 to 1/2 teaspoon crushed red pepper flakes

Cut chicken wings into three sections; discard wing tip section. In a large resealable plastic bag, combine remaining ingredients. Reserve 1 cup for basting and refrigerate. Add chicken to remaining marinade and turn to coat. Seal bag; refrigerate for 4 hours, turning occasionally. Drain and discard marinade.

Grill chicken, covered, over medium heat for 12-16 minutes, turning occasionally. Brush with reserved marinade. Grill, uncovered, for 8-10 minutes or until juices run clear, basting and turning several times. **Yield:** 6-8 servings.

■ ■ ■

Herbed Chicken Quarters

Garlic, basil, thyme, salt and cayenne pepper perfectly season chicken pieces.
—Erika Aylward, Clinton, Michigan

- 4 medium lemons, cut into wedges
- 1/2 cup vegetable oil
- 8 garlic cloves, minced
- 4 teaspoons minced fresh basil
- 2 teaspoons minced fresh thyme
- 2 teaspoons salt
- 1/2 teaspoon cayenne pepper
- 1 broiler/fryer chicken (about 3 pounds), quartered

Gently squeeze the juice from the lemons into a large resealable plastic bag; leave the lemon wedges in the bag. Add the oil, garlic, basil, thyme, salt and cayenne. Add the chicken and turn to coat. Seal bag and refrigerate for 24 hours, turning frequently.

Drain and discard the marinade. Grill chicken, covered, over medium heat, turning every 15 minutes, for 1 hour or until a meat thermometer reads 170° for breast meat quarters and 180° for leg quarters. **Yield:** 4 servings.

Apple Thyme Chicken

(Pictured above)

Apples and chicken may seem like an unusual combination, but they make a wonderful meal when grilled to perfection.
—Peter Halferty, Corpus Christi, Texas

- 6 tablespoons apple juice
- 6 tablespoons lemon juice
- 4-1/2 teaspoons cider vinegar
- 4-1/2 teaspoons vegetable oil
- 1-1/2 teaspoons dried thyme
- 4 boneless skinless chicken breast halves (4 ounces *each*)
- 2 medium Golden Delicious *or* other all-purpose apples, peeled and quartered
- 1 tablespoon honey

SAUCE:
- 2 teaspoons cornstarch
- 1/4 teaspoon dried thyme
- 3/4 cup apple juice

In a bowl, combine the first five ingredients; mix well. Pour half of the marinade into a large resealable plastic bag; add chicken. Seal bag and turn to coat; refrigerate for at least 2 hours. Cover and refrigerate remaining marinade.

Coat grill rack with nonstick cooking spray before starting the grill. Drain and discard marinade from chicken. Dip apples in reserved marinade; set aside. Combine the honey with the remaining marinade. Grill chicken, covered, over medium heat for 4-6 minutes on each side or until juices run clear, basting frequently with the honey marinade. Grill apples, uncovered, for 3-5 minutes, basting and turning frequently or until lightly browned.

In a saucepan, combine cornstarch, thyme and apple juice until blended. Bring to a boil; cook and stir for 2 minutes or until thickened. Slice grilled apples; stir into sauce. Serve with chicken. **Yield:** 4 servings.

Flattening Chicken

Flattening or pounding meat can serve several purposes. It is typically done for quicker, more even cooking and to produce an attractive appearance.

Before tender cuts of meat or poultry are flattened, it's best to put them inside a heavy-duty resealable plastic bag or between two sheets of heavy plastic wrap to prevent messy splatters. Use only the smooth side of a meat mallet to gently pound them to the desired thickness. This will prevent the meat from shredding.

When tougher cuts of meat need tenderizing, they are pounded with the ridged side of a meat mallet to break up the connective tissue.

Spicy Grilled Chicken

(Pictured above)

Very near the top of the list of foods I prepare for company is this chicken. It is a family favorite, too. Any leftovers are great in a salad or sandwich.
—Edith Maki, Hancock, Michigan

3/4 cup finely chopped onion
1/2 cup grapefruit juice
2 tablespoons olive oil
2 tablespoons soy sauce
1 tablespoon honey
1 garlic clove, minced
1-1/2 teaspoons salt
1-1/2 teaspoons rubbed sage
1-1/2 teaspoons dried thyme
1 teaspoon ground all spice
1 teaspoon garlic powder
1/2 teaspoon ground cinnamon
1/2 teaspoon ground nutmeg
1/4 teaspoon cayenne pepper
1/4 teaspoon pepper
6 boneless skinless chicken breast halves (1-1/2 pounds)

In a large resealable plastic bag, combine the first 15 ingredients; mix well. Reserve 1/3 cup for basting and refrigerate. Add chicken to remaining marinade and turn to coat. Seal bag; refrigerate overnight.

Drain and discard marinade. Grill chicken, uncovered, over medium heat for 3 minutes on each side. Baste with reserved marinade. Continue grilling for 6-8 minutes or until juices run clear, basting and turning several times. **Yield:** 6 servings.

Curry Grilled Chicken

(Pictured below)

Whenever I use this flavorful marinade, the chicken comes out tender and tangy every time. I've found that its mild curry flavor is equally good on pork. I know you and your family will enjoy this.
—Nancy Ode, Sherman, South Dakota

1/2 cup sugar
1/2 cup white vinegar
1/3 cup ketchup
   1 tablespoon Worcestershire sauce
1/2 teaspoon ground mustard
1/2 teaspoon paprika
1/2 teaspoon curry powder
1/2 teaspoon garlic salt
1/2 teaspoon salt
1/8 teaspoon pepper
   4 boneless skinless chicken breast halves (1-1/4 pounds)

In a blender, combine the first 10 ingredients; cover and process until blended. Pour into a large resealable plastic bag; add the chicken. Seal and refrigerate for 1-2 hours. Drain and discard marinade.

Grill the chicken, covered, over medium heat for 6 minutes on each side or until the juices run clear. **Yield:** 4 servings.

■ ■ ■

Lemon Barbecued Chicken

When we bought our first charcoal grill, we needed a recipe for barbecued chicken. We ended up combining two recipes to come up with this winning one. We use it often!
—Rodella Brown, Hanover, Pennsylvania

2/3 cup lemon juice
1/3 cup vegetable oil
1/3 cup white vinegar
  1 tablespoon soy sauce
  2 teaspoons sugar
  1 teaspoon salt
  1 teaspoon paprika
  1 teaspoon chili powder
1/2 teaspoon pepper
1/2 teaspoon garlic salt
  1 medium onion, chopped
  1 broiler/fryer chicken
    (3-1/2 to 4 pounds), cut up

Combine the first 11 ingredients; set aside 1/4 cup. Pour remaining marinade into a large resealable plastic bag. Add chicken; seal bag. Refrigerate at least 8 hours or overnight, turning occasionally. Drain, discarding marinade. Grill the chicken, covered, over medium heat for 45 minutes or until juices run clear, turning and basting with reserved marinade every 8-10 minutes. **Yield:** 6 servings.

■ ■ ■

Caribbean Chicken

(Pictured at right)

You'd be hard-pressed to find a marinade that's this flavorful from any store!
—Rusty Collins, Orlando, Florida

1/2 cup lemon juice
1/3 cup honey
  3 tablespoons vegetable oil
  6 green onions, sliced
  3 jalapeno peppers, seeded and
    chopped
  3 teaspoons dried thyme
3/4 teaspoon salt
1/4 teaspoon ground allspice
1/4 teaspoon ground nutmeg
  6 boneless skinless chicken breast
    halves (1-1/2 pounds)

Place the first nine ingredients in a blender or food processor; cover and process until smooth. Pour 1/2 cup into a small bowl for basting; cover and refrigerate. Pour remaining marinade into a large resealable plastic bag; add chicken. Seal bag and turn to coat; refrigerate for up to 6 hours.

Drain and discard marinade. Coat grill rack with nonstick cooking spray before starting the grill. Grill chicken, covered, over medium heat for 4-6 minutes on each side or until juices run clear, basting frequently with the reserved marinade. **Yield:** 6 servings.

Editor's Note: When cutting or seeding hot peppers, use rubber or plastic gloves to protect your hands. Avoid touching your face.

1/8 teaspoon ground allspice
4 boneless skinless chicken breast halves (1 pound)
1 tablespoon cornstarch
1/4 cup honey
1 medium navel orange, peeled and sectioned
3 cups hot cooked rice
2 teaspoons minced chives

In a bowl, combine first nine ingredients. Remove 1 cup; cover and chill. Place chicken in a large resealable plastic bag; add remaining marinade. Seal bag and turn to coat; refrigerate for 2-8 hours, turning occasionally. Drain and discard marinade.

Grill chicken, uncovered, over medium heat for 4 minutes on each side or until juices run clear. In a saucepan, combine cornstarch and reserved marinade until smooth. Stir in honey. Bring to a boil; cook and stir for 2 minutes or until thickened. Serve chicken with orange sections over rice; spoon sauce over top. Sprinkle with chives. **Yield:** 4 servings.

■ ■ ■

Glazed Herb Chicken

(Pictured above)

The orange flavor really comes through in the sauce that nicely coats this grilled chicken. I garnish it with fresh orange segments and snipped chives.
—Jill Smith, Irmo, South Carolina

1 can (14-1/2 ounces) chicken broth
3/4 cup orange juice concentrate
2 tablespoons red wine vinegar
2 teaspoons grated orange peel
2 garlic cloves, minced
1/2 teaspoon dried minced onion
1/8 to 1/4 teaspoon cayenne pepper
1/8 teaspoon dried thyme

Campfire Chicken Stew

My family loves it when I prepare these chicken stew packets on camping trips, but they're equally good on our backyard grill.
—Florence Kreis, Beach Park, Illinois

1 broiler/fryer chicken (3-1/2 to 4 pounds), cut up
3 to 4 medium potatoes, peeled and sliced
1 cup thinly sliced carrots
1 medium green pepper, sliced
1 can (10-3/4 ounces) condensed cream of mushroom soup, undiluted
1/4 cup water

1/2 teaspoon salt
1/4 teaspoon pepper

Grill the chicken, uncovered, over medium heat for 3 minutes on each side. Place two pieces of chicken each on four pieces of heavy-duty foil (about 18 in. x 12 in.). Divide the potatoes, carrots and green pepper between the four pieces of foil. Top each with 2 tablespoons soup, 1 tablespoon water, salt and pepper.

Fold the foil around the mixture and seal tightly. Grill, covered, over medium heat for 20 minutes; turn and grill 20-25 minutes longer or until the vegetables are tender and the chicken juices run clear. **Yield:** 4 servings.

■ ■ ■

Barbecued Picnic Chicken

(Pictured at right)

Cooked on a covered grill, poultry stays so tender and juicy. Everyone loves the zesty, slightly sweet homemade barbecue sauce.
—Priscilla Weaver, Hagerstown, Maryland

2 garlic cloves, minced
2 teaspoons butter
1 cup ketchup
1/4 cup packed brown sugar
1/4 cup chili sauce
2 tablespoons Worcestershire sauce
1 tablespoon celery seed
1 tablespoon prepared mustard
1/2 teaspoon salt
2 dashes hot pepper sauce
2 broiler/fryer chickens (3-1/2 to 4 pounds *each*), quartered

In a saucepan, saute the garlic in butter until tender. Add the next eight ingredients. Bring to a boil, stirring constantly. Remove from the heat and set aside.

Grill the chicken, covered, over medium heat for 30 minutes, turning occasionally. Baste with sauce. Grill 15 minutes longer or until a meat thermometer reads 170° for the breast meat quarters or 180° for the leg quarters, basting and turning several times. **Yield:** 8 servings.

The Italian dressing you use to pour on your salad makes a speedy, savory marinade! Place the chicken, meat, pork or vegetables in a resealable plastic bag. Add the dressing and marinate in the refrigerator for 30 minutes or more.

Drain and discard the marinade. Grill the chicken, meat, pork and vegetables according to the grilling charts found in each chapter of this book.

Rosemary Lime Chicken

(Pictured above)

I experimented with herbs and seasonings quite a bit before creating the final version of this entree.
—Nicole Harris, Greenbriar, Pennsylvania

    4 **boneless skinless chicken breast halves (5 ounces *each*)**
    2 **tablespoons vegetable oil**
 1/2 **cup white wine *or* chicken broth**
 1/4 **cup lime juice**
    2 **tablespoons minced fresh rosemary *or* 2 teaspoons dried rosemary, crushed**
 1/2 **teaspoon salt**
 1/4 **teaspoon pepper**

Flatten chicken to 1/2-in. thickness. In a large skillet, brown chicken in oil over medium-high heat. Add the remaining ingredients. Grill, covered, over medium heat for 5-7 minutes on each side or until chicken juices run clear. **Yield:** 4 servings.

■ ■ ■

Grilled Chicken Dinner

This complete meal grilled in a foil packet is a palate-pleasing and mess-free dinner for one.
—Floyd Hule, Apache Junction, Arizona

    1 **bone-in chicken breast half**
    1 **medium potato, peeled and quartered**
    1 **large carrot, cut into 2-inch pieces**
 1/2 **cup fresh vegetables (broccoli florets, peas *and/or* green beans)**
    1 **tablespoon onion soup mix**
 2/3 **cup condensed cream of chicken soup, undiluted**

Place chicken in the center of a piece of double-layered heavy-duty foil (about 18 in. square). Place vegetables around chicken. Sprinkle with soup mix. Top with soup. Fold foil around vegetables and chicken and seal tightly.

Grill, uncovered, over medium-low heat for 50-60 minutes or until chicken juices run clear and potato is tender. Open foil carefully to allow steam to escape. **Yield:** 1 serving.

■ ■ ■

Lemon-Lime Chicken

(Pictured below)

I've served this main dish numerous times for dinner guests and have received many compliments. In fact, my husband says this is the best chicken he's ever had!
—Dana Fulton, Stone Mountain, Georgia

6 **boneless skinless chicken breast halves (1-1/2 pounds)**
1/2 **cup packed brown sugar**
1/4 **cup cider vinegar**
3 **tablespoons** *each* **lemon juice and lime juice**
3 **tablespoons Dijon mustard**
3/4 **teaspoon garlic powder**
1/4 **teaspoon pepper**
1/2 **teaspoon salt**

Place chicken in a large resealable plastic bag. Combine remaining ingredients; pour over chicken. Seal bag and turn to coat; refrigerate at least 4 hours or overnight. Drain, discarding marinade. Grill chicken over medium-hot heat, turning once, until juices run clear, about 15-18 minutes. **Yield:** 4-6 servings.

■ ■ ■

Grilled Italian Chicken

This moist, tender chicken grills up in just minutes. With only two ingredients, the marinade couldn't be simpler.
—Joyce Pruitt, Jacksonville, Florida

1 **bottle (8 ounces) Italian salad dressing**
3 **tablespoons teriyaki sauce**
8 **boneless skinless chicken breast halves**

In a bowl, combine the salad dressing and teriyaki sauce. Remove 1/4 cup for basting; cover and refrigerate. Place the chicken in a large resealable plastic bag and add the remaining marinade. Seal bag and turn to coat; refrigerate for 8 hours or overnight, turning occasionally.

Drain and discard marinade. Grill chicken, covered, over medium heat for 3 minutes on each side. Baste with reserved marinade. Grill 3-4 minutes longer on each side or until juices run clear. **Yield:** 6 servings.

Grilled Chicken Cordon Bleu

(Pictured below)

You can assemble these bundles up to 8 hours in advance and keep them in the fridge. Then just place them on the grill when ready.
—Shawna McCutcheon
Homer City, Pennsylvania

6 **boneless skinless chicken breast halves (1-1/2 pounds)**
6 **slices Swiss cheese**
6 **thin slices deli ham**
3 **tablespoons olive oil**
3/4 **cup seasoned bread crumbs**

Flatten the chicken to 1/4-in. thickness. Place a slice of cheese and ham on each to within 1/4 in. of edges. Fold in half; secure with thin metal skewers or toothpicks. Brush with oil and roll in bread crumbs. Grill, covered, over medium-hot heat for 15-18 minutes or until juices run clear. **Yield:** 6 servings.

■ ■ ■

Chicken Pizza Packets

Basil, garlic, pepperoni and mozzarella give plenty of pizza flavor to chicken, green pepper, zucchini and cherry tomatoes in these individual foil dinners.
—Amber Zurbrugg, Alliance, Ohio

1 **pound boneless skinless chicken breasts, cut into 1-inch pieces**
2 **tablespoons olive oil**
1 **small zucchini, thinly sliced**
16 **pepperoni slices**
1 **small green pepper, julienned**
1 **small onion, sliced**
1/2 **teaspoon dried oregano**
1/2 **teaspoon dried basil**
1/4 **teaspoon salt**
1/4 **teaspoon garlic powder**
1/4 **teaspoon pepper**
1 **cup halved cherry tomatoes**
1/2 **cup shredded part-skim mozzarella cheese**
1/2 **cup shredded Parmesan cheese**

In a large bowl, combine first 11 ingredients. Coat four pieces of heavy-duty foil (about 12 in. square) with nonstick cooking spray. Place a quarter of chicken mixture in the center of each piece. Fold foil around mixture and seal tightly. Grill, covered, over medium-hot heat for 15-18 minutes or until chicken juices run clear.

Carefully open each packet. Sprinkle with tomatoes and cheeses. Seal loosely; grill 2 minutes longer or until cheese is melted. **Yield:** 4 servings.

Bombay Chicken

(Pictured at right)

This grilled dinner always turns out moist and tender. The marinade has a Middle Eastern flair, giving the dish a zesty flavor. It makes a beautiful presentation as well.
—June Thomas, Chesterton, Indiana

1-1/2 cups (12 ounces) plain yogurt
  1/4 cup lemon juice
    2 tablespoons chili powder
    2 tablespoons paprika
    2 tablespoons olive oil
1-1/2 teaspoons salt
  1/2 to 1 teaspoon cayenne pepper
  1/2 teaspoon garlic powder
  1/4 teaspoon ground ginger
  1/4 teaspoon ground cardamom
  1/8 teaspoon ground cinnamon
    4 to 5 pounds bone-in chicken thighs
       and legs, skin removed

In a large resealable plastic bag, combine the first 11 ingredients. Add the chicken; seal bag and turn to coat. Refrigerate overnight.

Coat grill rack with nonstick cooking spray before starting grill. Drain and discard marinade. Grill chicken, covered, over direct medium-hot heat for 15 minutes. Turn; grill for 10-15 minutes longer or until juices run clear. **Yield:** 8 servings.

■ ■ ■

Curried Peanut Chicken

This is a nice change from traditional grilled items. I sprinkle coconut and currants over a tasty combination of chicken and peppers.
—Jennifer Myers, Havertown, Pennsylvania

1-1/2 cups orange juice
  3/4 cup peanut butter

    2 tablespoons curry powder
    4 boneless skinless chicken breast
       halves
    2 medium sweet red peppers, cut in
       half
  1/4 cup flaked coconut, toasted
  1/4 cup dried currants
Hot cooked rice

In a bowl, combine the orange juice, peanut butter and curry powder. Pour a third of the marinade into a large resealable plastic bag; add chicken. Seal bag and turn to coat; refrigerate for 8 hours or overnight. Cover and refrigerate remaining marinade.

Drain and discard marinade from chicken. Grill chicken and peppers over medium heat for 8-10 minutes on each side or until chicken juices run clear and peppers are tender. Warm the reserved marinade. Cut chicken and peppers into 1/2-in. strips; sprinkle with coconut and currants. Serve with rice and reserved marinade. **Yield:** 4 servings.

Lemon Chicken Skewers

(Pictured above)

This easy-to-assemble recipe, with tender chunks of chicken and garden-fresh zucchini and cherry tomatoes, is always a hit when we have a party.
—Margaret Wagner Allen, Abingdon, Virginia

1/4 cup olive oil
3 tablespoons lemon juice
1 tablespoon white wine vinegar
2 garlic cloves, minced
2 teaspoons grated lemon peel
1 teaspoon salt
1/2 teaspoon sugar
1/4 teaspoon dried oregano
1/4 teaspoon pepper
1-1/2 pounds boneless skinless chicken breasts, into 1-1/2-inch pieces
3 medium zucchini, halved lengthwise and cut into 1-1/2-inch slices
3 medium onions, cut into wedges
12 cherry tomatoes

In a bowl, combine the first nine ingredients; set aside 1/4 cup for basting. Place chicken and vegetables in a large resealable plastic bag; add remaining marinade. Seal bag and turn to coat; refrigerate for 4 hours or overnight.

Drain and discard marinade. Alternately thread chicken and vegetables onto metal or soaked wooden skewers. Grill, covered, over medium heat for 6 minutes. Turn and baste with the reserved marinade. Cook 6 minutes longer or until chicken juices run clear. **Yield:** 6 servings.

■ ■ ■

Rosemary Chicken

A fast-to-fix overnight marinade with dried rosemary gives wonderful herb flavor to this tender chicken. The leftovers are delicious in a chicken salad.
—Marcia Morgan, Chevy Chase, Maryland

1 cup orange juice
1/4 cup olive oil
3 garlic cloves, minced
1 tablespoon dried rosemary, crushed
1 tablespoon dried thyme
8 boneless skinless chicken breast halves (2 pounds)

Combine the first five ingredients; pour half into a large resealable plastic bag. Refrigerate the remaining marinade for basting. Add chicken to bag; seal and toss to coat. Refrigerate for 8 hours or overnight. Drain and discard marinade.

Grill chicken, uncovered, over medium heat for 3 minutes on each side. Baste with reserved marinade. Continue cooking for 6-8 minutes or until meat juices run clear. **Yield:** 8 servings.

Grilled Chicken With Peaches

(Pictured below)

My grandmother gave me this recipe, which I lightened up. My children loved it when they were little, and now my grandchildren ask for it when they come over. The peaches are delicious hot off the grill.
—Linda McCluskey, Cullman, Alabama

  1 cup 100% peach spreadable fruit
  2 tablespoons olive oil
  4 teaspoons soy sauce
  1 tablespoon ground mustard
  1 garlic clove, minced
1/2 teaspoon salt
1/4 teaspoon pepper
1/4 teaspoon cayenne pepper
  8 bone-in skinless chicken breast halves (8 ounces *each*)
  8 medium ripe peaches, halved and pitted

Coat grill rack with nonstick cooking spray before starting grill for indirect heat. In a small bowl, combine the first eight ingredients; set aside. Grill chicken, covered, over indirect medium heat for 10 minutes on each side. Brush chicken with glaze. Grill 10-15 minutes longer or until juices run clear, turning every 5 minutes and brushing with glaze. Transfer to a serving platter and keep warm.

Grill peach halves cut side down over indirect heat for 2 minutes. Turn; brush with glaze and grill for 3-4 minutes longer or until tender. Serve grilled peaches with chicken. **Yield:** 8 servings.

Grilled Jerk Chicken

(Pictured below)

Jerk refers to a dry seasoning blend that originated in the Caribbean and that includes spices like allspice, ginger and cinnamon and a blend of peppers. Our Test Kitchen staff came up with this zesty jerk chicken recipe.

- 4 teaspoons curry powder
- 4 teaspoons ground cumin
- 4 teaspoons paprika
- 3 teaspoons ground ginger
- 3 teaspoons ground allspice
- 1 teaspoon salt
- 1 teaspoon cayenne pepper
- 1 teaspoon coarsely ground pepper
- 4 bone-in chicken breast halves with skin (8 ounces *each*)
- 4 chicken thighs with skin (4 ounces *each*)

In a small bowl, combine the first eight ingredients; rub over the chicken pieces. Cover and refrigerate for 1 hour. Grill the chicken, covered, over indirect medium heat for 30-40 minutes or until juices run clear. **Yield:** 4 servings.

■ ■ ■

Honey Orange Chicken

I couldn't get enough of the sweet-and-citrusy marinade flavoring this grilled chicken. So I saved some to drizzle on top.
—*Mary Hart Easterling, Santa Clarita, California*

- 1 cup chicken broth
- 1 cup orange juice
- 1/2 cup honey
- 1 tablespoon lemon juice
- 1 tablespoon cider vinegar
- 1 tablespoon soy sauce
- 1 teaspoon grated orange peel
- 1 teaspoon ground ginger
- 1/2 teaspoon salt
- 4 bone-in chicken breast halves (10 ounces *each*)
- 1 tablespoon cornstarch
- 2 tablespoons water
- 4 cups hot cooked rice

Chopped green onions, orange slices and parsley sprigs, optional

In a saucepan, combine the first nine ingredients. Bring to a boil. Remove from the heat; cool. Pour 1-1/3 cups marinade into a large resealable plastic bag; add chicken. Seal bag and turn to coat; refrigerate for 4-8 hours or overnight, turning occasionally. Cover and refrigerate remaining marinade.

Drain chicken, discarding marinade. Grill, covered, over medium heat for 12-15 minutes on each side or until juices run clear. Meanwhile, combine cornstarch and water in a small saucepan until smooth; stir in reserved marinade. Bring to a boil; cook and stir for 2 minutes or until thickened.

Remove and discard skin from chicken. Serve chicken over rice; drizzle with sauce. Garnish with green onions, orange slices and parsley if desired. **Yield:** 4 serving.

■ ■ ■

Herb Fryer Chicken

(Pictured above)

We use our grill all year long. Our boys love this chicken, and it's a hit with company, too. To really bring out the lemon flavor, pierce the chicken skin before marinating the meat overnight.
—Charlene Sylvia, Sandy, Utah

1/3 cup lemon juice
1/4 cup olive oil

1/4 cup minced fresh parsley
  2 tablespoons finely chopped onion
  3 garlic cloves, minced
  1 tablespoon grated lemon peel
  1 teaspoon minced fresh thyme
1/2 teaspoon salt
1/4 teaspoon pepper
  1 broiler/fryer chicken (3 pounds), cut up

In a large resealable plastic bag, combine the lemon juice, oil, parsley, onion, garlic, lemon peel, thyme, salt and pepper; add chicken. Seal bag and turn to coat; refrigerate overnight, turning occasionally. Drain and discard marinade.

Grill chicken, covered, over medium heat for 35-40 minutes or until juices run clear, turning every 15 minutes. **Yield:** 6 servings.

Montego Bay Chicken

(Pictured above)

You don't need high-fat ingredients to make this grilled chicken taste good. The marinade both flavors and tenderizes the meat. Rum extract and grape juice capture the flavor of the Caribbean.
—Julie DeMatteo, Clementon, New Jersey

    1/4 cup soy sauce
    1/4 cup orange juice
      2 tablespoons brown sugar
      2 garlic cloves, minced
      1 teaspoon hot pepper sauce
      1 teaspoon rum extract
    1/4 teaspoon ground ginger *or* 1
         teaspoon minced fresh gingerroot
      4 boneless skinless chicken breast
         halves (4 ounces *each*)

In a large resealable plastic bag, combine the first seven ingredients; add the chicken. Seal bag and turn to coat; refrigerate for at least 2 hours.

Drain and discard marinade. Coat grill rack with nonstick cooking spray before starting the grill. Grill chicken, uncovered, over indirect medium heat for 6-8 minutes on each side or until juices run clear. **Yield:** 4 servings.

Shrimp-Stuffed Chicken Breasts

(Pictured below)

Filled with a flavorful mix of shrimp, mayonnaise, onions and tarragon, these golden chicken breasts are special enough to serve at a family celebration or dinner party.
—Wendy McGowan, Poulsbo, Washington

      6 boneless skinless chicken breast
         halves (6 ounces *each*)
  2-1/2 cups frozen cooked salad shrimp,
         thawed
    1/2 cup chopped green onions
    1/2 cup mayonnaise
      1 tablespoon dried tarragon
      1 tablespoon lemon juice
    1/2 teaspoon Liquid Smoke, optional
      1 tablespoon vegetable oil
    1/4 teaspoon salt
    1/4 teaspoon pepper

Flatten chicken to 1/4-in. thickness. In a bowl, combine the shrimp, onions, mayonnaise, tarragon, lemon juice and Liquid Smoke if desired. Place about 1/3 cup down the center of each chicken breast half; fold chicken

Brush both sides of chicken with oil. Grill over medium heat, turning occasionally, for 10-14 minutes or until juices run clear.

Meanwhile, combine remaining ingredients in a small bowl. Spoon over warm chicken; serve immediately. Or, to serve cold, spoon sauce over chicken and refrigerate several hours or overnight. **Yield:** 4 servings.

■ ■ ■

Exotic Grilled Chicken

The marinade makes a savory statement in this grilled chicken recipe from our Test Kitchen home economists. It smells so good when cooking, your family and guests will be eager to try a piece.

- 1/4 cup soy sauce
- 3 tablespoons vegetable oil
- 2 tablespoons water
- 1 tablespoon dried minced onion
- 1 tablespoon sesame seeds
- 1-1/2 teaspoons sugar
- 2 garlic cloves, minced
- 1/2 teaspoon ground ginger
- 1/2 teaspoon salt
- 1/8 teaspoon cayenne pepper
- 1 broiler/fryer chicken (3 to 4 pounds), cut up

In a large resealable plastic bag, combine the first 10 ingredients. Set aside 1/4 cup for basting; cover and refrigerate. Add chicken to bag; seal bag and turn to coat. Refrigerate for 8 hours or overnight.

Drain and discard marinade from chicken. Grill chicken, skin side down, uncovered, over medium heat for 15 minutes on each side. Brush with reserved marinade. Grill for 5 minutes. Turn and baste again; grill 5 minutes longer or until meat juices run clear. Discard unused marinade. **Yield:** 4-6 servings.

over filling and secure with toothpicks.

Brush chicken with oil; sprinkle with salt and pepper. Grill, covered, over medium heat for 6-8 minutes on each side or until the juices run clear. Discard the toothpicks before serving. **Yield:** 6 servings.

■ ■ ■

Cool Cucumber Chicken

(Pictured above)

My husband really likes chicken, so when I need a delicious dish for a picnic, this is what I make.
—*Andria Barosi-Stampone*
Randolph, New Jersey

- 4 boneless skinless chicken breast halves (1-1/4 pounds)
- 2 tablespoons olive oil
- 1 medium cucumber, seeded and chopped
- 1/2 cup plain yogurt
- 2 tablespoons mayonnaise
- 1 tablespoon minced fresh dill
- 1/8 teaspoon pepper

Marinated Chicken Breasts

(Pictured above)

My sister shared this recipe with me, and it has been a big hit at Farm Bureau picnics and other get-togethers. I keep the ingredients on hand for fast weekday dinners.
—Eileen Schroeder, Montague, Michigan

> 1 cup sugar
> 1 cup water
> 1 cup soy sauce
> 1/4 cup pineapple juice
> 1/4 cup vegetable oil
> 1 teaspoon garlic powder
> 1 teaspoon ground ginger
> 8 boneless skinless chicken breast halves (about 2-1/2 pounds)

In a bowl, combine the first seven ingredients; remove 3/4 cup for basting; cover and refrigerate. In a large resealable plastic bag, place the chicken and remaining marinade. Seal bag and turn to coat; refrigerate for 4 hours or overnight.

Drain and discard marinade. Grill chicken, covered, over medium heat for 3 minutes on each side. Baste with reserved marinade. Grill 3-4 minutes longer on each side or until juices run clear, basting several times. **Yield:** 8 servings.

■ ■ ■

Grilled Raspberry Chicken

Raspberry vinaigrette and raspberry jam lend fruity flavor to this moist chicken dish I created.
—Gloria Warczak, Cedarburg, Wisconsin

> 1 cup plus 4-1/2 teaspoons raspberry vinaigrette, *divided*

2 tablespoons minced fresh rosemary *or* 2 teaspoons dried rosemary, crushed, *divided*
6 chicken thighs
6 chicken drumsticks
1/2 cup seedless raspberry jam
1-1/2 teaspoons lime juice
1/2 teaspoon soy sauce
1/8 teaspoon garlic powder

In a large resealable plastic bag, combine 1 cup vinaigrette and half of the rosemary. Add chicken. Seal bag and turn to coat; refrigerate for 1 hour. In a bowl, combine the jam, lime juice, soy sauce, garlic powder, and remaining vinaigrette and rosemary; set aside.

Drain and discard marinade. Place chicken skin side down on grill rack. Grill, covered, over indirect medium heat for 20 minutes. Turn; grill 10-20 minutes longer or until juices run clear, basting occasionally with raspberry sauce. **Yield:** 6 servings.

■ ■ ■

Honey Lemon Chicken

(Pictured at right)

When I told our daughter that we were grilling chicken, she asked to make a marinade. Now we use her combination of honey, lemon, garlic and seasonings every time we grill chicken.
—Tamara McFarlin, Mondovi, Wisconsin

1/2 cup lemon juice
1/3 cup honey
1/4 cup soy sauce
2 tablespoons finely chopped onion
4 garlic cloves, minced
2 teaspoons dried parsley flakes
2 teaspoons dried basil
1 teaspoon salt-free seasoning blend
1 teaspoon white pepper
1 teaspoon lime juice
6 boneless skinless chicken breast halves

In a bowl, combine the first 10 ingredients; mix well. Pour 2/3 cup marinade into a large resealable plastic bag; add the chicken. Seal bag and turn to coat; refrigerate for at least 4 hours or overnight. Cover and refrigerate the remaining marinade.

Drain and discard marinade from chicken. Coat grill rack with nonstick cooking spray before starting the grill. Grill chicken, uncovered, over medium heat 12-15 minutes or until juices run clear, turning once and basting occasionally with reserved marinade. **Yield:** 6 servings.

Chutney-Glazed Chicken

(Pictured below)

I like to garnish these grilled chicken breasts with fresh chives. They make a really delicious meal when served with a tossed salad and dinner rolls.
—Angie Ridgway, Fairfield, Nebraska

  1/2 cup mango chutney
    2 tablespoons sherry *or* apple juice
    2 tablespoons Dijon mustard
    1 teaspoon curry powder
    6 bone-in chicken breast halves
       (about 8 ounces *each*), skin removed

Coat grill rack with nonstick cooking spray before starting the grill for indirect heat. In a small bowl, combine the chutney, sherry or apple juice, mustard and curry powder. Grill the chicken meaty side down over indirect medium heat for 15 minutes. Turn; grill 15-20 minutes longer or until a meat thermometer reads 170°, basting occasionally with the chutney mixture. **Yield:** 6 servings.

■ ■ ■

Summertime Chicken Tacos

(Pictured above right)

Try these tempting tacos when you're looking for a change of pace from regular tacos.
—Susan Scott, Asheville, North Carolina

  1/3 cup olive oil
  1/4 cup lime juice
    4 garlic cloves, minced
    1 tablespoon minced fresh parsley
       or 1 teaspoon dried parsley flakes
    1 teaspoon ground cumin
    1 teaspoon dried oregano
  1/2 teaspoon salt
  1/4 teaspoon pepper
    4 boneless skinless chicken breast
       halves (1-1/4 pounds)
    6 flour tortillas (8 inches) *or* taco
       shells, warmed
Toppings of your choice

In a large resealable plastic bag, combine the first eight ingredients. Add chicken and turn to coat. Seal bag and refrigerate 8 hours or overnight, turning occasionally. Drain and discard marinade.

    Grill chicken, uncovered, over medium heat for 5-7 minutes on each side or until juices run clear. Cut into thin strips; serve in

tortillas or taco shells with desired toppings.
Yield: 6 servings.

■ ■ ■

Sesame Chicken Kabobs

(Pictured at right)

This colorful dish is a favorite of mine for entertaining. I marinate the chicken and cut up the peppers the night before. Then the next day, I just assemble the kabobs and grill.
—Cindy Novak, Antioch, California

1/3 **cup sherry *or* chicken broth**
1/3 **cup soy sauce**
  2 **green onions, chopped**
  3 **tablespoons apricot preserves**
  1 **tablespoon vegetable oil**
  2 **garlic cloves, minced**
1/2 **teaspoon ground ginger *or* 2 teaspoons minced fresh gingerroot**
1/2 **teaspoon hot pepper sauce**
  3 **teaspoons sesame seeds, toasted, *divided***
1-1/2 **pounds boneless skinless chicken breasts, cut into 1-inch cubes**
  1 **medium sweet red pepper, cut into 1-inch pieces**
  1 **medium sweet yellow pepper, cut into 1-inch pieces**

In a bowl, combine the sherry or broth, soy sauce, onions, preserves, oil, garlic, ginger, hot pepper sauce and 1-1/2 teaspoons sesame seeds. Pour 1/3 cup into another bowl for basting; cover and refrigerate. Pour the remaining marinade into a large resealable plastic bag; add the chicken. Seal the bag and turn to coat; refrigerate for 2-3 hours or overnight, turning occasionally.

Drain and discard marinade. On metal or soaked wooden skewers, alternately thread chicken and peppers. Grill, uncovered, over medium heat for 6 minutes, turning once. Baste with reserved marinade. Grill 5-10 minutes longer or until meat juices run clear, turning and basting frequently. Sprinkle with remaining sesame seeds. **Yield:** 6 servings.

·Turkey·

For a tasty twist next Thanksgiving, consider firing up the grill for Marinated Thanksgiving Turkey or Cider Marinated Turkey. Or throughout the year, turn to this chapter for a host of other turkey dishes your family will surely gobble up, like Teriyaki Turkey Tenderloin, Cranberry Turkey Cutlets and Turkey Lime Kabobs!

Marinated Thanksgiving Turkey

(Pictured at left)

My family enjoys this turkey because it cooks up tender, tasty and golden-brown. The marinade flavors the meat very well. I like grilling it since it adds that tempting barbecued flavor.
—Ken Churches, San Andreas, California

1-1/2 **cups chicken broth**
    2 **cups water**
    1 **cup soy sauce**
  2/3 **cup lemon juice**
    2 **garlic cloves, minced**
1-1/2 **teaspoons ground ginger**
    1 **teaspoon pepper**
    1 **turkey (12 to 13 pounds)**

Combine the first seven ingredients; reserve 1 cup for basting. Pour remaining marinade into a 2-gal. resealable plastic bag. Add the turkey and seal the bag; turn to coat. Refrigerate overnight, turning several times.

Drain and discard marinade. Heat grill according to manufacturer's directions for indirect cooking. Tuck wings under turkey; place breast side down on grill rack. Cover and grill for 1 hour.

Add 10 briquettes to coals; turn the turkey breast side up. Brush with reserved marinade. Cover and cook for 2 hours, adding 10 briquettes to maintain heat and brushing with marinade every 30 minutes until meat thermometer reads 185°. Cover; let stand 20 minutes before carving. **Yield:** 8 servings.

Barbecued Turkey Slices

(Pictured below)

At banquets, church dinners and even wedding buffets, this tantalizing turkey is a "must" for the table. It was a hit with the 100-plus guests at our family reunion. I've served it with cheesy potatoes and assorted summer salads. It's a snap to fix ahead of time and keeps well in the freezer.
—Jerry Olson, Ephraim, Utah

1/2 cup grapefruit *or* citrus soda
1/2 cup soy sauce
1/4 cup vegetable oil
2-1/2 teaspoons garlic powder
1 teaspoon prepared horseradish
2-1/2 pounds boneless skinless turkey breast, cut into 3/4-inch slices

In a large resealable plastic bag, combine the soda, soy sauce, oil, garlic powder and horse-radish. Add turkey slices. Seal bag and turn to coat; refrigerate for 6-8 hours or overnight.

Drain and discard the marinade. Grill the turkey, uncovered, over medium heat for 4-5 minutes on each side or until the turkey juices run clear. **Yield:** 8-10 servings.

Turkey Grilling Chart

Turkey breasts and turkey tenderloins are done at 170°; whole turkeys at 180° as measured in the thigh. Kabobs are done when juices run clear. Ground turkey patties are done at 165°. For direct grilling, turn meat halfway through grilling time. The cooking times given are a guideline. Check for doneness with a meat thermometer or other appropriate doneness test.

Cut	Weight or Thickness	Heat	Approximate Cooking Time
Whole, unstuffed	8 to 11 lbs.	medium/indirect	2 to 3 hours
	12 to 16 lbs.	medium/indirect	3 to 4 hours
Breast, bone-in	4 to 5 lbs.	medium/indirect	1-1/2 to 2 hours
Breast, boneless	1-1/4 to 1-3/4 lbs.	medium/indirect	1 to 1-1/4 hours
Tenderloins	8 oz.	medium/direct	15 to 20 minutes
Drumsticks or Thighs	1/2 to 1-1/2 lbs.	medium/indirect	45 to 75 minutes
Patties	4 oz. and 1/2 in.	medium/direct	10 to 12 minutes
Kabobs	1-in. cubes	medium/direct	10 to 15 minutes

Cranberry Turkey Cutlets

When our son-in-law brought home some wild turkey one year, we turned to this recipe. He took care of the grilling while I made the sauce, and we all enjoyed this healthy entree.
—Marguerite Shaeffer, Sewell, New Jersey

- 1 **cup thinly sliced onion**
- 2 **teaspoons vegetable oil**
- 2 **cups dried cranberries**
- 2 **cups orange juice**
- 1-1/2 **teaspoons balsamic vinegar** *or* **cider vinegar**
- 6 **turkey cutlets (4 ounces** *each* **and 1/2 inch thick)**
- 1/2 **teaspoon salt**
- 1/2 **teaspoon pepper**

In a large skillet, saute onion in oil until lightly browned, about 6 minutes. Stir in the cranberries, orange juice and vinegar. Bring to a boil over medium heat; cook and stir until sauce begins to thicken. Set aside.

Coat grill rack with nonstick cooking spray before starting the grill. Sprinkle the turkey cutlets with salt and pepper. Grill, covered, over indirect medium heat for 5-6 minutes on each side or until turkey juices run clear.

Top each cutlet with some of the cranberry sauce; grill 1-2 minutes longer. Serve with the remaining cranberry sauce. **Yield:** 6 servings.

Marinated Turkey Tenderloins

(Pictured above)

When they taste my grilled specialty, guests say, "This turkey melts in your mouth—and the flavor is fantastic!" The recipe includes a tangy marinade that was developed for our turkey producers' booth at the state fair one summer.
—Denise Nebel, Wayland, Iowa

1/4 **cup soy sauce**
1/4 **cup vegetable oil**
1/4 **cup apple juice**
　2 **tablespoons lemon juice**
　2 **tablespoons dried minced onion**
　1 **teaspoon vanilla extract**
1/4 **teaspoon ground ginger**
Dash *each* **garlic powder and pepper**
　2 **turkey breast tenderloins (1/2 pound** *each***)**

In a large resealable plastic bag, combine the soy sauce, oil, apple juice, lemon juice, onion, vanilla, ginger, garlic powder and pepper. Add turkey; seal bag and refrigerate for at least 2 hours. Drain and discard marinade.

Grill the turkey, covered, over medium heat for 8-10 minutes per side or until juices run clear. **Yield:** 4 servings.

■ ■ ■

Zesty Apricot Turkey

Grilled turkey is bound to be the centerpiece of any picnic. The poultry's fruity coating gets a little kick from hot pepper sauce...and would be a nice complement to other meats, too. This entree is so easy, you'll be munching in the sunshine in no time.
—Wendy Moylan, Crystal Lake, Illinois

1/3 **cup apricot preserves**
　1 **tablespoon white wine vinegar**
　1 **tablespoon honey**
1/2 **teaspoon grated lemon peel**
　1 **garlic clove, minced**
1/8 **teaspoon hot pepper sauce**

1 **boneless skinless turkey breast half (1 pound)**

In a microwave-safe dish, combine the first six ingredients. Microwave, uncovered, until the preserves are melted, about 1-2 minutes on high. Stir to blend. Set aside half to serve with turkey.

Grill turkey, covered, over indirect medium heat for 3 minutes on each side. Brush with remaining apricot sauce. Grill 7-10 minutes longer or until juices run clear and a meat thermometer reads 170°. Slice; serve with the reserved apricot sauce. **Yield:** 4 servings.

■ ■ ■

Turkey Lime Kabobs

(Pictured at right)

My husband loves to grill these deliciously different turkey kabobs, and everyone gets a kick out of the zingy taste from the limes and jalapenos. Its tongue-tingling combination of flavors makes this one company dish that always draws compliments.
—Shelly Johnston, Rochester, Minnesota

  3 **cans (6 ounces** *each***) orange juice concentrate, thawed**
1-1/4 **cups lime juice**
  1 **cup honey**
  4 **to 5 jalapeno peppers, seeded and chopped**
10 **garlic cloves, minced**
  3 **tablespoons ground cumin**
  2 **tablespoons grated lime peel**
  1 **teaspoon salt**
  2 **pounds boneless turkey, cut into 1-1/4-inch cubes**
  4 **medium sweet red** *or* **green peppers, cut into 1-inch pieces**
  1 **large red onion, cut into 1-inch pieces**
  3 **small zucchini, cut into 3/4-inch slices**
  8 **ounces fresh mushrooms**
  3 **medium limes, cut into wedges**

In a bowl, combine the first eight ingredients; mix well. Pour half of marinade into a large resealable plastic bag; add meat and turn to coat. Pour remaining marinade into another large resealable plastic bag. Add vegetables and turn to coat. Seal and refrigerate for 8 hours or overnight, turning occasionally.

Drain meat, discarding marinade. Drain vegetables, reserving marinade for basting. On metal or soaked wooden skewers, alternate meat, vegetables and lime wedges. Grill, uncovered, over medium heat for 4-5 minutes on each side. Baste with reserved marinade. Continue turning and basting for 10-12 minutes or until meat juices run clear and vegetables are tender. **Yield:** 8 servings.

Editor's Note: When cutting or seeding hot peppers, use rubber or plastic gloves to protect your hands. Avoid touching your face.

Brazilian-Style Turkey with Ham

(Pictured below)

Grilling is a different and fun way to prepare whole turkey. My mom has served this main dish for special occasions, "Christmas in July" and weddings at her home.
—*Carol Marriott, Centreville, Virginia*

    1 whole turkey (12 pounds)
4-1/2 teaspoons salt
    2 teaspoons pepper
    3 garlic cloves, minced
1-1/2 cups white vinegar
    1 cup olive oil
    4 medium tomatoes, seeded and
      chopped
    4 medium green peppers, seeded
      and chopped
  1/2 cup minced fresh parsley
    2 pounds smoked ham, thinly sliced

Remove giblets from turkey and discard. Place a turkey-size oven roasting bag inside a second roasting bag; add turkey. Place in a roasting pan. Combine the salt, pepper and garlic; rub over turkey.

In a bowl, combine the vinegar, oil, tomatoes, peppers and parsley. Pour over turkey and into cavity. Squeeze out as much air as possible from bag; seal and turn to coat. Refrigerate for 12-24 hours, turning several times. Drain and discard marinade. Skewer turkey openings; tie drumsticks together. Prepare grill for indirect heat, using a drip pan. Coat grill rack with nonstick cooking spray before starting the grill.

Grill turkey, covered, over indirect medium heat for 2 to 2-1/2 hours or until a meat thermometer reads 180°, tenting turkey with foil after about 1 hour. Let stand for 20 minutes before slicing. Meanwhile, warm the ham. Layer turkey and ham slices on a serving platter. **Yield:** 12 servings plus leftovers.

■ ■ ■

Cider Marinated Turkey

(Pictured above right)

Make Thanksgiving dinner memorable by serving this golden-brown turkey from our Test Kitchen staff. It's marinated in apple cider, kosher salt and spices.

    8 cups apple cider *or* unsweetened
      apple juice
  1/2 cup kosher salt
    2 bay leaves
    2 sprigs fresh thyme
    8 whole cloves
    5 garlic cloves
    1 teaspoon whole allspice, crushed
    2 medium navel oranges, quartered
    3 quarts cold water

1 turkey (12 pounds)
1 medium onion, quartered
2 medium carrots, halved and quartered
2 sprigs fresh sage *or* 1 tablespoon rubbed sage
1 tablespoon vegetable oil

In a large kettle, combine the first seven ingredients. Bring to a boil. Cook and stir until salt is dissolved. Stir in oranges. Remove from the heat. Add water; cool to room temperature.

Remove giblets from turkey; discard. Place a turkey-size oven roasting bag inside a second roasting bag; add turkey. Place in a roasting pan. Carefully pour cooled marinade into bag. Squeeze out as much air as possible; seal bag and turn to coat. Refrigerate for 12-24 hours; turn several times.

Drain and discard marinade. Rinse turkey under cold water; pat dry. Place onion, carrots and sage in cavity. Rub oil over skin. Skewer turkey openings; tie drumsticks together.

Coat grill rack with nonstick cooking spray before starting the grill. Prepare grill for indirect heat, using a drip pan. Place turkey over drip pan; grill, covered, over indirect medium heat for 2 to 2-1/2 hours or until a meat thermometer reads 180°, tenting turkey with foil after about 1 hour.

If desired, thicken pan juices for gravy. Remove and discard skin and vegetables in cavity before carving turkey. Serve with gravy. **Yield:** 12 servings plus leftovers.

Editor's Note: It is best not to use a prebasted turkey for this recipe. However, if you do, omit the salt in the recipe.

Fruity Turkey Breast

(Pictured above)

After marinating overnight, this turkey breast is grilled, then dressed up with a fast, fruity sauce. Our family loves it any time of year.
—*Ravonda Mormann, Raleigh, North Carolina*

- 2 boneless skinless turkey breast halves (about 2-1/2 pounds *each*)
- 1 cup cranberry juice
- 1/4 cup orange juice
- 1/4 cup olive oil
- 1 teaspoon salt
- 1 teaspoon pepper

SAUCE:
- 1 can (16 ounces) jellied cranberry sauce
- 1/4 cup lemon juice
- 3 tablespoons brown sugar
- 1 teaspoon cornstarch

Place turkey in a large resealable plastic bag. Combine the next five ingredients; pour over turkey. Seal and refrigerate for 8 hours or overnight, turning occasionally.

Drain and discard marinade. Grill turkey, covered, over indirect heat for 1-1/4 to 1-1/2 hours or until juices run clear and a meat thermometer reads 170°. Meanwhile, combine sauce ingredients in a saucepan; cook and stir over medium heat until thickened, about 5 minutes. Serve with the turkey. **Yield:** 10 servings.

Thawing a turkey in the refrigerator is the best and safest method. The turkey should be kept in its original wrapper during the thawing process. Allow up to 5 hours defrosting time per pound.

Teriyaki Turkey Tenderloins

(Pictured below)

These grilled tenderloins are fantastic because of the savory teriyaki and soy sauce mixture.
—Linda Gregg, Spartanburg, South Carolina

- 1/4 cup vegetable oil
- 1/4 cup soy sauce
- 1/4 cup teriyaki sauce
- 2 tablespoons red wine vinegar
- 1 tablespoon lime juice
- 1 tablespoon Dijon mustard
- 2 garlic cloves, minced
- 2 teaspoons coarsely ground pepper
- 1-1/2 teaspoons dried parsley flakes
- 1-1/2 teaspoons dried basil
- 1/2 teaspoon onion powder
- 2 pounds turkey tenderloins

In a 2-cup measuring cup, combine the first 11 ingredients. Pour 2/3 cup into a large resealable plastic bag; add turkey. Seal bag and turn to coat; refrigerate for 8 hours or overnight. Cover and refrigerate remaining marinade.

Before starting the grill, coat grill rack with nonstick cooking spray. Drain and discard marinade from turkey. Grill, covered, over medium heat for 7-9 minutes; baste with reserved marinade. Turn and grill 7-9 minutes longer or until juices run clear. **Yield:** 8 servings.

■ ■ ■

Apricot-Stuffed Turkey Breast

For a new take on turkey, give this recipe a try. It cooks on the grill, and it's stuffed with a sensational apricot mixture.
—Bonnie De Meyer, New Carlisle, Indiana

- 1 bone-in turkey breast half (2-1/2 pounds), skin removed
- 1-1/2 cups soft bread crumbs
- 1/2 cup diced dried apricots
- 1/4 cup chopped pecans, toasted
- 3 tablespoons water *or* unsweetened apple juice, *divided*
- 1 tablespoon vegetable oil
- 1/4 teaspoon dried rosemary, crushed
- 1/4 teaspoon garlic salt
- 1 tablespoon Dijon mustard

Remove bone from turkey. Cut a horizontal slit into thickest part of turkey to form a 5-in. x 4-in. pocket. In a bowl, combine the bread crumbs, apricots, pecans, 2 tablespoons water or juice, oil, rosemary and garlic salt; toss gently. Stuff into pocket of turkey. Secure opening with metal or soaked wooden skewers.

Grill, covered, over indirect heat for 30 minutes. Combine the mustard and remaining water; brush over the turkey. Grill 10 minutes longer or until golden brown and a meat thermometer inserted into the stuffing reads 165°. Let stand 10 minutes before slicing. **Yield:** 8 servings.

In a bowl, combine the chili sauce, lemon juice, sugar and bay leaves; mix well. Pour 1/4 cup marinade into a large resealable plastic bag; add the turkey. Seal bag and turn to coat; refrigerate for at least 2 hours or overnight. Cover and refrigerate remaining marinade.

Coat grill rack with nonstick cooking spray before starting the grill. Drain and discard marinade. Discard bay leaves from reserved marinade. On eight metal or soaked wooden skewers, alternately thread turkey and vegetables. Brush lightly with oil.

Grill, uncovered, over medium-hot heat for 3-4 minutes on each side or until juices run clear, basting frequently with reserved marinade and turning three times. **Yield:** 4 servings.

■ ■ ■

Grilled Turkey Kabobs

(Pictured above)

The turkey marinating overnight really gives the flavor a chance to soak in.
—*Marilyn Rodriguez, Fairbanks, Alaska*

- 1/3 cup chili sauce
- 2 tablespoons lemon juice
- 1 tablespoon sugar
- 2 bay leaves
- 1 pound turkey breast tenderloins, cut into 1-1/2 cubes
- 2 medium zucchini, cut into 1/2-inch slices
- 2 small green peppers, cut into 1-1/2 squares
- 2 small onions, quartered
- 8 medium fresh mushrooms
- 8 cherry tomatoes
- 1 tablespoon vegetable oil

Citrus Grilled Turkey Breast

(Pictured at right)

Instead of the usual outdoor barbecue, treat your guests to a sit-down dinner featuring this delicious grilled fare with a luscious herb and citrus gravy. It comes from our Test Kitchen staff.

- 1 bone-in turkey breast (4 to 5 pounds)
- 1/4 cup fresh parsley sprigs
- 1/4 cup fresh basil leaves
- 3 tablespoons butter
- 4 garlic cloves, halved
- 1/2 teaspoon salt
- 1 medium lemon, thinly sliced
- 1 medium orange, thinly sliced
- 1 tablespoon cornstarch
- 2 tablespoons water
- 1 cup orange juice
- 1 teaspoon grated orange peel
- 1 teaspoon grated lemon peel
- 1/4 teaspoon pepper

Using fingers, carefully loosen the skin from both sides of turkey breast. In a food processor or blender, combine the parsley, basil, butter, garlic and salt; cover and process until smooth. Spread under turkey skin; arrange lemon and orange slices over herb mixture. Secure skin to underside of breast with toothpicks.

Coat grill rack with nonstick cooking spray before starting the grill. Prepare grill for indirect heat, using a drip pan; place turkey over drip pan. Grill, covered, over indirect medium heat for 1-3/4 to 2-1/4 hours or until a meat thermometer reads 170° and juices run clear. Cover and let stand for 10 minutes.

Meanwhile, pour pan drippings into a measuring cup; skim fat. In a saucepan, combine the cornstarch and water until smooth.

Add the orange juice, orange peel, lemon peel, pepper and pan drippings. Bring to a boil; cook and stir for 2 minutes or until thickened. Discard the skin, lemon and orange slices from turkey breast. Remove herb mixture from turkey; stir into gravy. Slice turkey and serve with gravy. **Yield:** 8 servings with leftovers.

To collect drippings for making gravy when grilling a turkey, pour a little water into foil pan. Replenish water as needed to keep drippings from burning.

About 30 minutes before the bird should be done, remove the pan from under the turkey and make gravy while the turkey continues to cook.

Grilled Turkey Tenderloins

(Pictured above)

Turkey isn't just for Thanksgiving anymore. My family grills these tenderloins outside in summer and inside in winter. The friend who shared the recipe says the marinade is excellent with any poultry.
—Charlotte Casey, Barton, Vermont

1-1/2 **cups lemon-lime soda**
3/4 **cup vegetable oil**
3/4 **cup soy sauce**
1 **teaspoon prepared horseradish**
1/4 **teaspoon garlic powder**
1/4 to 1/2 **teaspoon Liquid Smoke, optional**
2-1/2 **pounds boneless skinless turkey breast tenderloins**

In a large resealable plastic bag, combine the first six ingredients. Add turkey; seal bag and turn to coat. Refrigerate for 8 hours or overnight, turning once.

Drain and discard marinade. Grill turkey, covered, over medium heat for 5-6 minutes on each side or until juices run clear. **Yield:** 10 servings.

Tarragon Mustard Turkey

(Pictured below right)

I adapted a chicken recipe for turkey breasts instead. It quickly became one of my husband's favorites for the grill.
—Ann Greene, Dowagiac, Michigan

　2　tablespoons lemon juice
　2　tablespoons vegetable oil
1/4　teaspoon pepper
　1　turkey breast tenderloin (1/2 pound)
4-1/2　teaspoons tarragon vinegar *or* cider vinegar
　2　tablespoons dry white wine *or* chicken broth
　1　teaspoon dried tarragon
1/4　cup butter, cubed
　2　tablespoons Dijon mustard

In a resealable plastic bag, combine the lemon juice, oil and pepper; add turkey. Seal bag and turn to coat; refrigerate for up to 2 hours.

In a small saucepan, combine the vinegar, wine or broth and tarragon. Bring to a boil; cook until reduced by half. Reduce heat; add butter and mustard. Stir until butter is melted; set aside and keep warm.

Drain and discard marinade. Grill turkey, uncovered, over medium heat for 5 minutes; turn and baste with mustard sauce. Cook 10-15 minutes more or until juices run clear, basting frequently. **Yield:** 2 servings.

■ ■ ■

Sausage Squash Kabobs

Expect a crowd to gather around the grill when these kabobs are cooking! The zesty honey-mustard glaze gives a lovely sheen to the sausage and veggies.
—Lisa Malynn Kent
North Richland Hills, Texas

　1　pound small red potatoes
　1　tablespoon water
1/2　cup honey
1/4　cup Dijon mustard
1/2　teaspoon grated orange peel
　1　pound turkey kielbasa, sliced 1/2 inch thick
　2　small yellow summer squash, sliced 1/2 inch thick
　2　small zucchini, sliced 1/2 inch thick

In a large microwave-safe bowl, combine potatoes and water. Cover and microwave on high for 6-8 minutes or until tender; drain and set aside. For glaze, combine the honey, mustard and orange peel in a small bowl.

Coat the grill rack with nonstick cooking spray before starting the grill. On eight metal or soaked wooden skewers, alternately thread the sausage, potatoes, yellow squash and zucchini; brush with half of the glaze. Grill kabobs, uncovered, over medium heat for 5-8 minutes on each side or until vegetables are tender and sausage is heated through, basting frequently with glaze and turning once. **Yield:** 4 servings.

·Pork·

From tenderloins and ribs to ham and sausage, there's a pork cut to cover all of your cooking needs! Tangy Ham Steak and Campfire Bundles liven up weekday dinners. For a casual get-together with friends, Apricot Sausage Kabobs and Orange-Ginger Pork Chops are simple yet special. Looking for a more elegant entree? Herb-Stuffed Pork Loin and Grilled Rosemary Pork Roast are sure to impress.

Grilled Pork with Pear Salsa

(Pictured at left)

My husband, Dave, and I have been in a dinner group with three other couples for a few years now. We often share our recipes. The pork was served by one of the couples, and I decided to "pear" it with this fabulous salsa. It's a winning combination.
—Suzan Ward, Coeur d'Alene, Idaho

1/4 cup lime juice
2 tablespoons olive oil
2 garlic cloves, minced
1-1/2 teaspoons ground cumin
1-1/2 teaspoons dried oregano
1/2 teaspoon pepper
2 pork tenderloins (about 1 pound *each*), cut into 3/4-inch slices

PEAR SALSA:
4 cups chopped peeled pears (about 4 medium)
1/3 cup chopped red onion
2 tablespoons chopped fresh mint *or* 2 teaspoons dried mint
2 tablespoons lime juice
1 tablespoon grated lime peel
1 jalapeno pepper, seeded and chopped
1 teaspoon sugar
1/2 teaspoon pepper

In a large resealable plastic bag, combine the lime juice, oil, garlic, cumin, oregano and pepper; add pork. Seal bag and turn to coat; refrigerate overnight.

Drain and discard marinade. Grill pork, uncovered, over indirect medium heat for 6-7 minutes on each side or until meat juices run clear. In a bowl, combine salsa ingredients. Serve with the pork. **Yield:** 6-8 servings.

Editor's Note: When cutting or seeding hot peppers, use rubber or plastic gloves to protect your hands. Avoid touching your face.

Zesty Grilled Pork Medallions

(Pictured above)

Some of our friends made up this marinade but weren't able to give me exact measurements. I experimented until I came up with this recipe, which tastes as good as theirs.
—Patty Collins, Morgantown, Indiana

    2 **cups salsa**
  1/4 **cup sugar**
4-1/2 **teaspoons sweet-and-sour sauce**
    1 **tablespoon vegetable oil**
    1 **tablespoon green taco sauce**
    2 **teaspoons balsamic vinegar**
Dash hot pepper sauce
    2 **pork tenderloins (about 1 pound *each*)**

In a bowl, combine the first seven ingredients; mix well. Set aside 1 cup for dipping; cover and refrigerate. Pour remaining marinade into a large resealable plastic bag; add the pork. Seal the bag and turn to coat; refrigerate overnight.

Drain and discard marinade. Grill pork, covered, over indirect medium heat for 30-40 minutes or until a meat thermometer reads 160°. Warm the dipping sauce; serve with sliced pork. **Yield:** 6-8 servings.

■ ■ ■

Sweet Pork Kabobs

The original version of this recipe called for beef. But I use pork for a change of pace. A delightful honey-sweetened marinade brings out the best in a healthy selection of vegetables and lean tenderloin cubes.
—Karen Salyer, Campobello, South Carolina

3/4 **cup apricot nectar**
  6 **tablespoons dry white wine**
    or lemon juice
  3 **tablespoons honey**

3 tablespoons lime juice
2 garlic cloves, minced
1-1/2 teaspoons dried thyme
1 pork tenderloin (1 pound), cut into 1-inch cubes
2 medium sweet potatoes (about 1 pound), peeled and cubed
2 medium zucchini, cut into 1/2-inch slices
16 dried apricots, halved

In a bowl, combine the first six ingredients; mix well. Pour 1/2 cup marinade into a large resealable plastic bag; add the pork. Seal bag and turn to coat; refrigerate for at least 8 hours or overnight.

Meanwhile, place sweet potatoes in a saucepan; cover with water. Cover and bring to a boil. Cook until tender, about 8-10 minutes; drain well. Pour remaining marinade into another resealable plastic bag. Add potatoes and zucchini. Seal bag and turn to coat; refrigerate for at least 8 hours or overnight.

Coat grill rack with nonstick cooking spray before starting the grill. Drain pork and discard marinade. Drain vegetables, reserving marinade for basting. On eight metal or soaked wood skewers, alternately thread pork, potatoes, zucchini and apricots.

Grill, uncovered, over medium heat for 3 minutes on each side. Baste with reserved marinade. Grill 4-5 minutes longer or until meat juices run clear, turning and basting frequently with reserved marinade. **Yield:** 4 servings.

Pork Grilling Chart

Pork, fresh pork sausages and ground pork are done at 160°. Cooked sausages are done when heated through. For direct grilling, turn meat halfway through grilling time. The cooking times given are a guideline. Check for doneness with a meat thermometer or other appropriate doneness test.

Cut	Weight or Thickness	Heat	Approximate Cooking Time
Loin or Rib Chop, bone-in	3/4 to 1 in.	medium/direct	8 to 10 minutes
	1-1/4 to 1-1/2 in.	medium/direct	12 to 18 minutes
Loin Chop, boneless	3/4 to 1 in.	medium/direct	8 to 10 minutes
	1-1/4 to 1-1/2 in.	medium/direct	12 to 18 minutes
Back Ribs or Spareribs	3 to 4 lbs.	medium/indirect	1-1/2 to 2 hours
Tenderloin	3/4 to 1 lb.	medium-hot/indirect	25 to 40 minutes
Loin Roast, bone-in or boneless	3 to 5 lbs.	medium/indirect	1-1/4 to 1-3/4 hours
Kabobs	1-in. cubes	medium/direct	10 to 15 minutes
Sausage, cooked	—	medium/direct	3 to 7 minutes or until heated through
Sausage, fresh	4 oz.	medium/indirect	20 to 30 minutes
Pork Patties	4 oz. and 1/2 in.	medium/direct	8 to 10 minutes

Pork with Tangy Mustard Sauce

(Pictured below)

About any side dish would accompany this entree well. Leftovers would be good in an omelet.
—Ginger Johnson, Farmington, Illinois

- 1 boneless pork loin roast (2-1/2 to 3 pounds)
- 2 teaspoons olive oil
- 1-1/4 teaspoons ground mustard
- 3/4 teaspoon garlic powder
- 1/4 teaspoon ground ginger
- 1/2 cup horseradish mustard
- 1/2 cup apricot *or* pineapple preserves

Rub roast with oil. Combine mustard, garlic powder and ginger; rub over roast. Place in a large resealable plastic bag; seal bag. Refrigerate overnight.

Grill roast, covered, over indirect medium heat for 60 minutes. Combine the horseradish mustard and preserves. Continue grilling for 15-30 minutes, basting twice with sauce, or until a meat thermometer reads 160°-170°. Let stand for 10 minutes before slicing. Heat remaining sauce to serve with roast. **Yield:** 10-12 servings.

Editor's Note: As a substitute for horseradish mustard, combine 1/4 cup spicy brown mustard and 1/4 cup prepared horseradish.

■ ■ ■

Oriental Pork Chops

The nicely seasoned marinade for these chops started as a marinade for poultry. This is now my favorite way to make pork.
—Annie Arnold, Plymouth, Minnesota

- 3 tablespoons soy sauce
- 3 tablespoons honey
- 1 tablespoon lemon juice
- 1 tablespoon olive oil
- 3 garlic cloves, minced
- 1/2 teaspoon ground ginger
- 4 boneless pork chops (1/2 to 3/4 inch thick)

In a large resealable plastic bag, combine the first six ingredients. Add pork and turn to coat. Seal bag and refrigerate for 4-8 hours. Grill, uncovered, over medium heat for 10-12 minutes or until juices run clear, turning once. **Yield:** 4 servings.

Dijon Grilled Pork Chops

(Pictured above)

My mom gave me the recipe for these savory chops with a sweet and tangy marinade. The apple juice and Dijon mustard complement the pork nicely. With a vegetable and some rice or pasta, you have a meal.
—*Babette Watterson, Atglen, Pennsylvania*

- 6 tablespoons Dijon mustard
- 6 tablespoons brown sugar
- 3 tablespoons unsweetened apple juice
- 3 tablespoons Worcestershire sauce
- 4 bone-in pork loin chops (8 ounces *each*)

In a bowl, combine the first four ingredients; mix well. Pour 2/3 cup marinade into a large resealable plastic bag; add the pork chops. Seal bag and turn to coat. Refrigerate for 8 hours or overnight. Cover and refrigerate remaining marinade for basting.

Coat grill rack with nonstick cooking spray before starting the grill. Drain marinade from pork. Grill, covered, over medium heat for 6-10 minutes on each side or until a meat thermometer reads 160°, basting occasionally with reserved marinade. **Yield:** 4 servings.

When buying pork, look for

meat that's pale pink with a small amount of marbling and white fat. The darker pink the flesh, the older the animal.

Contrary to popular belief, it is just fine for cooked pork to be slightly pink in the center. The best way to test pork's doneness is with a meat thermometer. The internal temperature should read 160°.

Honey Barbecued Ribs

(Pictured at right)

My family celebrates four birthdays in July, and these tender ribs are a must at our joint get-together. Honey adds wonderful flavor to the homemade sauce.
—Joyce Duff, Mansfield, Ohio

  3 pounds country-style pork ribs
1/2 teaspoon garlic salt
1/2 teaspoon pepper
  1 cup ketchup
1/2 cup packed brown sugar
1/2 cup honey
1/4 cup spicy brown mustard
  2 tablespoons Worcestershire sauce
1-1/2 teaspoons Liquid Smoke, optional

Place ribs in a large kettle or Dutch oven; sprinkle with garlic salt and pepper. Add enough water to cover; bring to a boil. Reduce heat; cover and simmer for 1 hour or until juices run clear and ribs are tender; drain.

Meanwhile, combine the remaining ingredients. Grill ribs, uncovered, over medium heat for 10-12 minutes, basting with sauce and turning occasionally. **Yield:** 4 servings.

Tenderizing Ribs

Before the Honey Barbecued Ribs (recipe below) are grilled, they're tenderized in boiling water. Another way to tenderize ribs so they're fall-off-the-bone tender is to place them on a rack in a shallow baking pan. Cover tightly with foil; bake at 350° for 1-1/2 hours.

Mango-Glazed Ham

I'm always looking for new ways to prepare ham... but many of my cookbooks have the same old tried-and-true glazes. When I tried this one, I knew I had hit the jackpot!
—Sandy Lewis, Appleton, Wisconsin

1-1/2 cups red wine vinegar
1/2 cup sugar
  1 teaspoon finely chopped jalapeno pepper
1/4 teaspoon ground ginger *or* 1 teaspoon grated fresh gingerroot
  1 medium ripe mango *or* 2 medium ripe peaches, peeled and cut into wedges

1 **bone-in fully cooked lean ham steak (about 2 pounds)**
1/8 **teaspoon pepper**

In a saucepan, combine the vinegar, sugar, jalapeno and ginger. Bring to a boil. Reduce heat; simmer, uncovered, for 25-30 minutes or until glaze is thick and caramelized. Strain and cool. Place mango in a food processor or blender; cover and process until smooth. Stir into glaze; set aside.

Coat grill with nonstick cooking spray before starting the grill. Sprinkle both sides of ham steak with pepper. Grill, covered, over medium heat for 10 minutes on each side or until heated through. Brush both sides of ham with mango glaze; grill 5 minutes longer. Serve ham with remaining glaze. **Yield:** 8 servings.

Editor's Note: When cutting or seeding hot peppers, use rubber or plastic gloves to protect your hands. Avoid touching your face.

Tangy Ham Steak

(Pictured below)

This glazed ham steak is a yummy, quick-and-easy main dish. On summer weekends back home, Dad does the grilling while Mom prepares the rest of the meal.
—Sue Gronholz, Columbus, Wisconsin

1/3 **cup spicy brown mustard**
1/4 **cup honey**
1/2 **teaspoon grated orange peel**
1 **fully cooked ham steak (about 2 pounds)**

In a small bowl, combine mustard, honey and orange peel. Brush over one side of ham. Grill, uncovered, over medium-hot heat for 7 minutes. Turn; brush with mustard mixture. Cook until well glazed and heated through, about 7 minutes. **Yield:** 6-8 servings.

Grilled Veggie Sausage Pizza

(Pictured below)

Last summer, I experimented with this crispy, thin-crust pizza. It met with such approval, guests were eager to try it in their own backyards.
—Faith Sommers, Bangor, California

     1 tablespoon active dry yeast
 1-1/3 cups warm water (110° to 115°)
     5 teaspoons sugar
     4 teaspoons vegetable oil
   1/4 teaspoon salt
   1/4 teaspoon garlic salt
   1/4 teaspoon dried oregano
 3-1/4 to 3-1/2 cups all-purpose flour
TOPPINGS:
   1/2 pound bulk Italian sausage
 1-1/2 cups pizza sauce
     2 cups (8 ounces) shredded part-skim
       mozzarella cheese
     1 cup sliced fresh mushrooms
   1/4 cup chopped sweet red pepper
   1/4 cup chopped green pepper

In a large mixing bowl, dissolve yeast in water. Add the sugar, oil, salt, garlic salt, oregano

and 1-1/2 cups flour. Stir in enough of the remaining flour to form a soft dough.

Turn onto a floured surface; knead until smooth and elastic, about 6-8 minutes. Place in a greased bowl, turning once to grease top. Cover and let rise in a warm place for 30 minutes.

Wrap foil over the outside bottom of two 12-in. pizza pans; grease pans and set aside. In a skillet, cook sausage over medium heat until no longer pink; drain and set aside. Divide dough in half. On a floured surface, roll each portion into a 13-in. circle. Transfer to prepared pans; build up edges slightly.

Spread pizza sauce over crusts; sprinkle with sausage, cheese, mushrooms and peppers. Grill, covered, over medium heat for 15-20 minutes or until bottom of crust is browned and cheese is melted. **Yield:** 2 pizzas (8 slices each).

■ ■ ■

Tropical Sausage Kabobs

I've prepared these yummy kabobs for family and friends for years. They're a favorite.
—Joan Hallford, North Richland Hills, Texas

     1 tablespoon cornstarch
     3 tablespoons Dijon mustard
   3/4 cup ginger ale
   1/3 cup honey
     1 pound fully cooked kielbasa *or*
       Polish sausage, cut into 1-inch
       chunks
     4 medium firm bananas, cut into
       1-inch slices
     2 fresh pineapples, peeled and cut
       into 1-inch chunks *or* 2 cans
       (20 ounces *each*) pineapple chunks,
       drained

In a small saucepan, combine the cornstarch and mustard until smooth. Gradually stir in gin-

ger ale and honey until well blended. Bring to a boil; cook and stir for 2 minutes or until thickened and bubbly.

Alternately thread sausage and fruit onto metal or soaked wooden skewers. Brush with mustard sauce. Grill, uncovered, over medium-hot heat for 4 minutes or until evenly browned, basting and turning several times. **Yield:** 4-6 servings.

■ ■ ■

Pork and Apple Skewers

(Pictured above)

Necessity was the "mother" of this recipe! I'd already marinated the pork before realizing we were short on kabob vegetables. In place of them, I used apples I had on hand. This has since become one of my most-requested dishes.
—Cheryl Plainte, Minot, North Dakota

3/4 cup barbecue sauce
1/2 cup pineapple juice
1/4 cup honey mustard
1/4 cup packed brown sugar
  2 tablespoons soy sauce
  2 tablespoons olive oil
1-1/2 pounds pork tenderloin, cut into 3/4-inch cubes
  5 medium unpeeled tart apples

In a large resealable plastic bag, combine the first six ingredients; mix well. Reserve 1/2 cup for basting and refrigerate. Add pork to remaining marinade and turn to coat. Seal bag; refrigerate for at least 1 hour.

Drain and discard marinade. Cut the apples into 1-1/2-in. cubes. Alternate pork and apples on metal or soaked wooden skewers. Grill, uncovered, over medium heat for 3 minutes on each side. Baste with the reserved marinade. Continue turning and basting for 8-10 minutes or until meat juices run clear and apples are tender. **Yield:** 6 servings.

Editor's Note: As a substitute for honey mustard, combine 2 tablespoons Dijon mustard and 2 tablespoons honey.

Herb-Stuffed Pork Loin

(Pictured above)

I serve this pork roast often when I'm entertaining company. It's especially good with garden-fresh herbs, but dried ones work nicely as well. It makes a stunning presentation.
—Michele Montgomery, Lethbridge, Alberta

- 1 **boneless pork loin roast (3 pounds)**
- 1/4 **cup Dijon mustard**
- 4 **garlic cloves, minced**
- 1/3 **cup minced chives**
- 1/4 **cup minced fresh sage** *or* 4 **teaspoons rubbed sage**
- 2 **tablespoons minced fresh thyme** *or* 2 **teaspoons dried thyme**
- 1 **tablespoon minced fresh rosemary** *or* 1 **teaspoon dried rosemary, crushed**
- 2-3/4 **teaspoons pepper,** *divided*
- 1 **teaspoon salt,** *divided*
- 1 **tablespoon olive oil**

Starting about a third in from one side, make a lengthwise slit down the roast to within 1/2 in. of the bottom. Turn roast over and make another lengthwise slit starting about a third in from the opposite side. Open roast so it lies flat; cover with plastic wrap. Flatten to 3/4-in. thickness; remove plastic wrap.

Combine the mustard and garlic; rub two-thirds of the mustard mixture over the roast. Combine the chives, sage, thyme, rosemary, 3/4 teaspoon pepper and 1/2 teaspoon salt. Sprinkle two-thirds of the herb mixture over the roast. Roll up jelly-roll style, starting with a long side; tie several times with kitchen string. Rub oil over the roast; sprinkle with the remaining salt and pepper.

Coat the grill rack with nonstick cooking spray before starting the grill. Grill, covered, over indirect medium heat for 1 hour. Brush the roast with the remaining mustard mixture and sprinkle with the remaining herbs. Grill 20-25 minutes longer or until a meat thermometer reads 160°. Let stand for 10 minutes before slicing. **Yield:** 12 servings.

■ ■ ■

Sweet 'n' Spicy Grilled Pork Chops

This started out as a mild sauce that I decided to spice up. You'll find it's easy to adjust the seasonings to suit your family's taste. I also like to use the sauce on boneless skinless chicken breasts.
—Gladys Peterson, Beaumont, Texas

- 1 **can (14-1/2 ounces) diced tomatoes, drained**
- 1 **can (10 ounces) diced tomatoes with chilies, undrained**
- 1/2 **cup raisins**

1/4 cup currant jelly
4-1/2 teaspoons cider vinegar
1/4 teaspoon *each* garlic powder, salt
and crushed red pepper flakes
12 boneless pork chops
(3/4 inch thick)

In a blender, combine the tomatoes, raisins, jelly, vinegar and seasonings; cover and process until smooth. Pour into a 1-qt. saucepan; bring to a boil. Reduce heat; simmer, uncovered, for 20 minutes or until thickened. Set aside 3/4 cup for serving.

Coat grill rack with nonstick cooking spray before starting grill. Grill pork chops, uncovered, over medium heat for 4 minutes. Turn; brush with sauce. Grill 4-6 minutes longer or until meat juices run clear. Serve with reserved sauce. **Yield:** 12 servings.

■ ■ ■

Molasses-Glazed Baby Back Ribs

(Pictured at right)

My husband sizzles up his luscious ribs recipe for our family of five at least once a month in summer. The sweet-and-sour barbecue sauce is the perfect condiment for the moist, tender meat. We enjoy these ribs with corn on the cob.
—Kim Braley, Dunedin, Florida

4-1/2 pounds pork baby back ribs
2 liters cola
1/2 teaspoon salt
1/2 teaspoon pepper
1/4 teaspoon garlic salt
1/4 teaspoon onion powder
1/4 teaspoon dried oregano
1/8 teaspoon cayenne pepper
BARBECUE SAUCE:
1/4 cup ketchup

1/4 cup honey
1/4 cup molasses
1 tablespoon prepared mustard
1/2 teaspoon salt
1/2 teaspoon cayenne pepper

Place the ribs in large resealable plastic bags; add cola. Seal bags and turn to coat; refrigerate for 8 hours or overnight, turning occasionally.

Drain and discard cola. Pat ribs dry with paper towels. Combine the salt, pepper, garlic salt, onion powder, oregano and cayenne; rub over ribs.

Prepare grill for indirect heat, using a drip pan. Place ribs over pan; grill, covered, over indirect medium heat for 1 hour, turning occasionally. In a small bowl, combine the barbecue sauce ingredients. Brush over ribs; grill 10-20 minutes longer or until meat is tender. **Yield:** 4 servings.

Peanutty Pork Kabobs

(Pictured above)

Cubes of pork tenderloin and green pepper chunks get a spicy treatment from a combination of peanut butter, brown sugar, ginger and red pepper flakes. Reserving half of this mixture to use as a basting sauce adds an extra boost of flavor.
—Ellen Koch, St. Martinville, Louisiana

1/2 **cup soy sauce**
1/4 **cup lime *or* lemon juice**
1/4 **cup peanut butter**
  2 **tablespoons brown sugar**
  2 **garlic cloves, minced**
  1 **teaspoon crushed red pepper flakes**
1/4 **teaspoon ground ginger**
  1 **pork tenderloin (about 1 pound), cut into 1-inch cubes**
  2 **medium green peppers, cut into 1-inch pieces**

In a large bowl, combine the first seven ingredients; mix well. Set aside 1/2 cup for basting; cover and refrigerate. Pour remaining marinade into a large resealable plastic bag; add pork and turn to coat. Seal bag and refrigerate for 2-3 hours, turning occasionally.

Drain and discard the marinade. On metal or soaked wooden skewers, alternate the pork and green peppers. Grill, uncovered, over medium heat for 6 minutes, turning once. Baste with the reserved marinade. Grill 8-10 minutes longer or until meat juices run clear, turning and basting frequently. **Yield:** 4 servings.

When grilling pork

tenderloin, you may want to tie it before grilling so that the more slender end can be tucked under, resulting in more even cooking.

Fold the last 4 to 5 inches of the slender end of the tenderloin under so that the tenderloin will be approximately the same thickness throughout. Cut strings approximately 12 inches in length and tie around tenderloin at 1 to 1-1/2 inch intervals.

Mandarin Pork

(Pictured below right)

I often serve this pork with fried rice and Chinese-style vegetables. It also makes a great appetizer by itself. Folks have fun dipping the nuggets into the two homemade sauces.
—*Flo Weiss, Seaside, Oregon*

  1 cup soy sauce
1/2 cup vegetable oil
  3 tablespoons honey
  1 tablespoon ground ginger
  1 tablespoon ground mustard
  1 garlic clove, minced
  2 pork tenderloins (3/4 to 1 pound *each*)
SWEET-AND-SOUR SAUCE:
1/2 cup orange marmalade
  2 tablespoons white vinegar
  1 tablespoon diced pimientos
1/8 teaspoon paprika
Dash salt
FIRE-HOT MUSTARD:
1/4 cup boiling water
1/4 cup ground mustard
1/2 teaspoon salt

Combine the first six ingredients in a large resealable plastic bag; add pork and turn to coat. Seal bag; refrigerate overnight, turning meat several times.

Meanwhile, combine sauce ingredients in a bowl; cover and chill. In another bowl, stir boiling water into mustard; add salt and stir until smooth. Cover and let stand at room temperature for 1 hour; chill.

Drain meat and discard marinade. Grill, covered, over medium heat, turning occasionally, for 18-20 minutes or until a meat thermometer reads 160°. Let stand for 5 minutes before slicing. Serve with sauce and mustard for dipping. **Yield:** 6-8 servings.

Apricot Sausage Kabobs

Basted with a simple sweet-sour sauce, these tasty kabobs make a quick meal that's elegant enough for company.
—*Susie Lindquist, Ellijay, Georgia*

3/4 cup apricot preserves
3/4 cup Dijon mustard
  1 pound fully cooked kielbasa or Polish sausage, cut into 12 pieces
12 dried apricots
12 medium fresh mushrooms
Hot cooked rice

In a small bowl, combine preserves and mustard; mix well. Remove 1/2 cup for serving; set aside. Alternate sausage, apricots and mushrooms on four metal or soaked wooden skewers. Grill, covered, over indirect medium heat for 15-20 minutes or until meat juices run clear. Turn frequently and baste with remaining apricot sauce. Warm the reserved sauce; serve with kabobs and rice. **Yield:** 4 servings.

Cut a pocket in each pork chop; sprinkle 1/4 teaspoon salt and 1/8 teaspoon pepper in pockets. Set aside. In a nonstick skillet, saute green pepper and onion in butter until tender. Transfer to a bowl. Add the bread cubes, corn, egg substitute, pimientos, cumin and remaining salt and pepper; mix well. Stuff into pork chops; secure with wooden toothpicks.

Before starting the grill, coat grill rack with nonstick cooking spray. Grill chops, covered, over medium indirect heat for 15-18 minutes on each side or until a meat thermometer inserted in stuffing reads 160°. **Yield:** 6 servings.

■ ■ ■

Corn-Stuffed Pork Chops

(Pictured above)

For an eye-catching entree, I grill pork chops filled with a colorful corn, pimiento and green pepper stuffing.
—Elizabeth Jussaume, Lowell, Massachusetts

  6 **bone-in center loin pork chops (1 inch thick, about 10 ounces *each*)**
3/4 **teaspoon salt, *divided***
1/4 **teaspoon pepper, *divided***
1/4 **cup chopped green pepper**
1/4 **cup chopped onion**
  1 **tablespoon butter**
1-1/2 **cups bread cubes, toasted**
1/2 **cup frozen corn, thawed**
1/4 **cup egg substitute**
  2 **tablespoons chopped pimientos**
1/4 **teaspoon ground cumin**

Grilled Rosemary Pork Roast

(Pictured below right)

When the family's coming or we're expecting guests for dinner, I often serve this delicious grilled pork roast—and it's always a winner! Chopped apple and sweet honey complement the rosemary and garlic.
—Christine Wilson, Sellersville, Pennsylvania

  3 **medium tart apples, peeled and chopped**
  1 **cup unsweetened apple cider *or* juice**
  3 **green onions, chopped**
  3 **tablespoons honey**
  1 **to 2 tablespoons minced fresh rosemary *or* 1 to 2 teaspoons dried rosemary, crushed**
  2 **garlic cloves, minced**
  1 **boneless pork loin roast (3 pounds)**

In a saucepan, combine the first six ingredients; bring to a boil. Reduce heat; simmer, uncovered, for 5 minutes. Cool slightly. Place pork roast in a large resealable plastic bag; add half of the marinade. Seal bag and refrigerate overnight, turning occasionally. Transfer the remaining marinade to a bowl; cover and refrigerate.

Drain and discard marinade. Grill roast, covered, over indirect medium-low heat for 1-1/2 to 2 hours or until a meat thermometer reads 160°, turning occasionally. Let stand for 10 minutes before slicing. Heat reserved marinade; serve with pork. **Yield:** 8 servings.

■ ■ ■

Glazed Country Ribs

(Pictured at right)

I like these ribs basted only with the mildly sweet glaze, but you can serve your favorite barbecue sauce on the side, too. They taste as good reheated as they do right off the grill.
—Tamrah Bird, Gaines, Michigan

3 pounds boneless country-style ribs
3/4 cup pineapple juice
1/2 cup vegetable oil
1/2 cup white wine *or* chicken broth
1/4 cup packed brown sugar
1 tablespoon Worcestershire sauce
6 garlic cloves, minced
1 teaspoon salt
1 teaspoon pepper
1 teaspoon dried rosemary, crushed

Pierce ribs several times with a fork; place in a large resealable plastic bag. In a bowl, combine all of the remaining ingredients; set aside 1/2 cup for basting. Pour the remaining marinade over the ribs. Seal bag and refrigerate for 8 hours or overnight, turning once.

Drain and discard marinade. Grill ribs, covered, over indirect medium heat for 10 minutes on each side. Baste with some of the reserved marinade. Grill 20-25 minutes longer or until meat juices run clear and meat is tender, turning and basting occasionally. **Yield:** 6 servings.

Kielbasa Apple Kabobs

(Pictured below)

Sausage makes these colorful kabobs deliciously different from most. The meaty chunks are skewered with tart apples and colorful peppers, then basted with a mild, sweet glaze.
—Edna Hoffman, Hebron, Indiana

1/4 cup sugar
1 tablespoon cornstarch
3/4 cup cranberry juice
2 tablespoons cider vinegar
2 teaspoons soy sauce
1 pound fully cooked kielbasa or
   Polish sausage, cut into
   1-1/2-inch pieces
2 medium tart apples, cut into
   wedges
1 medium sweet red pepper, cut into
   1-inch pieces
1 medium green pepper, cut into
   1-inch pieces

In a saucepan, combine sugar and cornstarch. Stir in cranberry juice, vinegar and soy sauce. Bring to a boil; cook and stir for 1-2 minutes or until thickened. On metal or soaked wooden skewers, alternately thread sausage, apples and peppers. Grill, uncovered, over indirect heat for 8 minutes or until heated through, turning and brushing with glaze occasionally. **Yield:** 8 servings.

■ ■ ■

Grilled Pork and Poblano Peppers

My husband and I entertain a lot in summer, and this has quickly become the most-requested dish. I usually serve it with Mexican rice and a tossed salad.
—Donna Gay Harris, Springdale, Arkansas

4 large poblano peppers
2 cups (8 ounces) shredded
   Monterey Jack cheese

4-1/2 teaspoons chili powder
1-1/2 teaspoons onion powder
1-1/2 teaspoons ground cumin
  1/2 teaspoon garlic powder
  1/4 teaspoon salt
  1/8 teaspoon aniseed, ground
  1/8 teaspoon cayenne pepper
   2 pork tenderloins (about 1
     pound *each*)

Cut the top off each pepper and set the tops aside. Remove the seeds. Stuff the peppers with cheese. Replace the tops and secure with toothpicks; set aside.

    Combine the seasonings; rub over the pork. Grill, covered, over medium-hot heat for 18 minutes or until a meat thermometer reads 160° and juices run clear. Place the peppers on the sides of the grill (not directly over coals); heat for 10 minutes or until browned. **Yield:** 6-8 servings.

■ ■ ■

Orange-Ginger Pork Chops

(Pictured above right)

Basting chops with this tangy sauce makes them extremely tender and savory. My family requests this dish for the terrific taste. I make it for them often because it's on the lighter side.
—Lynette Randleman, Cheyenne, Wyoming

  1 teaspoon ground ginger *or* 4
    teaspoons minced fresh gingerroot
  1 garlic clove, minced
  1 tablespoon vegetable oil
1/2 cup sherry *or* chicken broth
1/4 cup honey
1/4 cup soy sauce
  1 tablespoon sesame seeds
  1 tablespoon grated orange peel
3/4 teaspoon hot pepper sauce

  4 bone-in pork loin chops
    (6 ounces *each*)
  1 teaspoon cornstarch
  2 tablespoons water

In a saucepan, cook the ginger and garlic in oil for 1 minute; remove from the heat. Stir in the sherry or broth, honey, soy sauce, sesame seeds, orange peel and hot pepper sauce; mix well. Pour 1/2 cup into a small bowl and set aside. Pour the remaining marinade into a large resealable plastic bag; add the pork chops. Seal bag and turn to coat; refrigerate for at least 1 hour.

    Meanwhile, in a saucepan, combine the cornstarch and water until smooth; add the reserved marinade. Bring to a boil; cook and stir for 1 minute or until thickened.

    Drain and discard marinade from the pork. Coat grill rack with nonstick cooking spray before starting the grill. Grill chops, covered, over medium heat for 4 minutes. Turn; baste with sauce. Grill 15-20 minutes longer or until juices run clear, basting occasionally. Serve with any remaining sauce. **Yield:** 4 servings.

Pork Chops with Mango Relish

(Pictured below)

A delicate marinade flavors these pork chops with the fragrant seasonings of India and tenderizes the meat at the same time. The colorful relish would be delicious alongside any grilled entree.
—Linda Lacek, Winter Park, Florida

- 2 tablespoons plain yogurt
- 2 teaspoons honey
- 2 garlic cloves, minced
- 1 teaspoon white wine vinegar
- 1/2 teaspoon ground cumin
- 1/4 teaspoon salt
- 1/4 teaspoon ground turmeric
- 1/8 teaspoon ground cloves
- 1/8 teaspoon ground cinnamon
- 1/8 teaspoon cayenne pepper
- Dash ground ginger *or* 1/2 teaspoon minced fresh gingerroot
- 4 boneless pork loin chops (4 ounces *each*)

MANGO RELISH:
- 1 large mango *or* 2 small peaches, peeled and diced
- 3/4 cup chopped red onion
- 3/4 cup chopped seeded tomatoes
- 4 teaspoons chopped seeded jalapeno pepper
- 2 teaspoons lime juice
- 1/4 teaspoon salt

In a large resealable plastic bag, combine the first 11 ingredients. Add pork. Seal bag and turn to coat; refrigerate for at least 2 hours. Meanwhile, combine the relish ingredients in a bowl. Let stand at room temperature for 1 hour; refrigerate until serving.

Drain and discard marinade. Coat grill rack with nonstick cooking spray before starting the grill. Grill pork chops, covered, over medium heat for 6-10 minutes on each side or until a meat thermometer reads 160°. Serve with mango relish. **Yield:** 4 servings.

Editor's Note: When cutting or seeding hot peppers, use rubber or plastic gloves to protect your hands. Avoid touching your face.

■ ■ ■

Bratwurst Supper

This meal-in-one grills to perfection in a heavy-duty foil bag. Loaded with chunks of bratwurst, red potatoes, mushrooms and carrots, it's easy to season with onion soup mix, a little soy sauce and pepper.
—Janice Meyer, Medford, Wisconsin

- 3 pounds uncooked bratwurst links
- 3 pounds small red potatoes, cut into wedges
- 1 pound baby carrots
- 1 large red onion, sliced and separated into rings
- 2 jars (4-1/2 ounces *each*) whole mushrooms, drained
- 1/4 cup butter, cubed

1 envelope onion soup mix
2 tablespoons soy sauce
1/2 teaspoon pepper

Cut bratwurst links into thirds. Place the bratwurst, potatoes, carrots, onion and mushrooms in a heavy-duty foil bag (17 in. x 15 in.). Dot with butter. Sprinkle with the soup mix, soy sauce and pepper. Seal tightly and turn to coat.

Grill, covered, over medium heat for 45-55 minutes or until vegetables are tender and sausage is no longer pink, turning once. **Yield:** 12 servings.

■ ■ ■

Grilled Pork with Avocado Salsa

(Pictured above right)

I love the zesty taste of this moist, grilled tenderloin. The cumin, avocado and jalapeno give it Southwestern flair. It's an easy, elegant way to prepare pork.
—Josephine Devereaux Piro
Easton, Pennsylvania

1/2 cup chopped sweet onion
1/2 cup lime juice
1/4 cup chopped seeded
   jalapeno peppers
2 tablespoons olive oil
4 teaspoons ground cumin
2 pork tenderloins (3/4 pound *each*),
   cut into 3/4-inch slices
SALSA:
2 medium ripe avocados,
   peeled and chopped
2 plum tomatoes, seeded and
   chopped
1 small cucumber, seeded and
   chopped
2 green onions, chopped
2 tablespoons minced fresh cilantro

1 tablespoon honey
1/4 teaspoon salt
1/4 teaspoon pepper
3 tablespoons jalapeno pepper jelly

In a small bowl, combine the first five ingredients. Pour 1/2 cup marinade into a large resealable plastic bag; add the pork. Seal bag and turn to coat; refrigerate for up to 2 hours. Reserve 1/3 cup of the remaining marinade. Place the rest of the marinade in a large bowl; add the avocados, tomatoes, cucumber, green onions, cilantro, honey, salt and pepper. Cover and refrigerate until serving.

In a small saucepan, combine the jelly and reserved marinade. Bring to a boil; cook and stir for 2 minutes or until slightly thickened.

Coat grill rack with nonstick cooking spray before starting the grill. Drain and discard marinade from pork. Grill, uncovered, over medium heat for 4-6 minutes on each side or until juices run clear, brushing occasionally with jelly mixture. Serve with avocado salsa. **Yield:** 6 servings.

Editor's Note: When cutting or seeding hot peppers, use rubber or plastic gloves to protect your hands. Avoid touching your face.

Pineapple Pork Kabobs

(Pictured above)

Our Test Kitchen staff came up with this perfectly portioned recipe that quickly cooks on the grill. The slightly sweet marinade pairs well with the pork and peppers. Round out the meal with fresh fruit.

  1 **can (8 ounces) unsweetened pineapple chunks**
  2 **tablespoons plus 1-1/2 teaspoons cider vinegar**
  2 **tablespoons brown sugar**
Dash pepper
 1/2 **pound pork tenderloin, cut into 1-inch pieces**
 1/2 **small sweet red pepper, cut into 1-inch chunks**
 1/2 **small green pepper, cut into 1-inch chunks**
Hot cooked rice, optional

Drain pineapple, reserving juice; refrigerate the pineapple. In a bowl, combine the pineapple juice, vinegar, brown sugar and pepper. Pour half of the marinade into a large resealable plastic bag; add the pork. Seal and turn to coat; refrigerate for 4 hours. Cover and refrigerate remaining marinade for basting.

Drain and discard marinade from pork. On metal or soaked wooden skewers, alternately thread the pork, pineapple and peppers. Grill kabobs, covered, over medium heat for 10-15 minutes or until vegetables are tender and meat is no longer pink, turning and basting occasionally with reserved marinade. Serve with rice if desired. **Yield:** 2 servings.

Small, tender pork

cuts like tenderloin, ribs, ham slices, thick-cut chops and sausage are ideal for grilling because they won't become tough or dried out over the high heat. For best results, leaner cuts should be marinated before grilling.

Barbecued Spareribs

All of us—my husband, our two sons and I—love to eat barbecued ribs. But the closest rib restaurant to us is in Denver, which is 150 miles away. So I came up with this recipe. It's now our traditional meal on the Fourth of July.
—Jane Uphoff, Idalia, Colorado

- 1 tablespoon ground mustard
- 1 tablespoon chili powder
- 1/2 teaspoon cayenne pepper
- 1/4 teaspoon garlic powder
- 3 pounds pork spareribs
- 2/3 cup ketchup
- 1/2 cup water
- 1/2 cup chopped onion
- 1/4 cup lemon juice
- 2 tablespoons vegetable oil
- 1 teaspoon dried oregano
- 1 teaspoon Liquid Smoke, optional
- 1/2 teaspoon salt
- 1/4 teaspoon pepper

Combine the first four ingredients; rub over ribs. For sauce, combine the remaining ingredients; mix well and set aside.

Grill ribs, covered, over indirect, medium-low heat for 1 hour, turning occasionally. Add 10 briquettes to coals. Grill 30 minutes longer, basting both sides several times with sauce, or until meat is tender. **Yield:** 4 servings.

■ ■ ■

Marinated Ham Steaks

It's a snap to combine this zippy marinade…and you can vary the marinating time to fit your day's activities.
—Maribeth Edwards, Follansbee, West Virginia

- 1-1/2 cups pineapple juice
- 1/4 cup packed brown sugar
- 2 tablespoons butter, melted
- 1 to 2 tablespoons ground mustard
- 1 garlic clove, minced
- 1/4 teaspoon paprika
- 2 fully cooked ham steaks (1 pound *each*)

In a large resealable plastic bag, combine the first six ingredients; mix well. Add ham and turn to coat. Seal bag and refrigerate for at least 2 hours, turning occasionally.

Drain and reserve marinade. Place marinade in a saucepan; bring to a rolling boil. Grill ham, uncovered, over medium-hot heat for 3-4 minutes on each side, basting often with marinade. **Yield:** 6 servings.

■ ■ ■

Grilled Ham Slices

A simply spiced marinade gives mild, sweet flavor to these tender grilled ham slices. It's very good served with scrambled eggs for brunch. We round out the meal with melon balls and buttered toast.
—Rita Deere, Evansville, Indiana

- 2 fully cooked ham slices (about 1 pound *each*)
- 1 cup pineapple juice
- 1 cup sherry *or* apple juice
- 1/4 cup butter, melted
- 1 tablespoon ground mustard
- 1/4 teaspoon ground cloves

Place ham in a large resealable plastic bag. In a bowl, combine the remaining ingredients; mix well. Remove 1/2 cup for basting; cover and refrigerate. Pour remaining marinade over ham; seal bag and turn to coat. Refrigerate for 8 hours or overnight.

Drain and discard marinade. Grill ham, uncovered, over medium-hot heat for 3-4 minutes on each side until heated through, basting frequently with the reserved marinade. **Yield:** 6 servings.

Zesty Grilled Chops

(Pictured above)

My sister gave me the recipe for this easy five-ingredient marinade. It keeps the meat so moist and tasty…now this is the only way my husband wants his pork chops prepared.
—Bernice Germann, Napoleon, Ohio

3/4 **cup soy sauce**
1/4 **cup lemon juice**
  1 **tablespoon chili sauce**
  1 **tablespoon brown sugar**
1/4 **teaspoon garlic powder**
  6 **rib** *or* **loin pork chops**
    (3/4 inch thick)

In a large resealable plastic bag or shallow glass container, combine the first five ingredients; mix well. Remove 1/4 cup for basting and refrigerate. Add pork chops to remaining marinade; turn to coat. Cover and refrigerate for 3 hours or overnight, turning once.

Drain chops, discarding marinade. Grill, covered, over medium-hot heat for 4 minutes. Turn; baste with reserved marinade. Grill 4-7 minutes longer or until juices run clear. **Yield:** 6 servings.

■ ■ ■

Marinated Pork Strips

This is a good recipe for grilling, especially if you're having company. While it looks like you spent time on it, it's actually easy to prepare.
—Karen Peterson, Hainesville, Illinois

  5 **tablespoons soy sauce**
1/4 **cup ketchup**
  3 **tablespoons vinegar**
  3 **tablespoons chili sauce**
  3 **tablespoons sugar**
  2 **teaspoons salt**
1/8 **teaspoon pepper**
  3 **garlic cloves, minced**
  2 **cans (12 ounces** *each***)**
    lemon-lime soda
  2 **pounds pork tenderloin,**
    cut lengthwise into 1/2-inch strips

In a large bowl, combine the first nine ingredients. Place pork in a heavy resealable plastic bag; add the marinade. Seal the bag and turn to coat. Refrigerate overnight.

Drain and discard marinade. Thread pork onto metal or soaked wooden skewers. Grill over hot heat for 12 minutes, turning once, or until meat juices run clear. **Yield:** 6-8 servings.

Thin cut pork chops can easily be overcooked, resulting in dry meat. For tender, juicy pork chops from the grill, buy chops that are about 3/4 or 1 inch thick.

It's also important to preheat the grill so that the meat's juices will be quickly sealed in.

Pork with Watermelon Salsa

(Pictured above)

A colorful combination of fruit makes a sweet salsa that's ideal to serve along side grilled pork. Our Test Kitchen staff developed this one-of-a-kind recipe.

- 1 cup seeded chopped watermelon
- 1/2 cup chopped strawberries
- 1/2 cup chopped kiwifruit
- 1/4 cup chopped peaches
- 3 tablespoons lime juice
- 4 teaspoons honey
- 1/2 teaspoon grated lime peel
- 1 to 2 mint leaves, chopped
- 1/2 cup peach preserves
- 3 pork tenderloins (3/4 pound *each*)

For salsa, combine first eight ingredients in a bowl; set aside. In a saucepan or microwave, heat the preserves for 1 minute. Grill pork, covered, over indirect medium heat for 5 minutes. Turn; brush with some of the preserves.

Grill 8-9 minutes longer or until meat juices run clear and a meat thermometer reads 160°, basting occasionally with preserves. Serve with salsa. **Yield:** 6-8 servings (1-1/4 cups salsa).

Lime-Glazed Pork Chops

(Pictured above)

A wonderful sweet-sour citrus glaze makes these tender chops tangy and tasty. Quick and easy to prepare, the grilled chops are perfect for picnics and barbecues.
—*Jacqui Correa, Landing, New Jersey*

1/3 cup orange marmalade
 1 jalapeno pepper, seeded and finely chopped
 2 tablespoons lime juice
 1 teaspoon grated fresh gingerroot
 4 bone-in pork loin chops (8 ounces *each*)
 4 teaspoons minced fresh cilantro
Lime wedges

In a small saucepan, combine the first four ingredients. Cook and stir over medium heat for 5 minutes or until marmalade is melted. Set aside.

Coat grill rack with nonstick cooking spray before starting the grill. Grill chops, covered, over medium heat for 6-7 minutes on each side or until juices run clear, brushing with the glaze during the last 5 minutes of grilling. Sprinkle with cilantro and serve with lime wedges. **Yield:** 4 servings.

Editor's Note: When cutting or seeding hot peppers, use rubber or plastic gloves to protect your hands. Avoid touching your face.

Campfire Bundles

(Pictured below)

A family camping trip's where I created this recipe. I'd brought along a hodgepodge of ingredients, so I just threw them all together in a foil packet. Everyone said that the bundles were delicious. Ever since, I've grilled them at home with equally good results.
—Lauri Krause, Jackson, Nebraska

- 1 large sweet onion, sliced
- 1 *each* large green, sweet red and yellow peppers, sliced
- 4 medium potatoes, sliced 1/2 inch thick
- 6 medium carrots, sliced 1/4 inch thick
- 1 small cabbage, sliced
- 2 medium tomatoes, chopped
- 1 to 1-1/2 pounds fully cooked Polish sausage, cut into 1/2-inch pieces
- 1/2 cup butter
- 1 teaspoon salt
- 1/2 teaspoon pepper

Place vegetables in order listed on three pieces of double-layered heavy-duty foil (about 18 in. x 18 in.). Add sausage; dot with butter. Sprinkle with salt and pepper. Fold foil around the mixture and seal tightly.

Grill, covered, over medium heat for 30 minutes. Turn and grill 30 minutes longer or until vegetables are tender. **Yield:** 6 servings.

■ ■ ■

Marinated Chops 'n' Onion

The first time I made this spicy dish, my husband commented on how moist the pork was, so I knew it was a keeper. It gets eye-appeal from red onion slices that turn a pretty pink when they're cooked.
—Connie Brueggeman, Sparta, Wisconsin

- 3/4 cup lime juice
- 1 teaspoon salt
- 1/4 to 1/2 teaspoon cayenne pepper
- 4 pork chops (1/2 inch thick)
- 1 large red onion, sliced

In a large resealable plastic bag, combine the lime juice, salt and cayenne. Add the pork chops and onion; turn to coat. Seal bag. Refrigerate for at least 2 hours.

Drain, reserving marinade and onion. Grill chops, covered, over medium-hot heat for 8-10 minutes on each side or until meat juices run clear. Place the marinade and onion in a saucepan; bring to a rolling boil. Serve with the chops. **Yield:** 4 servings.

Relatives and friends will fall for these fish and seafood favorites…hook, line and sinker! Cast aside any doubt that dinner guests will be impressed and dish out hearty helpings of salmon, tuna, halibut, orange roughy, catfish and more! For the seafood lovers in your family, shrimp and scallop selections will net you unending compliments.

Lemon Grilled Salmon

(Pictured at left)

Mom proudly serves this tender, flaky fish to family and guests. A savory marinade that includes dill gives the salmon mouth-watering flavor. Since it can be grilled or broiled, we enjoy it year-round.
—Lisa Kivirist, Browntown, Wisconsin

2 teaspoons snipped fresh dill
  or 3/4 teaspoon dill weed
1/2 teaspoon lemon-pepper seasoning
1/2 teaspoon salt
1/4 teaspoon garlic powder
1 salmon fillet (1-1/2 pounds)
1/4 cup packed brown sugar
3 tablespoons chicken broth
3 tablespoons vegetable oil
3 tablespoons soy sauce
3 tablespoons finely chopped
  green onions
1 small lemon, thinly sliced
2 onion slices, separated into rings

Sprinkle dill, lemon-pepper, salt and garlic powder over salmon. Place in a large resealable plastic bag. Combine brown sugar, broth, oil, soy sauce and green onions; pour over the salmon. Seal bag and refrigerate for 1 hour, turning once.

Drain and discard marinade. Place salmon skin side down on grill over medium heat; arrange lemon and onion slices over the top. Cover and cook for 15-20 minutes or until fish flakes easily with a fork. **Yield:** 6 servings.

Grilled Tuna with Pineapple Salsa

(Pictured above)

When I spent some time in Honolulu, I came upon this tropical treatment for tuna. I still prepare the pineapple salsa as a tangy-sweet garnish for everything from grilled fish to pork and poultry.
—*Beveylon Concha, Chesapeake, Virginia*

1/2	medium fresh pineapple, peeled and cut into 1/2-inch slices
1	small onion, diced
2	jalapeno peppers, seeded and diced
2	tablespoons minced fresh cilantro
2	tablespoons lime juice
4	tuna steaks (6 ounces *each*)
1	tablespoon olive oil
1/4	teaspoon salt
1/4	teaspoon pepper

Grill pineapple slices, uncovered, over medium heat for 5-7 minutes on each side. Remove and chill pineapple for 30 minutes. Dice chilled pineapple. In a bowl, combine the pineapple, onion, jalapeno peppers, cilantro and lime juice. Refrigerate for 1 hour or until chilled.

Brush tuna with oil. Sprinkle with salt and pepper. Grill, covered, over medium heat for 5 minutes on each side or until the fish flakes easily with a fork. Serve with salsa. **Yield:** 4 servings.

Editor's Note: When cutting or seeding hot peppers, use rubber or plastic gloves to protect your hands. Avoid touching your face.

■ ■ ■

Grilled Salmon Steaks

(Pictured at right)

Salmon is a fish that's rich in nutrients. Seasoned with herbs and lemon juice, these flame-broiled steaks are excellent. Sprinkle the hot coals with rosemary for additional flavor.
—*Robert Bishop, Lexington, Kentucky*

Fish & Seafood Grilling Chart

Fish is done when it turns opaque in the thickest portion and flakes into sections. Scallops are done when they turn opaque, and shrimp are done when they turn pink. Watch closely to avoid overcooking. For direct grilling, turn steaks, whole fish, shrimp and scallops halfway through grilling time. Fillets generally do not need to be turned. To ease turning, use a grill basket. The cooking times given are a guideline. Check for doneness with a meat thermometer or other appropriate doneness test.

Cut	Weight or Thickness	Heat	Approximate Cooking Time (in minutes)
FISH			
Fillets or steaks	1/4 to 1/2 in.	high/direct	3 to 5
	1/2 to 1 in.	high/direct	5 to 10
Dressed fish	1 lb.	medium/direct	10 to 15
	2 to 2-1/2 lbs.	medium/indirect	20 to 30
Kabobs	1-in. cubes	medium/direct	8 to 12
SHELLFISH			
Scallops, Sea	1 lb.	medium/direct	5 to 8
Shrimp, medium	1 lb.	medium/direct	5 to 8

- **3 tablespoons dried rosemary, crushed, *divided***
- **1 tablespoon rubbed sage**
- **1/4 teaspoon white pepper**
- **1 tablespoon lemon juice**
- **1 tablespoon olive oil**
- **6 salmon steaks (6 ounces *each*)**

In a bowl, combine 4-1/2 teaspoons rosemary, sage, pepper, lemon juice and oil. Brush over both sides of salmon steaks. Coat grill rack with nonstick cooking spray before starting the grill. Sprinkle the remaining rosemary over hot coals for added flavor.

 Place salmon on grill rack. Grill, covered, over medium heat for 5 minutes. Turn; grill 7-9 minutes longer or until fish flakes easily with a fork. **Yield:** 6 servings.

Shrimp and Vegetable Kabobs

(Pictured above)

These colorful kabobs from our Test Kitchen home economists pair special shrimp and garden-fresh vegetables for a memorable main dish that's often requested. You can use whatever veggies you like.

1/2 cup Italian salad dressing
1 tablespoon minced fresh parsley
1 teaspoon dried basil
2 medium yellow squash, cut into 1-inch pieces
8 cherry tomatoes
1 medium green pepper, cut into 1-inch chunks
8 medium fresh mushrooms, optional
1 pound uncooked medium shrimp, peeled and deveined
2 cups hot cooked rice

In a small bowl, combine the salad dressing, parsley and basil. Alternate the vegetables and shrimp on eight metal or soaked wooden skewers. Grill, uncovered, over medium

Success with Skewers

When threading food on a skewer, allow 2 inches at one end so you can handle them while on the grill. To assure that everything cooks evenly, don't crowd food on skewers. It's best to allow about 1/4 inch between items to promote thorough, uniform cooking.

heat for 3 minutes, turning once. Baste with dressing mixture. Grill 3-4 minutes longer or until shrimp turn pink and vegetables are tender, turning and basting frequently. Serve with rice. **Yield:** 4 servings.

■ ■ ■

Lemon-Pepper Catfish

Nothing beats a supper of grilled catfish after a hard day's work. It's my family's choice during the summer.
—Regina Rosenberry
Greencastle, Pennsylvania

6 tablespoons lemon juice
1/4 cup butter, melted
2 teaspoons Worcestershire sauce
4 catfish fillets (about 5 ounces *each*)
1/2 teaspoon salt
1/2 teaspoon lemon-pepper seasoning

In a shallow glass container, combine the lemon juice, butter and Worcestershire sauce; mix well. Add catfish and turn to coat. Cover and refrigerate for 1 hour, turning occasionally.

Coat grill rack with nonstick cooking spray before starting the grill. Drain and discard marinade. Sprinkle catfish with salt and lemon-pepper. Grill, covered, over medium heat for 12-14 minutes or until fish flakes easily with a fork, turning once. **Yield:** 4 servings.

Honey-Mustard Grilled Trout

This easy-to-prepare dish is a favorite with my family. We like the honey-mustard sauce so much, I make a double batch and keep some in the fridge to use as dressing.
—Charlene Cronin, Kenner, Louisiana

> 1/4 cup mayonnaise
> 1 tablespoon cider vinegar
> 1 tablespoon prepared mustard
> 1 tablespoon honey
> 1/8 teaspoon cayenne pepper
> 4 large onions, cut into 1/2-inch slices
> 6 trout fillets (6 ounces *each*)

Coat grill rack with nonstick cooking spray before starting the grill. In a bowl, combine the first five ingredients. Place onions cut side down on grill rack with sides touching. Arrange fillets on onion slices. Cover and grill over medium-hot heat for 5 minutes. Baste with mustard mixture. Cook 5-6 minutes longer or until fish flakes easily with a fork, basting frequently. Discard onion slices. **Yield:** 6 servings.

Orange Roughy Bundles

(Pictured below)

Each meal-in-one packet contains zucchini, red pepper and a flaky full-flavored fish fillet. It cooks in no time.
—Margaret Wilson, Hemet, California

> 4 fresh *or* frozen orange roughy fillets (6 ounces *each*), thawed
> 1/4 cup grated Parmesan cheese
> 1/8 to 1/4 teaspoon cayenne pepper
> 2 medium zucchini, cut into 1/4-inch slices
> 1 small sweet red pepper, julienned
> 1/2 teaspoon salt

Place each fillet on a piece of heavy-duty foil (about 12 in. square). Sprinkle with the Parmesan cheese and cayenne. Top with zucchini, red pepper and salt. Fold foil over vegetables and seal tightly. Grill, covered, over indirect heat for 8-10 minutes or until fish flakes easily with a fork. **Yield:** 4 servings.

Barbecued Alaskan Salmon

We eat salmon all summer long, and this is our favorite way to fix it. The mild sauce—brushed on as the fish grills—really enhances the taste.
—Janis Smoke, King Salmon, Alaska

> 2 tablespoons butter
> 2 tablespoons brown sugar
> 1 to 2 garlic cloves, minced
> 1 tablespoon lemon juice
> 2 teaspoons soy sauce
> 1/2 teaspoon pepper
> 4 salmon steaks (1 inch thick)

In a small saucepan, combine the first six ingredients. Cook and stir until sugar is dissolved. Meanwhile, grill salmon, covered, over medium-hot heat for 5 minutes. Turn salmon; baste with the butter sauce. Grill 7-9 minutes longer, turning and basting occasionally, or until the salmon flakes easily with a fork. **Yield:** 4 servings.

Southwestern Catfish

(Pictured below left)

Catfish fillets are rubbed with a blend that includes chili powder, cumin, coriander, cayenne and paprika, then topped with homemade salsa. A green salad, garlic bread and sweet potatoes round out the meal nicely.
—Bruce Crittenden, Clinton, Mississippi

> 3 medium tomatoes, chopped
> 1/4 cup chopped onion
> 2 jalapeno peppers, seeded and finely chopped
> 2 tablespoons white wine vinegar
> 3 teaspoons salt, *divided*
> 3 teaspoons paprika
> 3 teaspoons chili powder
> 1 to 1-1/2 teaspoons ground cumin
> 1 to 1-1/2 teaspoons ground coriander
> 3/4 to 1 teaspoon cayenne pepper
> 1/2 teaspoon garlic powder
> 4 catfish fillets (6 ounces *each*)

For salsa, in a bowl, combine the tomatoes, onion, jalapenos, vinegar and 1 teaspoon salt. Cover and refrigerate for at least 30 minutes.

Combine the paprika, chili powder, cumin, coriander, cayenne, garlic powder and remaining salt; rub over catfish.

Coat grill rack with nonstick cooking spray before starting the grill. Grill fillets, uncovered, over medium heat for 5 minutes on each side or until fish flakes easily with a fork. Serve with salsa. **Yield:** 4 servings.

Editor's Note: When cutting or seeding hot peppers, use rubber or plastic gloves to protect your hands. Avoid touching your face.

Grilled Halibut Steaks

(Pictured above)

This recipe called for salmon, but I substituted another fish with delicious results. It saves me time in the kitchen because my husband grills it.
—Lisa Rowley, North East, Maryland

- 3/4 **cup butter, softened**
- 1 **tablespoon lemon juice**
- 1-1/2 **teaspoons dried minced onion**
- 1-1/2 **teaspoons garlic salt**
- 1-1/2 **teaspoons dried parsley flakes**
- 3/4 **teaspoon dill weed**
- 1/4 **teaspoon sugar**
- 1/4 **teaspoon pepper**
- 4 **halibut** *or* **swordfish steaks,**
  1 inch thick

In a small bowl, combine the first eight ingredients; let stand for 30 minutes. If grilling the fish, coat grill rack with nonstick cooking spray before starting the grill. Spread 1 tablespoon herbed butter over each halibut steak.

Grill fish, buttered side down, covered, over medium heat for 5-1/2 minutes. Spread 1 tablespoon of the herbed butter over each halibut steak; turn and spread with the remaining butter. Grill 5-6 minutes longer or until fish the flakes easily with a fork. **Yield:** 4 servings.

Facts for grilling fish:

- To keep fish from sticking, brush the grill rack lightly with vegetable oil or coat with nonstick cooking spray before starting the grill. Do the same thing if using a grilling basket.

- Add flavor to grilled seafood by sprinkling fresh rosemary, oregano or tarragon onto the hot coals.

- Grilled seafood will cook more evenly if the pieces are placed about 3/4 inch apart on the rack.

- Be careful not to over-marinate seafood. It's naturally tender and may fall apart.

Apple Halibut Kabobs

(Pictured below)

At first, I was hesitant to try this recipe, but I'm very glad I did. The apple and halibut flavors complement one another so well.
—*Marilyn Rodriguez, Fairbanks, Alaska*

- **1/2 cup dry white wine** *or* **unsweetened apple juice**
- 2 **tablespoons lime juice**
- 2 **tablespoons olive oil**
- 2 **tablespoons diced onion**
- 1 **teaspoon salt**
- 1/2 **teaspoon dried thyme**
- 1/4 **teaspoon pepper**
- 1-1/2 **pounds halibut, cut into 1-inch cubes**
- 1 **small red onion, cut into 1-inch pieces**
- 1 **medium Golden Delicious apple, cut into 1-inch pieces**
- 1 **medium sweet red pepper, cut into 1-inch pieces**

In a bowl, combine the first seven ingredients; mix well. Pour half into a large resealable plastic bag; add halibut. Seal bag and turn to coat. Pour remaining marinade into another large resealable plastic bag; add the onion, apple and red pepper. Seal bag and turn to coat. Refrigerate fish and apple mixture for 4-6 hours, turning occasionally.

Coat grill rack with nonstick cooking spray before starting the grill. Drain fish, discarding marinade. Drain fruit and vegetables, reserving marinade for basting.

On eight metal or soaked wooden skewers, alternately thread fish, onion, apple and red pepper. Grill, covered, over medium heat for 2-3 minutes on each side or until fish flakes easily with a fork, and fruit and vegetables are tender, turning once. Baste frequently with reserved marinade. **Yield:** 4 servings.

Drain and discard marinade. Alternately thread shrimp and scallops on metal or soaked wooden skewers. Grill, uncovered, over medium-hot heat for 6 minutes, turning once. Brush with reserved marinade. Grill 8-10 minutes longer or until shrimp turn pink and scallops are opaque. **Yield:** 4 servings.

■ ■ ■

Zesty Jumbo Shrimp

At your next barbecue, toss these zippy marinated shrimp on the grill. Dress up the great flavor with a hint of orange and several dashes of ginger and red pepper. Cooked rice and a salad complete the meal.
—Grace Yaskovic, Lake Hiawatha, New Jersey

2 tablespoons soy sauce
1 tablespoon orange juice
1 tablespoon olive oil
1/2 teaspoon sugar
1 garlic clove, minced
Dash crushed red pepper flakes
Dash ground ginger
2/3 pound jumbo shrimp, peeled and deveined
12 cherry tomatoes
Hot cooked rice, optional

In a bowl, combine first seven ingredients. Cover and refrigerate 2 tablespoons for basting. Pour remaining marinade into a large resealable plastic bag; add shrimp. Seal bag and turn to coat; refrigerate for at least 1 hour.

Drain and discard marinade from shrimp. Alternately thread shrimp and tomatoes onto metal or soaked wooden skewers. Coat grill rack with nonstick cooking spray before starting the grill. Grill kabobs, uncovered, over medium heat for 3 minutes on each side or until shrimp turn pink, basting occasionally with reserved marinade. Serve over rice if desired. **Yield:** 2 servings.

Tangy Shrimp And Scallops

(Pictured above)

Shrimp and scallops together make this a special dish for company. I serve these appealing kabobs over pasta with a green salad and garlic bread.
—Lauren Llewellyn, Raleigh, North Carolina

28 large shrimp (about 1-1/2 pounds), peeled and deveined
28 sea scallops (about 1/2 pound)
1/2 cup butter
7 tablespoons lemon juice
5 tablespoons Worcestershire sauce
1 to 2 teaspoons garlic powder
1 teaspoon paprika

Place shrimp and scallops in a large resealable plastic bag. In a microwave-safe bowl, combine the butter, lemon juice, Worcestershire sauce, garlic powder and paprika. Microwave at 50% power for 1-1/2 minutes or until butter is melted. Stir to blend; set aside 1/3 cup for basting. Pour remaining marinade over shrimp and scallops. Seal bag and turn to coat; refrigerate for 1 hour, turning occasionally.

Sweet-and-Sour Skewered Shrimp

(Pictured above)

This recipe is a summertime favorite. We fix it often on our portable grill when we go boating. My husband thinks it's great. It's the sauce that makes it!
—Rena Malek, Dubuque, Iowa

1/2 cup barbecue sauce
1/4 cup pineapple preserves
1/4 cup lemon juice
  4 teaspoons soy sauce
1/2 teaspoon ground ginger
 30 large fresh shrimp (about 2 pounds), shelled and deveined
  1 to 2 large green peppers, cut into 1-inch pieces
1/2 pound fresh mushrooms, halved

Combine the barbecue sauce, preserves, lemon juice, soy sauce and ginger in a small saucepan; bring to a boil over medium heat, stirring frequently. Remove from the heat; cool. Set aside 1/2 cup for basting. Place remaining sauce in a large resealable plastic bag; add shrimp. Seal bag; refrigerate for 30 minutes.

Drain and discard marinade. Thread shrimp, green peppers and mushrooms alternately on metal or soaked bamboo skewers. Grill, uncovered, over medium-hot heat for 2 minutes on each side. Brush with reserved sauce. Continue grilling for 4-8 minutes or until shrimp are pink throughout, turning and basting several times. **Yield:** 6 servings.

■ ■ ■

Haddock with Citrus Salsa

I'd prepared old favorites for 30 years when the latest emphasis on health-conscious cooking led me to find new recipes, like this mouth-watering way to serve fish.
—Sally Roberts, Port St. Lucie, Florida

  4 medium navel oranges, peeled and sectioned

1/2 cup chopped red onion
1/4 cup lime juice
1/4 cup minced fresh cilantro
1/4 teaspoon crushed red pepper
   flakes
 1 garlic clove, minced
 1 teaspoon grated orange peel
3/4 teaspoon salt, *divided*
1-1/8 teaspoons pepper, *divided*
 2 teaspoons ground coriander
 2 teaspoons ground cumin
 1 pound haddock fillets

For salsa, in a bowl, combine the oranges, onion, lime juice, cilantro, pepper flakes, garlic, orange peel, 1/4 teaspoon salt and 1/8 teaspoon pepper. Cover and chill.

Combine coriander, cumin and remaining salt and pepper; rub over both sides of fillets. Grill, covered, over medium-hot heat for 5-6 minutes on each side or until fish flakes easily with a fork. Serve with citrus salsa. **Yield:** 4 servings.

Garlic Lime Salmon

(Pictured below)

I use the grill to cook these delicious fillets. The moist, tender fish is mildly seasoned, so the leftovers (if there are any!) work well in other recipes.
—Gail Uchwat, Sand Springs, Oklahoma

1/2 cup vegetable oil
 1 medium onion, diced
 2 tablespoons lime juice
 1 teaspoon grated lime peel
 1 garlic clove, minced
 2 salmon fillets (about 1-1/2
    pounds *each*)
Lime slices, optional

In a jar with a tight-fitting lid, combine the oil, onion, lime juice, peel and garlic; shake well. Place salmon skin side down on grill over medium heat. Cover and cook for 20 minutes or until fish flakes easily with a fork, basting every 5 minutes with lime mixture. Garnish with lime slices if desired. **Yield:** 6 servings.

Crispy Catfish

(Pictured below)

Grilling is my family's favorite way to fix meals. Because my husband savors well-prepared foods, this recipe quickly became one of his most requested.
—Rhonda Dietz, Garden City, Kansas

3/4 **cup finely crushed saltines (22 crackers)**
  1 **teaspoon seasoned salt**
1/2 **teaspoon celery salt**
1/2 **teaspoon garlic salt**
  4 **catfish fillets (about 8 ounces *each*)**
1/3 **cup butter, melted**

In a shallow dish, combine the first four ingredients. Pat fillets dry; dip in butter, then coat with crumb mixture. Coat grill rack with nonstick cooking spray before starting grill. Grill fillets, covered, over medium-hot heat for 10 minutes or until fish flakes easily with a fork, carefully turning once. **Yield:** 4 servings.

Most store-bought

catfish is farm-raised and mild in flavor. The white flesh of catfish has a medium-form texture and a low fat content. When buying catfish, look for pure-white fillets and avoid those with a gray tinge or browning.

Seafood Skewers

My guests are always impressed when I make these special shrimp and scallop kabobs. They taste great and look spectacular when I garnish the plate with orange slices and fresh parsley.
—Carolyn Grier, Aurora, Illinois

1/4 **cup olive oil**
1/4 **cup chili sauce**
  2 **garlic cloves, minced**
1/2 **teaspoon hot pepper sauce**
Pepper to taste
 16 **uncooked large shrimp (about 1/2 pound), peeled and deveined**
  8 **sea scallops (about 1/2 pound)**
Hot cooked rice

In a large resealable plastic bag, combine the first five ingredients. Add shrimp and scallops. Seal bag and turn to coat. Refrigerate for at least 1 hour. Discard marinade. Place shrimp and scallops on four metal or soaked bamboo skewers. Grill, covered, over medium heat for 5 minutes on each side or until shrimp turn pink. Serve over rice. **Yield:** 4 servings.

Maple-Glazed Grilled Salmon

(Pictured above)

When I made up my mind to serve my family more nutritious fare, I decided to use more fish.
—Kate Selner, St. Paul, Minnesota

- 3/4 **cup maple syrup**
- 2 **tablespoons ketchup**
- 1 **tablespoon brown sugar**
- 1 **tablespoon cider vinegar**
- 1 **tablespoon Worcestershire sauce**
- 1/2 **teaspoon salt**
- 1/2 **teaspoon ground mustard**
- 1/8 **teaspoon hot pepper sauce**
- 1 **salmon fillet (2 pounds)**

In a bowl, combine the first eight ingredients; mix well. Pour 1/2 cup into a large resealable plastic bag; add the salmon. Seal bag and turn to coat; refrigerate for up to 2 hours. Cover and refrigerate the remaining marinade.

Before starting the grill, coat grill rack with nonstick cooking spray. Drain and discard marinade from salmon. Grill salmon skin side up over medium-hot heat for 2-4 minutes. Transfer to a double thickness of heavy-duty foil (about 17 in. x 21 in.). Spoon some of the reserved marinade over salmon. Fold foil around fillet and seal tightly. Grill 5-6 minutes longer or until fish flakes easily with a fork. Brush with remaining marinade. **Yield:** 8 servings.

Testing for Doneness

For fish fillets, check for doneness by inserting a fork at an angle into the thickest portion of the fish and gently parting the meat. When it flakes into sections, it is cooked completely. Whole fish or steaks are done when the flesh is easily removed from the bones. Cooked fish is opaque in color and the juices are milky white.

Grilled Sole with Nectarines

(Pictured below)

I found this recipe and adapted it to suit my family's tastes. We enjoy the great herbs on this grilled fish.
—Mary Rhoden, Waldport, Oregon

- 4 sole fillets (6 ounces *each*)
- 2 medium nectarines *or* peaches, peeled and sliced
- 1/2 cup sliced green onions
- 1-1/2 teaspoons chopped fresh tarragon *or* 1/2 teaspoon dried tarragon
- 1/4 teaspoon salt
- 1/8 teaspoon pepper
- 1 teaspoon butter, melted

Place each fillet on a double thickness of heavy-duty foil (about 18 in. x 12 in.). Arrange nectarines around the fillets. Sprinkle with the green onions, tarragon, salt, pepper and butter. Fold foil around the fish and seal tightly. Grill, covered, over medium heat for 7-8 minutes or until the fish flakes easily with a fork. **Yield:** 4 servings.

Flavorful Flounder

When my grandparents lived in the Florida Keys, they ate fish often. The Parmesan cheese in this fast recipe adds just the right flavor to the flounder.
—Tammy Sanborn, Alto, Michigan

- 2 pounds flounder *or* sole fillets
- 2 tablespoons lemon juice
- 1/2 cup grated Parmesan cheese
- 1/4 cup butter, melted
- 3 tablespoons mayonnaise
- 3 tablespoons chopped green onions
- 1/4 teaspoon salt

Coat a piece of heavy-duty foil (about 14 in. x 14 in.) with nonstick cooking spray. Place fillets on foil; brush with lemon juice. Crimp foil, forming edges. Place foil flat on the grill (do not seal).

Grill, covered, over medium-hot heat for 4 minutes. Combine Parmesan cheese, butter, mayonnaise, onions and salt; brush over the fillets. Grill 3-4 minutes longer or until fish flakes easily with a fork. **Yield:** 4-6 servings.

■ ■ ■

Herbed Orange Roughy

The simple seasonings in this recipe enhance the pleasant, mild flavor of orange roughy. It's a quick and easy way to prepare fish that my whole family enjoys. I know yours will, too.
—Sue Kroening, Mattoon, Illinois

- 2 tablespoons lemon juice
- 1 tablespoon butter, melted
- 1/2 teaspoon dried thyme
- 1/2 teaspoon grated lemon peel
- 1/4 teaspoon salt
- 1/4 teaspoon paprika
- 1/8 teaspoon garlic powder

4 orange roughy, red snapper, catfish *or* trout fillets (6 ounces *each*)

In a shallow glass container, combine the first seven ingredients; dip fillets. Grill, covered, over hot heat for 10 minutes or until fish flakes easily with a fork. **Yield:** 4 servings.

■ ■ ■

Shrimp Kabobs

(Pictured above)

My family always asks me to prepare these tangy and juicy kabobs during our beach getaways.
—Cheryl Williams, Evington, Virginia

1 can (8 ounces) tomato sauce
1 cup chopped onion
1/2 cup water
1/4 cup packed brown sugar
1/4 cup lemon juice
3 tablespoons Worcestershire sauce
2 tablespoons vegetable oil
2 tablespoons prepared mustard
1/2 teaspoon salt
1/2 teaspoon pepper
1 can (20 ounces) unsweetened pineapple chunks
1 pound uncooked medium shrimp, peeled and deveined (about 32)
1 medium green pepper, cut into chunks
1 medium onion, cut into chunks
3 cups hot cooked rice

In a saucepan, combine the first 10 ingredients. Bring to a boil. Reduce heat; simmer, uncovered, for 15 minutes.

Drain pineapple, reserving 2 tablespoons juice (save remaining juice for another use); set pineapple aside. Stir reserved juice into sauce. Pour half into a bowl for basting; cover and refrigerate. Pour remaining sauce into a large resealable plastic bag; add shrimp. Seal bag and turn to coat; chill for 2-3 hours.

Drain and discard marinade. Alternately thread shrimp, pineapple, green pepper and onion on eight metal or soaked wooden skewers.

Coat grill rack with nonstick cooking spray before starting the grill. Grill kabobs, covered, over medium heat for 5 minutes on each side or until shrimp turn pink, basting occasionally with reserved sauce. Serve over rice. **Yield:** 4 servings.

Salmon with Citrus Salsa

(Pictured above)

This grilled salmon is a surefire winner! It makes a perfect light summer supper.
—Nancy Shirvani, Terryville, Connecticut

1/2 cup raspberry vinegar
1/4 cup soy sauce
  2 tablespoons minced fresh cilantro
1-1/2 teaspoons ground ginger *or* 2 tablespoons minced fresh gingerroot
  1 tablespoon olive oil
1/2 teaspoon hot pepper sauce
1/8 teaspoon pepper
  4 salmon fillets (6 ounces *each*)

CITRUS SALSA:
3/4 cup pink grapefruit segments, cut into bite-size pieces
1/2 cup orange segments, cut into bite-size pieces
  1 tablespoon raspberry vinegar
  1 tablespoon honey
  1 teaspoon minced fresh cilantro
1/8 teaspoon ground ginger *or* 1 teaspoon minced fresh gingerroot
1/8 teaspoon hot pepper sauce

In a large resealable plastic bag, combine the first seven ingredients; add salmon. Seal bag and turn to coat; refrigerate for 2 hours. Meanwhile, in a bowl, combine salsa ingredients. Cover and refrigerate.

  Drain and discard marinade. Coat grill rack with nonstick cooking spray before starting grill. Place salmon, skin side down, on grill. Grill, covered, over medium heat for 15-20 minutes or until fish flakes easily with a fork. Serve with salsa. **Yield:** 4 servings.

Teriyaki Tuna Steaks

(Pictured below)

*After sampling tuna at a Japanese restaurant,
I decided to try my hand at the recipe.
It took a little trial and error, but I was
please with the results.*
—Michelle Dennis, Clarks Hill, Indiana

- 1/4 **cup soy sauce**
- 3 **tablespoons brown sugar**
- 3 **tablespoons olive oil**
- 2 **tablespoons white wine vinegar**
- 2 **tablespoons sherry** *or*
  chicken broth
- 2 **tablespoons unsweetened
  pineapple juice**
- 2 **garlic cloves, minced**
- 1-1/2 **teaspoons ground ginger** *or* **2
  tablespoons minced fresh
  gingerroot**
- 4 **tuna steaks (6 ounces** *each***)**

In a bowl, combine the first eight ingredients; mix well. Remove 1/3 cup to a small bowl for basting; cover and refrigerate. Pour remaining marinade into a large resealable plastic bag; add tuna. Seal bag and turn to coat; refrigerate for up to 1 hour.

Coat grill rack with nonstick cooking spray before starting the grill. Drain and discard marinade. Grill tuna, uncovered, over medium heat for 5-6 minutes on each side or until fish flakes easily with a fork, basting frequently with reserved marinade. **Yield:** 4 servings.

When buying frozen fish,

make sure it is solidly frozen and the wrapping isn't damaged. There should be no odor or icy spots.

Allow about 24 hours to thaw one pound of fish. To quick-thaw, place the fish in its packaging in cold water. Allow about an hour for 1 pound.

After thawing, pat the fish dry with paper towels before using.

Marinated Catfish Fillets

(Pictured below)

When we hosted a group of young people from Canada, we wanted to give them a true taste of the South. They raved about this dish.
—Pauletta Boese, Macon, Mississippi

- 6 catfish fillets (about 8 ounces *each*)
- 1 bottle (16 ounces) Italian salad dressing
- 1 can (10-3/4 ounces) condensed tomato soup, undiluted
- 3/4 cup vegetable oil
- 3/4 cup sugar
- 1/3 cup white vinegar
- 3/4 teaspoon celery seed
- 3/4 teaspoon salt
- 3/4 teaspoon pepper
- 3/4 teaspoon ground mustard
- 1/2 teaspoon garlic powder

Place fillets in a large resealable plastic bag; cover with salad dressing. Seal bag; refrigerate for 1 hour, turning occasionally. Drain and discard marinade. Combine remaining ingredients; mix well. Remove 1 cup for basting. (Refrigerate remaining sauce for another use.)

Grill fillets, covered, over medium-hot heat for 3 minutes on each side. Brush with the basting sauce. Continue grilling for 6-8 minutes or until fish flakes easily with a fork, turning once and basting several times. **Yield**: 6 servings.

Editor's Note: Reserved sauce may be used to brush on grilled or broiled fish, chicken, turkey or pork.

Basil-Marinated Fish

Combined with oil, a sprinkling of other herbs and a little zesty lemon peel, basil vinegar makes a delightfully mild and pleasant marinade for orange roughy or halibut. Never made an herb vinegar? It's easy! Our Test Kitchen staff came up with a super simple recipe with just two ingredients.

BASIL VINEGAR:
- 1 cup fresh basil leaves, crushed
- 2 cups white wine vinegar

FISH:
- 1/4 cup Basil Vinegar (recipe above)
- 2 tablespoons olive oil
- 1 tablespoon *each* chopped fresh basil, thyme, oregano and parsley *or* 1 teaspoon *each* dried basil, thyme, oregano and parsley flakes
- 2 garlic cloves, minced
- 1 teaspoon grated lemon peel
- 1/2 teaspoon salt
- 1/4 teaspoon pepper
- 2 orange roughy *or* halibut fillets (1 pound)

Place crushed basil leaves in a sterilized pint jar. Heat vinegar just until simmering; pour over basil. Cool to room temperature. Cover and let stand in a cool dark place for 24 hours; strain and discard basil.

In a large resealable plastic bag, combine 1/4 cup basil vinegar, oil, herbs, garlic, lemon peel, salt and pepper. Add fillets; seal bag and turn to coat. Refrigerate for 30 minutes, turning once or twice. Drain and discard marinade.

Coat grill rack with nonstick cooking spray before starting grill. Grill fillets, covered, over medium-hot heat for 7-10 minutes or until fish flakes easily with a fork. **Yield:** 4 servings.

Caesar Salmon Fillets

(Pictured above)

Not only is this my husband's favorite meal, but it's a dish dinner guests enjoy as well.
—Joan Garneau, Ellenton, Florida

- 4 salmon fillets (6 ounces *each*)
- 1/2 cup Caesar salad dressing
- 1/4 cup soy sauce
- 1 garlic clove, minced

Place salmon fillets in a large resealable plastic bag; add the salad dressing. Seal bag and turn to coat; refrigerate for at least 2 hours.

Drain and discard marinade. Coat grill rack with nonstick cooking spray before starting the grill. Place salmon skin side down on grill rack. Grill, covered, over medium heat for 5 minutes.

In a small bowl, combine soy sauce and garlic; brush over salmon. Grill 10-15 minutes longer or until fish flakes easily with a fork, basting occasionally. **Yield:** 4 servings.

Grilled Spiced Fish

(Pictured below)

These moist, flaky fillets provide a welcome change of pace at summer cookouts. I pepper a savory herb rub with cayenne, then work it into the fish. Even steak lovers will be smacking their lips.
—*Chris McBee, Xenia, Ohio*

4 red snapper *or* orange roughy fillets (6 ounces *each*)
1 tablespoon olive oil
2 teaspoons paprika
1 teaspoon salt
1 teaspoon onion powder
1 teaspoon garlic powder
1/2 teaspoon cayenne pepper
1/4 teaspoon white pepper
1/4 teaspoon *each* dried oregano, basil and thyme

Brush fish with oil. In a small bowl, combine the seasonings; sprinkle over fish and press into both sides. Cover and refrigerate for 30-60 minutes. Coat grill rack with nonstick cooking spray before starting the grill. Grill fillets uncovered, over medium heat for 3-4 minutes on each side or until fish flakes easily with a fork. **Yield:** 4 servings.

■ ■ ■

Maritime Grilled Fish

Sweet honey and zippy red pepper flakes accent the herb-enhanced marinade I use for grilled fish. It's also good on chicken. My family thinks it's fantastic.
—*Julie Craghead, Peoria, Illinois*

1/4 cup dry white wine *or* chicken broth
1/4 cup soy sauce
3 tablespoons honey
1 tablespoon olive oil
3 to 4 garlic cloves, minced
1/4 teaspoon crushed red pepper flakes
1/8 teaspoon pepper
1/8 teaspoon *each* dried basil, thyme and rosemary, crushed
1/8 teaspoon dill weed
4 orange roughy fillets (6 ounces *each*)

In a large resealable plastic bag, combine the wine, soy sauce, honey, oil, garlic and seasonings; add the fish. Seal bag and turn to coat; refrigerate for up to 1 hour.

Coat the grill rack with nonstick cooking spray before starting the grill. Drain and discard marinade. Grill the fish, covered, over medium heat for 5-6 minutes on each side or until the fish flakes easily with a fork. **Yield:** 4 servings.

A no-fat dill sauce

to serve alongside salmon is so simple to prepare! Just stir some minced fresh dill or dried dill into your favorite fat-free ranch salad dressing. It tastes great!

Citrus-Ginger Tuna Steaks

(Pictured above)

We had tuna steaks similar to this in Hawaii. I tried mixing different ingredients before coming up with this recipe. Now that I am retired, I have lots of time to experiment and prepare meals...but this tuna, with its seasoned marinade, takes only minutes to make.
—Fran Roff, Rochester, New York

1/2 cup olive oil
1/4 cup white wine vinegar
2 tablespoons soy sauce
1 tablespoon lemon juice
1 tablespoon lime juice
2 garlic cloves, minced
1 tablespoon minced fresh gingerroot
2 tuna steaks (8 ounces *each*)

In a bowl, combine the first seven ingredients. Pour 1/2 cup marinade into a large resealable plastic bag; add tuna steaks. Seal bag and turn to coat; refrigerate for 2-4 hours. Cover and refrigerate remaining marinade.

Drain and discard marinade from tuna. Coat grill rack with nonstick cooking spray before starting grill. Grill tuna, uncovered, for 5-7 minutes on each side or until fish flakes easily with a fork. Serve with the reserved marinade. **Yield:** 2 servings.

Halibut with Zesty Peach Salsa

(Pictured below)

Our Test Kitchen staff came up with a fun way to serve halibut by marinating it in citrus juices and brown sugar, then topping it with a refreshing peach salsa.

1/3 cup orange juice
  2 tablespoons canola oil
  2 tablespoons lime juice
  1 tablespoon brown sugar
  2 teaspoons grated lime peel
  1 garlic clove, minced
1/2 teaspoon salt
  4 halibut steaks (6 ounces *each*)

SALSA:
  2 cups chopped fresh *or*
     frozen peaches
1/4 cup chopped sweet red pepper
1/4 cup chopped red onion
  1 jalapeno pepper, seeded
     and chopped
  2 tablespoons orange juice
  1 tablespoon minced fresh cilantro
  2 teaspoons lime juice
1/4 teaspoon salt

In a bowl, combine the first seven ingredients; mix well. Remove 1/4 cup for basting; cover and refrigerate. Pour remaining marinade into a large resealable plastic bag; add the halibut. Seal bag and turn to coat; refrigerate for 2 hours. In a bowl, combine salsa ingredients; cover and refrigerate until serving.

Coat grill rack with nonstick cooking spray before starting the grill. Drain and discard marinade from fish. Grill, uncovered, over medium heat for 4-6 minutes on each side or until fish flakes easily with a fork, basting occasionally with reserved marinade. Serve with peach salsa. **Yield:** 4 servings.

Editor's Note: When cutting or seeding hot peppers, use rubber or plastic gloves to protect your hands. Avoid touching your face.

Drain and discard marinade. Place salmon skin side down on grill. Grill, covered, over medium-hot heat for 5 minutes. Baste with reserved marinade. Grill 10-15 minutes longer or until fish flakes easily with a fork, basting frequently. **Yield:** 4-6 servings.

■ ■ ■

Creole Catfish Fillets

I rub catfish fillets with a nice mixture of seasonings before cooking them quickly on the grill.
—*Dave Bremstone, Plantation, Florida*

>   3 tablespoons plain yogurt
>   2 tablespoons finely chopped onion
>   1 tablespoon mayonnaise
>   1 tablespoon Dijon mustard
>   1 tablespoon ketchup
> 1/2 teaspoon dried thyme
> 1/4 teaspoon grated lemon peel
>   1 teaspoon paprika
> 1/2 teaspoon onion powder
> 1/4 teaspoon salt
> 1/8 teaspoon cayenne pepper
>   4 catfish fillets (4 ounces *each*)
>   4 lemon wedges

In a bowl, combine the first seven ingredients. Cover and refrigerate until serving. In another bowl, combine the paprika, onion powder, salt and cayenne; rub over both sides of fillets.

Grill, covered, in a grill basket coated with nonstick cooking spray over medium-hot heat, or broil 6 in. from the heat for 5-6 minutes on each side or until fish flakes easily with a fork. Serve with lemon wedges and yogurt sauce. **Yield:** 4 servings.

Gingered Honey Salmon

(Pictured above)

Ginger, garlic powder and green onion blend nicely in an easy marinade that gives pleasant flavor to salmon.
—*Dan Strumberger, Farmington, Minnesota*

> 1/3 cup orange juice
> 1/3 cup soy sauce
> 1/4 cup honey
>   1 green onion, chopped
>   1 teaspoon ground ginger
>   1 teaspoon garlic powder
>   1 salmon fillet (1-1/2 pounds and 3/4 inch thick)

Coat grill rack with nonstick cooking spray before starting the grill. In a bowl, combine the first six ingredients; mix well. Set aside 1/3 cup for basting; cover and refrigerate. Pour remaining marinade into a large resealable plastic bag; add salmon. Seal bag and turn to coat. Refrigerate for 30 minutes, turning once or twice.

·Lamb·

Go out on a limb next time you plan a barbecue and serve family and friends flavorful lamb. With its versatility and delicate flavor, lamb appeals to all palates. And these days, grocery stores offer a variety of cuts to suit your needs. Pick up a pack of chops and fire up the grill! Or buy boneless lamb for quick and tasty kabobs. To turn an ordinary meal into something special, reach for a rack or leg of lamb.

Greek Lamb Kabobs

(Pictured at left)

We have a gas grill and use it year-round, especially to make these tender juicy kabobs. The lamb marinates overnight, and the attractive skewers can be quickly assembled the next day.
—Kathy Herrola, Martinez, California

1/2 cup lemon juice
4 teaspoons olive oil
2 tablespoons dried oregano
6 garlic cloves, minced
1 pound boneless lean lamb, cut into 1-inch cubes
16 cherry tomatoes
1 large green pepper, cut into 1-inch pieces
1 large onion, cut into 1-inch wedges

In a bowl, combine the lemon juice, oil, oregano and garlic; mix well. Remove 1/4 cup for basting; cover and refrigerate. Pour the remaining marinade into a large resealable plastic bag; add the lamb. Seal bag and turn to coat; refrigerate for at least 8 hours or overnight, turning occasionally.

Coat grill rack with nonstick cooking spray before starting the grill. Drain and discard marinade from lamb. On eight metal or soaked wooden skewers, alternately thread lamb, tomatoes, green pepper and onion. Grill kabobs, uncovered, over medium heat for 3 minutes on each side. Baste with reserved marinade. Grill 8-10 minutes longer or until meat reaches desired doneness (for medium-rare, a meat thermometer should read 145°; medium, 160°; well-done, 170°). Turn and baste frequently. **Yield:** 4 servings.

Lamb with Spinach and Onions

(Pictured above)

Grilling is a wonderful way to prepare lamb. The marinade and on-the-side onion sauce in this recipe enhance the meat's naturally terrific taste.
—Sarah Vasques, Milford, New Hampshire

- 1/2 cup lime juice
- 1/4 cup dry red wine *or* 1 tablespoon red wine vinegar
- 1 small onion, chopped
- 2 tablespoons minced fresh rosemary *or* 2 teaspoons dried rosemary, crushed
- 2 tablespoons olive oil
- 2 tablespoons Worcestershire sauce
- 3 garlic cloves, minced
- 1 tablespoon minced fresh thyme *or* 1 teaspoon dried thyme
- 1/4 teaspoon pepper

Dash Liquid Smoke, optional
- 12 rib lamb chops (1 inch thick)

ONION SAUCE:
- 2 tablespoons finely chopped green onions
- 1 teaspoon butter
- 1 cup balsamic vinegar
- 1 cup dry red wine *or* 1/2 cup beef broth and 1/2 cup grape juice
- 1/2 cup loosely packed fresh mint leaves, chopped
- 1 tablespoon sugar
- 1 large sweet onion, cut into quarters

Olive oil
Salt and pepper to taste
SPINACH:
- 1/4 cup finely chopped green onions
- 3 garlic cloves, minced
- 3 tablespoons olive oil
- 3 tablespoons butter
- 12 cups fresh baby spinach

Salt and pepper to taste

In a large resealable plastic bag, combine the first 10 ingredients; add lamb chops. Seal bag and turn to coat; refrigerate for 8 hours or overnight.

In a saucepan, saute green onions in but-

Lamb Grilling Chart

Lamb chops and steaks are done when a meat thermometer reads 145° for medium-rare, 160° for medium and 170° for well-done. Ground lamb is done at 160°. For direct grilling, turn meat halfway through grilling time. The cooking times given are a guideline. Check for doneness with a meat thermometer or other appropriate doneness test.

Cut	Weight or Thickness	Heat	Approximate Cooking Time
Rib or Loin Chops	1 in.	medium/direct	10 to 18 minutes
Leg of Lamb, bone-in	5 to 7 lbs.	medium-low/indirect	1-3/4 to 2-3/4 hours
Leg of Lamb, boneless	3 to 4 lbs.	medium-low/indirect	1-1/2 to 2-1/2 hours
Rack of Lamb	1 to 1-1/2 lbs.	medium/direct	25 to 35 minutes
Kabobs	1-in. cubes	medium/direct	8 to 12 minutes

ter until tender. Add vinegar and wine or broth and grape juice; bring to a boil. Add mint and sugar. Reduce heat; simmer, uncovered, for 30 minutes or until sauce is reduced to 3/4 cup. Strain; discard mint. Set sauce aside.

Thread onion wedges onto metal or soaked wooden skewers. Brush with oil; sprinkle with salt and pepper. Discard marinade from lamb. Grill chops, covered, over medium-hot heat for 5-6 minutes on each side or until meat reaches desired doneness (for medium-rare, a meat thermometer should read 145°; medium, 160°; well-done, 170°). Grill onion skewers for 2-3 minutes or until tender.

In a large skillet, saute green onions and garlic in oil and butter until tender. Add the spinach, salt and pepper; saute for 2-3 minutes or until spinach just begins to wilt and is heated through. Place on a serving platter. Remove onion from skewers; place onion and lamb chops over spinach. **Yield:** 6 servings.

When purchasing lamb, select lean lamb cuts that are cold and firm. Avoid packages with tears and any meat that looks dried out or does not smell fresh. Look for lamb with little excess liquid in the package. Ground lamb, tenderloin and rib, loin and sirloin chops are terrific for grilling.

Refrigerate lamb and use within 3 days or freeze lamb for longer storage. Ground lamb can be frozen for 3 months; cuts can be frozen for 6 months.

Grilled Lamb Kabobs

(Pictured at right)

My sister-in-law, who lives in Florida, sends fresh fruit every year at Christmas. I've invented various recipes for using it. We get plenty of snow here, but our grill is always put to good use!
—*Kathleen Boulanger, Williston, Vermont*

  1-1/4 cups grapefruit juice
    1/3 cup honey
      2 tablespoons minced fresh mint
    3/4 teaspoon salt
    3/4 teaspoon ground coriander
    3/4 teaspoon pepper
      1 pound boneless lamb, cut into
        1-inch cubes

CITRUS SALSA:
      4 medium navel oranges, *divided*
      2 medium pink grapefruit
    1/2 cup mango chutney
      1 to 2 tablespoons minced fresh mint
      2 medium onions, cut into wedges
      1 large sweet red pepper, cut into
        1-inch pieces

In a bowl, combine the first six ingredients; mix well. Pour 1 cup into a large resealable plastic bag; add the lamb. Seal bag and turn to coat; refrigerate for 1-4 hours. Cover and refrigerate remaining marinade.

For salsa, peel and section two oranges and grapefruit, then coarsely chop fruit. In a bowl, combine the chopped fruit, chutney and mint. Cover and refrigerate.

Coat grill rack with nonstick cooking spray before starting the grill. Peel remaining oranges; cut each into eight wedges. Drain and discard marinade from lamb. On eight metal or wooden soaked skewers, alternately thread onions, orange wedges, red pepper and lamb. Grill, uncovered, over medium heat for 4-5 minutes on each side or until meat reaches desired doneness and vegetables are tender, basting occasionally with reserved marinade. Serve kabobs with salsa. **Yield:** 4 servings.

◼ ◼ ◼

Lemon Herb Lamb Chops

This recipe comes from my aunt, who thought we'd enjoy it because we like lamb. She was right.
—*Mildred Sherrer, Bay City, Texas*

  1/4 cup olive oil
    1 tablespoon lemon juice
    1 garlic clove, minced
    1 teaspoon grated lemon peel
  1/4 teaspoon salt
  1/4 teaspoon dried basil
  1/4 teaspoon dried rosemary, crushed
  1/4 teaspoon pepper
    2 bone-in lamb loin chops
      (6 ounces *each*)

In a large resealable plastic bag, combine the first eight ingredients; add the chops. Seal bag and turn to coat; refrigerate for at least 2 hours or overnight.

Drain and discard marinade. Grill, covered, over medium-hot heat for 5-6 minutes on each side or until meat reaches desired doneness (for medium-rare, a meat thermometer should read 145°; medium, 160°; well-done, 170°). **Yield:** 1-2 servings.

■ ■ ■

Dijon Leg of Lamb

(Pictured below)

*This special entree is
always on our Easter table.*
—*Christy Porter, Centennial, Colorado*

- 1 **cup Dijon mustard**
- 1/2 **cup soy sauce**
- 2 **tablespoons olive oil**
- 1 **tablespoon chopped fresh
  rosemary or 1 teaspoon
  dried rosemary, crushed**
- 1 **teaspoon ground ginger**
- 1 **garlic clove, minced**
- 1 **boneless leg of lamb (4 to 5 pounds)**

In a bowl, whisk the first six ingredients. Remove 2/3 cup; cover and refrigerate for serving. Cut leg of lamb horizontally from the long side to within 1 in. of opposite side. Open meat so it lies flat; trim and discard fat. Place lamb in a large resealable plastic bag; add remaining mustard sauce. Seal bag and turn to coat. Refrigerate overnight.

Drain and discard marinade. Coat grill rack with nonstick cooking spray before starting the grill. Prepare grill for indirect medium heat, using a drip pan.

Place lamb over drip pan. Grill, covered, for 50-70 minutes or until meat reaches desired doneness (for medium-rare, a meat thermometer should read 145°; medium, 160°; well-done, 170°). Let stand for 10 minutes before slicing. Warm reserved mustard sauce; serve with lamb. **Yield:** 8-10 servings.

In a saucepan, combine the first eight ingredients. Simmer, uncovered, for 15-20 minutes. Meanwhile, grill lamb chops, turning once, over medium-hot heat for 5-6 minutes on each side or until meat reaches desired doneness (for medium-rare, a meat thermometer should read 145°; medium, 160°; well-done, 170°). Brush with sauce during the last few minutes of grilling. Serve with sour cream. **Yield:** 2 servings.

■ ■ ■

Grilled Rack of Lamb

Whenever my husband and I really want to impress guests, we make this rack of lamb.
—Gail Cawsey, Sequim, Washington

> 2 **cups apple cider** *or* **juice**
> 2/3 **cup cider vinegar**
> 2/3 **cup thinly sliced green onions**
> 1/2 **cup vegetable oil**
> 1/3 **cup honey**
> 1/4 **cup steak sauce**
> 2 **teaspoons dried tarragon**
> 2 **teaspoons salt**
> 1/2 **teaspoon pepper**
> 4 **racks of lamb (1-1/2 to 2 pounds** *each***)**

In a saucepan, combine the first nine ingredients. Bring to a boil. Reduce heat; simmer, uncovered, for 20 minutes. Remove 1 cup for basting; cover and refrigerate. Pour the remaining marinade into a large resealable plastic bag; add lamb. Seal bag and turn to coat; refrigerate for 2-3 hours or overnight, turning once or twice.

Coat grill rack with nonstick cooking spray before starting the grill. Drain and discard the marinade. Cover rib ends of lamb with foil. Grill, covered, over medium heat for 15 minutes. Baste with reserved marinade. Grill 5-10 minutes longer, basting occasionally, or until meat reaches desired doneness (for medium-rare, a meat thermometer should read 145°; medium, 160°; well-done, 170°). **Yield:** 4-6 servings.

Southwestern Grilled Lamb

(Pictured above)

Jalapeno peppers are quite abundant in this area of the country, and there are numerous ranches here that raise lambs. People seem to be eating food that's a little hotter nowadays, so I think this recipe will appeal to them.
—Margaret Pache, Mesa, Arizona

> 1 **cup salsa**
> 1/2 **cup chopped onion**
> 1/4 **cup molasses**
> 1/4 **cup fresh lime juice (about 2 limes)**
> 1/4 **cup chicken broth**
> 2 **garlic cloves, minced**
> 1 **to 3 tablespoons chopped seeded jalapeno peppers**
> 2 **teaspoons sugar**
> 4 **lamb chops (1 inch thick)**
> **Sour cream**

Beefy Lamb Kabobs

A lemon-olive oil marinade gives these tasty kabobs a nice tang. They're great for summer parties. In bad weather and during the winter, we cook them in a 400-degree oven for 25 to 40 minutes.
—Weda Mosellie, Phillipsburg, New Jersey

- 1/4 cup minced fresh parsley
- 2 tablespoons olive oil
- 4 teaspoons salt
- 2 teaspoons pepper
- 2 teaspoons lemon juice
- 2 pounds boneless lamb, cut into 1-1/2-inch cubes
- 1 pound boneless beef sirloin steak, cut into 1-1/2-inch cubes
- 6 small onions, cut into wedges
- 2 medium sweet red peppers, cut into 1-inch pieces
- 16 large fresh mushrooms
- 6 pita breads (6 inches), cut into wedges

In a small bowl, combine the first five ingredients. Place the lamb and beef in a large resealable plastic bag; add half of the marinade. Place the vegetables in another large resealable plastic bag; add the remaining marinade. Seal bags and turn to coat; refrigerate for 1 hour.

On eight metal or soaked wooden skewers, alternately thread the lamb, beef, onions, red peppers and mushrooms. Grill, covered, over medium-hot heat for 5-6 minutes on each side or until meat reaches desired doneness and vegetables are tender. Serve with pita bread. **Yield:** 8 servings.

Grilled Lamb With Veggies

Our Test Kitchen staff teamed lean lamb chops with a medley of vegetables to make a special meal.

- 1/2 cup apple juice
- 1/2 cup honey
- 2 tablespoons dried minced onion
- 2 tablespoons red wine vinegar
- 2 tablespoons tomato paste
- 2 garlic cloves, minced
- 1 teaspoon Worcestershire sauce
- 1/2 teaspoon pepper
- 3 medium potatoes
- 1 *each* medium green, sweet red and yellow pepper, julienned
- 2 sirloin lamb chops (about 1-1/2 pounds), trimmed

In a saucepan, combine the first eight ingredients; bring to a boil. Reduce heat; simmer, uncovered, for 5 minutes. Cut each potato into 16 wedges. Divide the potatoes and peppers between two pieces of heavy-duty foil (about 18 in. square). Top each with 1/2 cup sauce; set remaining sauce aside. Fold foil over vegetables and seal tightly.

Grill vegetable packets and lamb chops, covered, over medium-hot heat for 5 minutes. Turn chops; baste with remaining sauce. Grill 5 minutes longer. Turn and baste. Grill for 2 minutes or until a meat thermometer reads 145° for medium-rare, 150° for medium or 160° for well-done. Serve with vegetables. **Yield:** 2 servings.

Mouth-watering marinades and rubs

(for example, Teriyaki Marinade and Mediterranean Herb Rub) add special spark to a variety of meats before they're cooked on the grill. Sauces like Seafood Butter Sauce and Baste or Jamaican Barbecue Sauce are slathered on while the food is cooking—and at the table as well. You can also complement main courses with classic condiments such as Sweet-Sour Freezer Pickles, Three-Pepper Chutney and Special Hamburger Sauce.

Spiced Cranberry Ketchup

(Pictured at left)

Here's a condiment that makes grilled chicken and turkey sing!
We also like it with hamburgers.
—Gilda Lester, Wilmington, North Carolina

2-1/4 cups fresh *or* frozen cranberries
  1/2 cup water
  1/4 cup chopped green onions
    2 bay leaves
  3/4 cup plus 2 tablespoons sugar
  1/4 cup white wine vinegar
  1/4 cup balsamic vinegar
1-1/2 teaspoons Dijon mustard
  1/2 teaspoon ground cinnamon
  1/4 teaspoon salt
  1/4 teaspoon ground allspice
  1/4 teaspoon ground cloves
  1/8 teaspoon ground cumin

In a small saucepan, combine the cranberries, water, onions and bay leaves. Cook over medium heat until the berries pop, about 15 minutes. Cool slightly. Discard bay leaves. Press cranberry mixture through a fine mesh strainer; discard cranberry skins.

Return mixture to pan. Stir in the remaining ingredients. Bring to a boil. Reduce heat; simmer, uncovered, for 8-10 minutes or until thickened. Cool. Cover and refrigerate (mixture will thicken more upon refrigeration). **Yield:** 1 cup.

Barbecue Seasoning

(Pictured below)

I use this rub on country-style ribs, pork chops and chicken. You'll likely have the seasonings on hand to make a batch, and if you don't use it all, it will keep for the next time.
—Rose Rainier, Sheridan, Wyoming

- 1/4 **cup beef bouillon granules**
- 1/4 **cup chili powder**
- 1/4 **cup paprika**
- 1 **tablespoon sugar**
- 1 **tablespoon garlic salt**
- 1 **tablespoon onion salt**
- 1 **teaspoon celery salt**
- 1 **teaspoon cayenne pepper**
- 1 **teaspoon pepper**
- 1/2 **teaspoon curry powder**
- 1/2 **teaspoon dried oregano**

In a small bowl, combine all of the ingredients. Store in an airtight container in a cool dry place for up to 6 months. Use as a rub for ribs, chicken or pork. **Yield:** 1 cup.

Three-Pepper Chutney

(Pictured above)

This sweet chutney is as tasty on pork, beef and poultry as it is on grilled hot dogs and hamburgers. We also use it in place of mayonnaise on sandwiches.
—Lisa Louw, Alachua, Florida

- 1-1/2 **cups packed brown sugar**
- 1-1/2 **cups cider vinegar**
- 3 *each* **medium green and sweet red peppers, chopped**
- 3 **jalapeno peppers, seeded and chopped**
- 1 **medium onion, chopped**
- 1 **teaspoon salt**

In a large saucepan, combine all ingredients. Bring to a boil. Reduce heat; simmer, uncovered, for 1-1/2 to 2 hours or until thickened. Pour into a serving bowl. Cover and refrigerate for 1-2 hours or until chilled. **Yield:** 2 cups.

Editor's Note: When cutting or seeding hot peppers, use rubber or plastic gloves to protect your hands. Avoid touching your face.

Speedy Chicken Marinade

This is the best "fooler" recipe I've ever used. It takes just a few minutes but looks like you fussed. You can even place frozen chicken breasts in the marinade and allow them to defrost and marinate in the fridge overnight.
—Nan Haring, Portage, Michigan

- 1 **envelope zesty Italian salad dressing mix**
- 1/4 **cup red wine vinegar**
- 1/4 **cup soy sauce**

Combine all ingredients and pour over 1-1/2 to 2 pounds of boneless chicken breasts. Cover and refrigerate for several hours. Remove chicken from the marinade and grill over hot heat 5-6 minutes per side or until juices run clear. **Yield:** about 1/2 cup.

■ ■ ■

Teriyaki Marinade

You'll rely on this tried-and-true beef marinade year after year, meal after meal. It's versatile enough you can use it on chicken, pork, fish and even vegetables.
—Charlie and Ruthie Knote
Cape Girardeau, Missouri

- 1/2 **cup soy sauce**
- 3 **tablespoons sugar**
- 2 **tablespoons dry cooking sherry**
- 1/2 **teaspoon garlic powder**
- 1/2 **teaspoon ground ginger**

Combine all ingredients; mix well. Pour over beef; cover and refrigerate for 2 to 24 hours. **Yield:** 1/2 cup.

Marinades add flavor and can tenderize meat. However, marinades only penetrate about 1/2 inch deep, so the flavor is on the outer surface of the food. Meat and poultry need at least 1 to 4 hours to marinate, but many cuts can be marinated overnight, which is a convenience for the busy cook. You can make up the marinade one evening and marinate the food until the next night, or add the food in the morning and marinate until you are ready to cook it that night.

Most fish and seafood only need 15 to 30 minutes and can be marinating while other items are being prepared for dinner. Marinating too long may cause the meat texture to break down and become mushy.

An easy way to marinate is to use a resealable plastic bag. Pour the marinade into the bag, add the meat or vegetables and partially seal the bag. Squeeze out as much air as possible, then completely seal the bag. Place on a tray to contain any leakage. Any food marinated for more than 30 minutes must be placed in the refrigerator.

For food safety reasons, if you want to use some of the marinade for basting or for a dipping sauce, we recommend that some of the fresh marinade be reserved for this purpose before marinating the food. Any marinade that came in contact with uncooked meat, poultry or seafood should be discarded and not reused.

Cranberry Tomato Chutney

(Pictured below)

The unique flavor of this chutney complements turkey, pork and duck. To make a quick appetizer, process 1-1/2 cups chutney in the blender, pour over cream cheese and serve with crackers.
—*Kathy Garnes, Laurel, Maryland*

      5 cups fresh *or* frozen cranberries
      1 can (28 ounces) crushed tomatoes
      1 cup golden raisins
   3/4 cup sugar
      1 teaspoon salt
   3/4 teaspoon ground ginger

In a large saucepan, combine all ingredients. Bring to a boil. Reduce heat; cover and simmer for 20-25 minutes or until cranberries and raisins are tender, stirring occasionally. Cool. Cover and refrigerate for 2-3 days before serving. **Yield:** 6 cups.

Homemade Steak Sauce

I think this one-of-a-kind steak sauce tastes better than the commercial brands. The ruby red grapefruit juice adds a tang that sets it apart from traditional steak sauces. It's even great on pork.
—*Judy Neil, Royal Oak, Michigan*

   1/4 cup chopped onion
      1 tablespoon olive oil
      2 tablespoons honey
   1/4 cup beef broth
   1/4 cup Worcestershire sauce
   1/4 cup soy sauce
   1/4 cup ruby red grapefruit juice
      3 tablespoons tomato paste
      2 tablespoons balsamic vinegar
      2 tablespoons cider vinegar
      2 tablespoons raisins
      2 teaspoons garlic powder
 1-1/2 teaspoons coarsely crushed pepper
   3/4 teaspoon dried thyme
   1/2 teaspoon salt

In a nonstick saucepan over medium heat, cook onion in oil until tender. Add honey; cook and stir for 2 minutes. Stir in broth, Worcestershire sauce, soy sauce, grapefruit juice, tomato paste and vinegars until blended. Stir in the raisins, garlic powder, pepper, thyme and salt. Bring to a boil.

Reduce heat; simmer, uncovered, for about 20 minutes or until sauce is reduced to about 1-1/4 cups. Cool to room temperature. Transfer to a blender; cover and process until smooth. Cover and refrigerate. **Yield:** 1-1/4 cups.

Sweet 'n' Tangy Barbecue Sauce

(Pictured at right)

Jalapeno pepper, cayenne and chili powder lend a bit of a bite to this low-sodium sauce from our Test Kitchen home economists. Use it on pork, chicken, beef ribs and more.

    1 large onion, chopped
    1 jalapeno pepper, seeded
      and chopped
    1 tablespoon olive oil
1-1/2 cups water
    1 can (6 ounces) tomato paste
  1/2 cup packed brown sugar
  1/2 cup cider vinegar
  1/4 cup honey
    2 tablespoons chili powder
    1 tablespoon molasses
    2 teaspoons chicken bouillon granules
    1 teaspoon garlic powder
  1/2 teaspoon onion powder
  1/2 teaspoon ground cumin
  1/4 teaspoon pepper
  1/4 teaspoon cayenne pepper
  1/2 to 1 teaspoon Liquid Smoke,
      optional

In a saucepan, cook onion and jalapeno in oil over medium heat until tender and lightly browned. Add the next 13 ingredients. Bring to a boil. Reduce heat; simmer, uncovered, for 30 minutes or until thickened, stirring occasionally. Remove from the heat. Stir in Liquid Smoke if desired. Store in the refrigerator for up to 2 weeks. **Yield:** 2-1/2 cups.

Editor's Note: When cutting or seeding hot peppers, use rubber or plastic gloves to protect your hands. Avoid touching your face.

Cucumber Sauce
(Pictured at right)

We like lots of garlic in our cooking, and will serve this traditional Tsatziki with grilled lamb and chicken.
—*Efy Leonardi, Massapequa, New York*

- 4 cups (32 ounces) plain yogurt
- 1 medium cucumber, peeled, seeded and grated
- 1/2 teaspoon salt
- 1/4 cup olive oil
- 1/4 cup white vinegar
- 2 garlic cloves, minced

Line a fine mesh strainer with two layers of cheesecloth. Place yogurt in strainer over a bowl. Cover and refrigerate for at least 4 hours or overnight.

Drain and discard liquid in bowl; set yogurt aside. Place cucumber in a colander over a plate; sprinkle with salt. Let stand for 15 minutes; discard liquid. In a small bowl, whisk oil and vinegar until blended. Stir in the garlic, yogurt and cucumber. **Yield:** about 2-1/2 cups.

■ ■ ■

Special Hamburger Sauce

This thick sauce is the secret to making children happy. It turns an ordinary burger into their favorite fast-food version.
—*Cairol Ostrander, Bainbridge, Georgia*

- 1 cup mayonnaise
- 1/3 cup creamy French dressing
- 1/4 cup sweet pickle relish
- 1 tablespoon sugar
- 1 teaspoon dried minced onion

Salt and pepper to taste

In a bowl, combine all ingredients. Store in the refrigerator. **Yield:** 1-1/2 cups.

Mediterranean Herb Rub

You'll want to try this robust rub on fish, poultry or pork. Or sprinkle on cooked veggies.
—*Jacqueline Thompson Graves
Lawrenceville, Georgia*

- 1 tablespoon dried thyme
- 1 tablespoon dried oregano
- 1-1/2 teaspoons poultry seasoning
- 1 teaspoon dried rosemary, crushed
- 1 teaspoon dried marjoram
- 1 teaspoon dried basil
- 1 teaspoon dried parsley flakes
- 1/8 teaspoon pepper

In a small bowl, combine all ingredients. Store in an airtight container in a cool dry place for up to 6 months. **Yield:** 1/4 cup.

Rubs are a combination of herbs and spices that are rubbed onto meat, fish or poultry. They are quick to make and an easy way to add a flavor boost to a plain piece of meat.

Crisp Onion Relish

I take this special relish to picnics as a condiment for hamburgers and hot dogs.
—Marie Patkau, Hanley, Saskatchewan

- 4 medium sweet onions, halved and thinly sliced
- 1/2 cup sugar
- 1/3 cup water
- 1/3 cup cider vinegar
- 1 cup mayonnaise
- 1 teaspoon celery seed

Place onions in a large bowl. In a small bowl, combine the sugar, water and vinegar; stir until sugar is dissolved. Pour over onions. Cover and refrigerate for at least 3 hours. Drain. Combine mayonnaise and celery seed; add to onions and mix well. Store in the refrigerator. **Yield:** about 6 cups.

Sweet-Sour Freezer Pickles

(Pictured at right)

Now you can have all the goodness of crunchy sweet-sour pickles without going to the trouble of canning them. A batch of these puckery slices can keep in the freezer for up to 6 weeks.
—Jean Vance, Charlotte, North Carolina

- 10 to 12 medium pickling cucumbers (about 2 pounds), thinly sliced
- 3 medium onions, thinly sliced
- 1 large green pepper, chopped
- 3 tablespoons salt, *divided*
- 2 cups sugar
- 1 cup white vinegar
- 1 tablespoon celery seed

In a large container, combine the cucumbers, onions, green pepper and 2 tablespoons salt. Cover with crushed ice; mix well. Refrigerate

for 8 hours. Drain; rinse and drain again.

In a saucepan, combine the sugar, vinegar, celery seed and remaining salt. Bring to a boil; cook and stir for 1 minute. Spoon over cucumber mixture. Pour into jars or freezer containers. Cool.

Top with lids. Cover and freeze for up to 6 weeks. Thaw at room temperature for 4 hours before serving. **Yield:** 4 pints.

Zippy Dry Rub

This spicy blend has broad appeal since the rub can be used on all meats or added to rice while it's cooking for flavor boost.
—Gaynelle Fritsch, Welches, Oregon

- 1 tablespoon salt
- 1 teaspoon mustard seed
- 1 teaspoon pepper
- 1 teaspoon chili powder
- 1 teaspoon paprika
- 1/2 teaspoon ground cumin
- 1/2 teaspoon dried coriander
- 1/4 teaspoon garlic powder

In a small bowl, combine all ingredients. Store in an airtight container. Rub desired amount onto the surface of uncooked meat. Cover and refrigerate for at least 4 hours before grilling. **Yield:** about 2-1/2 tablespoons.

Jamaican Barbecue Sauce

(Pictured below)

Since visiting Jamaica, I've become a big fan of jerk chicken and fish. I eventually came up with my own version of that zesty island flavoring. It's a great sauce for ribs, whether you're grilling them or making them in the oven. It makes me feel like I'm on vacation!
—Lee Ann Odell, Boulder, Colorado

1 bacon strip, halved
1/2 cup chopped onion
2 tablespoons chopped green onion
1 tablespoon chopped jalapeno pepper
1 cup ketchup
1/2 cup chicken broth
1/2 cup molasses
2 tablespoons cider vinegar
2 tablespoons lemon juice
1 tablespoon soy sauce
1 tablespoon Worcestershire sauce
1 tablespoon prepared mustard
1 tablespoon minced fresh thyme
1 teaspoon salt
1/2 teaspoon pepper
1/4 to 1/2 teaspoon ground cinnamon
1/4 to 1/2 teaspoon ground nutmeg

In a saucepan, cook bacon over medium heat until crisp. Discard bacon or save for another use. In the drippings, saute the onions and jalapeno until tender. Stir in the remaining ingredients. Bring to a boil. Remove from the heat; cool. **Yield:** 2 cups.

Editor's Note: When cutting or seeding hot peppers, use rubber or plastic gloves to protect your hands. Avoid touching your face.

Seafood Butter Sauce and Baste

The delicate flavors in this buttery baste complement succulent seafood.
—Charlie and Ruthie Knote
Cape Girardeau, Missouri

1/2 cup butter
1/2 teaspoon dried rosemary
1/2 teaspoon dried tarragon
3/4 teaspoon salt
 1 tablespoon lemon juice

Melt the butter in a small saucepan. Add the remaining ingredients. Brush on seafood; baste occasionally during grilling. This may also be served warm as a nice dipping sauce for shrimp, crawfish, crab and lobster. **Yield:** 1/2 cup.

Basting foods during grilling adds a subtle layer of taste to your finished food. Baste only the cooked sides of the food to avoid contamination from the raw side. This also keeps the basting liquid from burning during grilling.

- Basting sauces containing tomato or sugar should be used towards the end of grilling since they tend to burn on the food. To prevent burning, brush on thick or sweet sauces during the last 10-15 minutes of cooking, basting and turning every few minutes.

- Be aware that basting sauces containing oil or butter tend to cause flare-ups when meat is grilled.

Sweet 'n' Spicy BBQ Sauce

(Pictured above)

I developed this sauce to serve with a stromboli steak sandwich. Over time, I started using it as a sauce for chicken and chops.
—Dorothy Ross, Jackson, Ohio

 2 cups packed brown sugar
 2 cups ketchup
 1 cup water
 1 cup cider vinegar
 1 cup finely chopped onion
 1 can (8 ounces) tomato sauce
 1 cup corn syrup
 1 cup molasses
 1 can (6 ounces) tomato paste
 2 tablespoons Worcestershire sauce
 1 tablespoon garlic-pepper blend
 1 tablespoon Liquid Smoke, optional
 1 tablespoon prepared mustard
 1 teaspoon onion salt
 1 teaspoon celery salt

In a large saucepan, combine all ingredients. Bring to a boil. Reduce heat; simmer, uncovered, for 15 minutes or until the flavors are blended. Remove from the heat; cool. **Yield:** about 2 quarts.

·Desserts·

Guests will be pleasantly surprised when you fire up the grill once again after enjoying the meal's main course. Now's your chance to impress them with a grill-side dessert! Enhance the natural sweetness of fruit by preparing Red-Hot Apples, Banana Boats or Grilled Peaches with Berry Sauce. For chocolate lovers, you can't go wrong with Cookout Caramel S'mores or Chocolate Dessert Wraps.

Grilled Fruit Kabobs

(Pictured at left)

Instead of making a traditional fruit salad, why not try these quick-and-easy kabobs? They cook on the grill in a matter of minutes, so you'll have a refreshing fruit dessert in no time. Plus, they're fun to eat!
—Mrs. Travis Baker, Litchfield, Illinois

1/2 **fresh pineapple, trimmed and cut into 1-inch chunks**
3 **medium fresh nectarines, cut into 1-inch chunks**
3 **medium fresh pears, cut into 1-inch chunks**
3 **medium fresh peaches, cut into 1-inch chunks**
3 to 4 **plums, cut into 1-inch chunks**
10 **apricots, halved**
Honey *or* corn syrup

Thread the pineapple, nectarines, pears, peaches, plums and apricots alternately onto metal or soaked wooden skewers. Grill, uncovered, over medium-hot heat until fruit is heated through, about 6 minutes, turning often. Brush with honey or corn syrup during the last minute of grilling time. **Yield:** 4-6 servings.

over medium heat for 1-2 minutes on each side or until golden brown, brushing occasionally with remaining pineapple juice mixture. Top each slice of cake with a pineapple ring and scoop of ice cream; drizzle with caramel topping. Serve immediately. **Yield:** 6 servings.

■ ■ ■

Pineapple Doughnut Dessert

(Pictured below)

When we can't go camping, we sometimes pitch a tent in the backyard for the kids and grill this simple treat.
—Christy Hinrichs, Parkville, Missouri

- 5 **cake doughnuts**
- 3 **tablespoons butter, softened**
- 2/3 **cup packed brown sugar**
- 1 **can (20 ounces) sliced pineapple, drained**
- 10 **maraschino cherries**

Cut doughnuts in half horizontally; spread with butter. For each packet, place two doughnut halves cut side up on a 12-in. square of heavy-duty foil. Sprinkle each with about 1 tablespoon brown sugar. Top with a pineapple slice; place a cherry in the center. Seal foil tightly. Grill over indirect medium heat for 2-4 minutes or until heated through. **Yield:** 10 servings.

Dessert from the Grill

(Pictured above)

I complete grilled meals with this light, refreshing dessert. By the time we're done eating, the coals have cooled to the right temperature. I brush slices of pineapple and pound cake with a yummy sauce, toast them on the grill and top 'em with ice cream and convenient caramel sauce.
—Becky Gillespie, Boulder, Colorado

- 1 **can (20 ounces) sliced pineapple**
- 1 **tablespoon butter**
- 1/2 **teaspoon brown sugar**
- 1/4 **teaspoon vanilla extract**
- 1/8 **teaspoon ground cinnamon**
- 1/8 **teaspoon ground nutmeg**
- 6 **slices pound cake**

Vanilla ice cream
Caramel ice cream topping

Drain pineapple, reserving 1/3 cup juice and six pineapple rings (save remaining juice and pineapple for another use). In a microwave-safe dish, combine butter, brown sugar, vanilla, cinnamon, nutmeg and reserved pineapple juice. Microwave, uncovered, on high for 1-2 minutes or until bubbly. Brush half of the mixture on both sides of pineapple rings and cake slices. Grill pineapple and cake, uncovered,

Fruit Grilling Chart

Grilled fruits are tasty, nutritious finales to meals throughout the year. Grill fruit until tender. Turn halfway through grilling time. Before grilling fruit, wash it under cool, running water and use a vegetable brush if needed. Remove any blemished areas.

Type	Weight or Thickness	Heat	Approximate Cooking Time (in minutes)
Apples	1/2-in. slices	medium/direct	4 to 6
Apricots	pitted, halved	medium/direct	6 to 8
Bananas	halved lengthwise	medium/direct	6 to 8
Peaches	pitted, halved	medium/direct	8 to 10
Pears	halved	medium/direct	8 to 10
Pineapple	1/2-in. rings	medium/direct	7 to 10

Cinnamon Flat Rolls

I shared this recipe when 4-H leaders requested an activity for younger members. The kids had a ball rolling out the dough and enjoying the sweet, chewy results.
—Ethel Farnsworth, Yuma, Arizona

- 1 **package (16 ounces) frozen dinner rolls, thawed**
- 5 **tablespoons vegetable oil**
- 1/2 **cup sugar**
- 1 **tablespoon ground cinnamon**

On a floured surface, roll each dinner roll into a 5-in. circle. Brush with oil. Grill, uncovered, over medium heat for 1 minute on each side or until golden brown (burst any large bubbles with a fork). Combine sugar and cinnamon; sprinkle over rolls. **Yield:** 1 dozen.

Red-Hot Apples

I use red-hot candies to turn ordinary apples into something cinnamony and sensational. The tender treats bake on the grill during dinner.
—Helen Shubert, Hays, Kansas

- 4 **medium tart apples, cored**
- 4 **teaspoons brown sugar**
- 1/4 **cup red-hot candies**
Vanilla ice cream, optional

Place each apple in the center of a piece of heavy-duty foil (12 in. square). Spoon 1 teaspoon sugar and 1 tablespoon red-hot candies into the center of each apple. Fold foil around apple and seal tightly.

Grill, covered, over medium-hot heat for 30 minutes or until apples are tender. Carefully transfer apples and syrup to bowls. Serve warm with ice cream if desired. **Yield:** 4 servings.

Grilled Apple Crisp

(Pictured below)

The first time I tasted this old-fashioned apple crisp, I couldn't believe it was made on the grill. Topped with a scoop of ice cream, the warm dessert will earn you rave reviews.
—Margaret Hanson-Maddox, Montpelier, Indiana

  10 **cups thinly sliced peeled tart apples (about 8 medium)**
   1 **cup old-fashioned oats**
   1 **cup packed brown sugar**
 1/4 **cup all-purpose flour**
   3 **teaspoons ground cinnamon**
   1 **teaspoon ground nutmeg**
 1/4 **teaspoon ground cloves**
 1/4 **cup cold butter**
Vanilla ice cream

Place the apple slices on a double thickness of heavy-duty foil (about 24 in. x 12 in.). In a small bowl, combine the oats, brown sugar, flour, cinnamon, nutmeg and cloves; cut in butter until mixture is crumbly. Sprinkle over apples.

Fold foil around the apple mixture and seal tightly. Grill, covered, over medium heat for 20-25 minutes or until the apples are tender. Serve warm with ice cream. **Yield:** 6 servings.

Marshmallow Fruit Kabobs

Here's a way to slip more fruit into your family's diet! The sauce can be made ahead of time. Kids will have a great time helping to assemble the kabobs, too.
—Claudia Ruiss, Massapequa, New York

1-1/2 **cups fresh *or* frozen raspberries, thawed**
 1/3 **cup orange juice**
   1 **tablespoon confectioners' sugar**
   2 **medium firm bananas, cut into 3/4-inch slices**
   2 **cups cubed fresh pineapple**
   2 **large fresh plums, cut into 3/4-inch pieces**
  24 **large marshmallows**
   1 **tablespoon lemon juice**
   1 **tablespoon honey**

Mash and strain raspberries, reserving juice. Discard the seeds. In a bowl, combine the orange juice, sugar and raspberry juice. Set aside.

Coat grill rack with nonstick cooking spray before starting the grill. On 12 metal or soaked wooden skewers, alternately thread fruit and marshmallows. Combine lemon juice and honey; brush over fruit. Grill kabobs over indirect medium heat for 1-2 minutes on each side or until marshmallows are golden. Serve kabobs with raspberry sauce. **Yield:** 6 servings.

Cookout Caramel S'mores

(Pictured above)

These gooey treats make a great finish to an informal meal. Toasting the marshmallows extends our after-dinner time together, giving us something fun to do as a family.
—Martha Haseman, Hinckley, Illinois

- 8 **large marshmallows**
- 2 **teaspoons chocolate syrup**
- 8 **graham crackers (2-1/2-inch square)**
- 2 **teaspoons caramel ice cream topping**

Using a long-handled fork, toast marshmallows 6 in. from medium-hot heat until golden brown, turning occasionally.

Drizzle chocolate syrup over four graham crackers; top each with two toasted marshmallows. Drizzle with caramel topping. Cover with remaining graham crackers. **Yield:** 4 servings.

Peach Pie Bundles

With just six ingredients, this recipe is simple yet so satisfying. The sweetness of the peaches is the perfect follow-up to grilled burgers.
—Janet Barnard, Toronto, Ontario

- 2 **cups frozen unsweetened sliced peaches, thawed**
- 4 **teaspoons all-purpose flour**
- 4 **teaspoons sugar**
- 1/2 **cup graham cracker crumbs**
- 1/4 **cup packed brown sugar**
- 4 **teaspoons cold butter**

Place the peaches in a bowl. Combine flour and sugar; sprinkle over peaches and toss to coat. In a small bowl, combine cracker crumbs and brown sugar; cut in butter until mixture is crumbly.

For each bundle, place half of the peach mixture on a double thickness of heavy-duty foil (about 18 in. x 12 in.). Sprinkle crumb mixture over peaches. Fold foil around mixture and seal tightly. Grill, covered, over medium heat for 5-10 minutes or until peaches are tender. **Yield:** 2 servings.

Grilled Peaches with Berry Sauce

(Pictured below)

This unusual dessert is as pretty as it is delicious. Topped with brown sugar and cinnamon, the peaches come off the grill sweet and spicy. The raspberry sauce adds a refreshing touch.
—Nancy Johnson, Connersville, Indiana

1/2 of a 10-ounce package frozen raspberries in syrup, slightly thawed
1-1/2 teaspoons lemon juice
2 medium fresh peaches, peeled and halved
5 teaspoons brown sugar
1/4 teaspoon ground cinnamon
1/2 teaspoon vanilla extract
1 teaspoon butter

In a blender or food processor, process raspberries and lemon juice until pureed. Strain and discard seeds. Cover and chill.

Place the peach halves, cut side up, on a large piece of heavy-duty foil (about 18 in. x 12 in.). Combine brown sugar and cinnamon; sprinkle into peach centers. Sprinkle with vanilla; dot with butter. Fold foil over peaches and seal.

Grill over medium-hot heat for 15 minutes or until heated through. To serve, spoon the raspberry sauce over peaches. **Yield:** 4 servings.

■ ■ ■

Banana Boats

When I was a church youth leader, I introduced many young campers to this scrumptious meal ending. It's wonderful because each person can add their choice of yummy toppings to this warm dessert. They taste almost like banana splits.
—Sandy Vanderhoff, Waldron, Arkansas

4 medium unpeeled ripe bananas
2 tablespoons flaked coconut
2 tablespoons chopped maraschino cherries
2 tablespoons raisins
2 tablespoons peanut butter chips
1/2 cup miniature marshmallows

Cut banana peels lengthwise about 1/2 in. deep and to within 1/2 in. of each end. Open peel to form a pocket. Combine coconut and cherries; spoon into pockets of two bananas. Combine raisins and peanut butter chips; fill remaining bananas. Divide marshmallows between bananas. Wrap each in an 18-in. x 12-in. piece of heavy-duty foil.

Grill, uncovered, over medium heat for 10-15 minutes or until marshmallows are melted and golden brown. **Yield:** 4 servings.

■ ■ ■

Chocolate Dessert Wraps

(Pictured at right)

The filled tortillas take just minutes on the grill and get a chewy consistency from marshmallows.
—Laurie Gwaltney, Indianapolis, Indiana

  1/2 **cup creamy peanut butter**
    4 **flour tortillas (8 inches)**
    1 **cup miniature marshmallows**
  1/2 **cup miniature semisweet chocolate chips**
Vanilla ice cream
Chocolate shavings, optional

Spread 2 tablespoons of peanut butter on each tortilla. Sprinkle 1/4 cup marshmallows and 2 tablespoons chocolate chips on half of each tortilla. Roll up, beginning with the topping side. Wrap each tortilla in heavy-duty foil; seal tightly.

Grill, covered, over low heat for 5-10 minutes or until heated through. Unwrap tortillas and place on dessert plates. Serve with ice cream. Garnish with chocolate shavings if desired. **Yield:** 4 servings.

Editor's Note: Crunchy peanut butter is not recommended for this recipe.

Warm Apple Topping

My husband and I love preparing entire meals on the grill. We created this unique dessert for my mother, who can't eat most grain products. She was thrilled with the sweet topping spooned over vanilla ice cream.
—Sharon Manton, Harrisburg, Pennsylvania

    3 **medium tart apples, peeled**
  1/3 **cup raisins**
    1 **tablespoon lemon juice**
  1/3 **cup packed brown sugar**
  1/4 **teaspoon ground cinnamon**
  1/4 **teaspoon ground cloves**
  1/8 **teaspoon salt**
  1/8 **teaspoon ground nutmeg**
    2 **tablespoons cold butter**
  1/3 **cup finely chopped walnuts**
Vanilla ice cream

Cut each apple into 16 wedges; place all on an 18-in. square piece of heavy-duty foil. Sprinkle with raisins; drizzle with lemon juice. In a bowl, combine the brown sugar, cinnamon, cloves, salt and nutmeg; cut in the butter. Stir in the walnuts. Sprinkle over apples and raisins.

Fold foil around apple mixture and seal tightly. Grill over indirect medium heat for 18-22 minutes or until apples are tender. Serve over ice cream. **Yield:** 3 cups.

■Alphabetical Index■

This index lists every recipe in alphabetical order so you can easily find your favorites by name.

■ General Index ■

*This index lists every recipe by food category and/or major ingredient,
so you can easily locate recipes to suit your needs.*

■Reference Index■

This index lists the many helpful hints found throughout the book. Also, be sure to review the Grilling Basics beginning on page 4.